RACE TO WIN

ALSO BY ROGER MARSHALL

Designed to Win
Designed to Cruise

RACE TO WIN

by Roger Marshall

W · W · Norton & Company   New York and London

FIRST EDITION

Library of Congress Cataloging in Publication Data
Marshall, Roger.
    Race to win.
    1. Yacht racing.   I. Title.
GV826.5.M37   1980   797.1′4   79–24284
ISBN 0–393–03236–1

1 2 3 4 5 6 7 8 9 0

Preface

For the past several years I have been fortunate to have my writings published in a number of sailing magazines around the world—*SAIL* in the United States, and *Yachts and Yachting* in England, *Australian Sailing*, and *Kazi* in Japan. This book is a collection of the best of these writings. It contains material on topics as diverse as designing efficient deck layouts, developing polar curves, reducing aerodynamic drag, and controlling broaching. Yet all are related under the common subject of yacht racing.

In selecting and organizing the articles for this book, I discovered that they naturally fell into four basic areas. Each area is critical to successful competition; each contributes to the racing edge. The first is obviously good design. As an architect, I am constantly concerned with the problems of designing for better speed and efficiency. Some of my ideas on subjects from hull, keel and stern design to deck layouts and racing accommodations are included in Part I. Second, as a sailor, I know that no skipper can expect to win without good preparation. Reducing drag, tuning your rig, even improving your crew's fitness, can all make significant contributions to winning long before your boat crosses the starting line. These and other topics concerned with race preparation are discussed in Part II. Of course, what occurs *during* a race is as important as what occurs before it. Knowing the best techniques for tacking, spinnaker handling, helming, and so forth is essential in top competition. Consequently, Part III is devoted to improving performance on the race course. And finally, Part IV touches on the critical topic of boat maintenance. As most racing sailors realize, winning is next to impossible if hulls, decks, sails, rigging, and basic equipment are in poor condition.

When compiling a book of articles such as this, certain difficulties inevitably arise. One is the problem of repetition. Because these articles were written over a fairly long period of time, some contained similar information. Where possible I have tried to edit out this duplication and insert cross-references instead. But some repetition unavoidably remains. Please understand the reason for it. Another potential problem with a book of this sort is currency. To give readers a collection of articles that is as up-to-date as possible, I have reviewed each selection for dated material, and have rewritten where new developments demanded it.

I am very much aware of the debt I owe to the excellent magazine editors with whom I have worked—especially Charles Mason III, at *SAIL*, but also Peter Cook at *Yachts and Yachting*, Bob Ross at *Australian Sailing*, and T. Suzuki at *Kazi*. From them I have had much encouragement, help, and advice and I give them my thanks. Thanks also go to my wife Mary, whose editorial skills improved each of my articles and whose criticisms helped to turn my scrawled first drafts into finished manuscript. There are many other people whose comments, thoughts, and stimulation have given me the germ of an idea for a new article. Space does not permit me to mention all of them, but Jack Baringer, Keith Ludlow, Bruce McPherson, Humphrey Sullivan; and Chris Wick have been immeasurably helpful. Most of these people do not realize the ideas they have given me, but without them many of my articles would have been much the poorer. My appreciation to all.

ROGER MARSHALL

Jamestown, R.I.

Contents

Part III:
Improving Performance on the Racecourse   149

Part IV:
Racing Boat Maintenance   233

Part II

Designing for Speed and Efficiency

Introduction

Many people think of racing design as a subject strictly for experts. Although they may talk a great deal about design, there is little they feel competent to do without consulting a naval architect. This attitude is partly justified. Many design subjects, such as hull design or keel shapes, should not be left to enthusiastic amateurs. A number of the chapters in this section deal with such topics. They are intended to make the average owner a more knowledgeable consumer of the yacht designer's trade.

Yet an owner need not step back and leave all design matters to professionals. With a little know-how, there is much a person can do himself to increase the efficiency of his present design. A deck layout, for instance, can be improved significantly in the hands of a skillful owner. So too can interior arrangements, such as a galley layout or a navigator's area. With the aim of taking some of the mystery out of rudimentary design problems, a number of other chapters in this section are directed to the do-it-yourselfer.

1 Racing Hulls

Skim through the racing sections of current sailing magazines and you're sure to find a wide array of hull shapes. Logically it might seem that racing hulls should look much more alike. After all, they are all designed to sail as fast as possible. Why, then, does one designer choose a fat stern while another widens the bow? Is one right and the other wrong? Not necessarily. Hull shapes are the result of a number of decisions, many of which involve tradeoffs and interpretations. Let's begin by considering how basic hull dimensions affect a boat's performance. Then we will take a look at some of the external variables—such as expected wind and sea conditions, building materials, or an owner's preferences—which can critically influence design choices.

Hull Dimensions and Performance

The fastest hull is usually the one whose designer fully understands how changes in key dimensions will affect speed and performance. The most important of these dimensions are probably length, beam, and draft.

THE EFFECT OF LENGTH. The length of a boat directly affects its potential speed. This is because a boat travels at the speed of the waves it creates, and the longer the boat, the longer and faster the wave system it can produce. Essentially, a boat reaches maximum speed when the waves that carry it along extend from the bow to the stern.

To understand the relationship between boat length, wave-length, and speed potential, imagine a boat sailing at very low speeds. Numerous small waves can be seen cresting along the sides of the hull. Boat speed is directly related to the length of these waves—that is, to the distance between the crests.

Now, as the boat moves faster, the wavelengths it produces in crease, and the boat begins to encounter greater and greater resist-ance due to its own wave making. Eventually, maximum hull speed is reached when the boat is sailing on a single wave, with one crest supporting the bow and the other slightly aft of the stern. At this point, if the wavelength is L, then maximum hull speed equals 1.34 $x\sqrt{L}$. Of course, most boats do not sail at maximum speed all of the time. Average speed is somewhere between 0.8 and 1.1 x $\sqrt{L}$. This means that the wavelengths a boat typically creates are shorter than its hull length.

Because of its importance to speed, length in one way or another has been part of almost every rating rule formula. This is true of the modern International Offshore Rule (IOR) formula, which uses a rated length.

THE EFFECT OF BEAM. Increases in beam can improve sailing per-formance in various ways. An increase in beam at the waterline increases frontal resistance, but it also increases stability. Conse-quently, less ballast is needed to support the sail area. This, in turn, means that the boat will be faster, since the same sail area is push-ing a lighter hull through the water. An increase in overall beam, without increasing beam waterline (BWL), can also have ad-vantages. For one thing, it increases hull volume and therefore allows a better interior accommodation. And on a racing boat it can help to position crew weight further outboard to enhance stability.

Beam has almost always been included in rating rules. In the British rule of 1855, for example, now known as the Thames Meas-urement, beam (B) was penalized three times: $(L\text{-}B)$ x B x $\frac{1}{2}$ B. Designers of that era responded by reducing beam drastically and producing deep heavily ballasted boats with length/beam (L/B) ratios often as high as 6. Compare this to today's ratios of 2.5 to 3.5!

THE EFFECT OF DRAFT. As just explained, an increase in beam usually means that a boat can be made lighter, which in turn reduces hull depth. When overall draft is limited, this reduction in hull depth allows a designer to use a deeper keel. Theoretically at least, such a keel should be more efficient for upwind sailing.

A significant trend in IOR boats has been an increase in beam, coupled with a reduction in hull depth. When average beam/mid depth immersed area (B/MDIA) for the last few years is plotted on a graph, this trend is very apparent.

COEFFICIENTS AND RATIOS. In yacht design, a change in one area of a boat inevitably affects another. How, then, does a designer know when key dimensions are properly balanced? One way is to analyze a series of coefficients and ratios.

The most important coefficient is the prismatic, which is the underwater hull volume divided by the underwater portion of the largest sectional area times the length. (See figure 1.1a.) The average prismatic is on the order of 0.5. Some designers use the entire hull plus the keel and rudder when calculating the prismatic coefficient, while others use the hull alone, without any appendages. But however it is arrived at, the prismatic essentially serves the same purpose. It gives the designer a feel for the fullness or fineness of the hull. Another frequently used coefficient is the block coefficient—the underwater volume of the hull divided by length on the waterline (*LWL*)

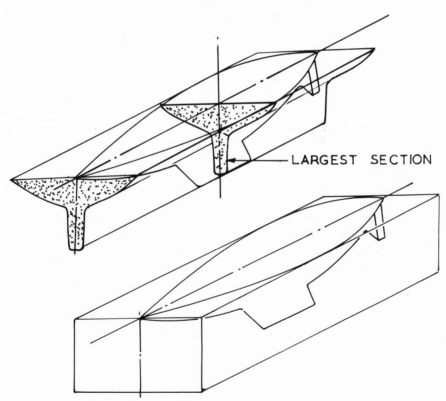

LARGEST SECTION

Figure 1.1a Calculating the prismatic coefficient: the underwater hull volume as a proportion of the volume of the largest section, multiplied by the length.

Figure 1.1b Calculating the block coefficient: the underwater hull volume as a proportion of the surrounding block.

Figure 1.2 The long, slim, heavy displacement hull of the twelve-meter *Enterprise*. It is designed to a rule in which sail area varies directly with displacement.

times beam waterline (*BWL*) times depth or draft. (See figure 1.lb.) This gives a general idea of the cargo-carrying capacity of the hull and is more significant for powerboats.

The most important ratios a designer consults are the displacement/length ratio and the sail area/length ratio. The first of these is the displacement in tons divided by 0.01 times *LWL* cubed:

$$\frac{\text{Disp}/2240}{(LWL/100)^3}.$$

It is typically on the order of 200 to 300. Some authorities estimate that this ratio must be under 150 for a boat to plane. Yet another useful ratio is the sail area/displacement ratio, or $\sqrt{(SA)}/\sqrt[3]{}($volume of displacement$)$. At first glance, this may not seem to affect the hull. But if a high ratio is required, then the beam or the ballast must be increased to carry the sail area. If the ballast is increased, displacement must also increase. So you can see that the displacement/length ratio and the sail area/displacement ratio closely interact.

Variable Factors Affecting Hull Design

So far we have outlined the ways in which key hull dimensions affect a boat's performance, and we have looked at some of the coefficients and ratios used to evaluate different designs. But there are other factors that must be considered when designing a racing hull. These are the external variables that can make one hull shape so different from another. Among the most important are the requirements of local wind and sea conditions, the particular building materials being used, the racing rule by which the boat will be rated, and the owner's as well as the designer's preferences.

WIND CONDITIONS. Average wind strength in the area where a boat will be sailed obviously affects hull design. If winds are predominantly heavy, sufficient stability must be achieved by increasing the beam at the waterline or by putting more lead in the keel, thus increasing displacement. Prevailing wind direction, too, can influence the ideal hull. A boat intended to sail mainly upwind will differ in both hull shape and displacement from a boat intended to sail mainly off the wind. Compare, for example, a twelve meter with a design for the Transpac Race.

SEA CONDITIONS. Expected sea conditions are also a factor, although they are often closely related to wind conditions. A boat intended to sail into a seaway will usually be fairly fine in the bow, carrying that fineness a long way aft. In contrast, a boat intended to surf down rollers will probably have a slightly fuller bow in order to get more dynamic lift.

BUILDING MATERIALS. Different building materials have different weights, which a hull must be designed to carry. A fifty-foot ferroconcrete boat, for instance, might weigh or displace some 60,000 pounds, whereas a fifty-foot cold-molded boat might displace only half that amount. Obviously the same hull would not be suitable for both.

Figure 1.3   The hull of *Finnistere*, once described as short, fat, and fast. Approximately the size of a modern one-tonner but weighing twice as much, it was designed to the CCA rule.

Figures 1.4a and 1.4b
Two views of *Circus Maximus.*
The long, light hull has
occasionally exceeded
twenty knots. The boat was
designed strictly for speed,
with little attention to IOR
parameters, so the rating is
extremely high.

THE RATING RULE. Rating rules influence hull shape tremendously. Even back in the days of the English plank on edge and the American sandbaggers we can see the effect of rating rules on hull design. Today, under the IOR, hull shapes are influenced by a rated beam taken at a predetermined distance below the sheerline, by the beam on the waterline, by various depths measured in the middle of the boat and in the forward quarter, and also by girth stations at the bow and stern. Measurement points are often emphasized or deemphasized to obtain a lower rating, and they can critically affect the speed potential of the hull.

OWNER'S PREFERENCES. The owner's specific requirements do not usually extend to the hull shape. He may, however, prefer a particular type of rudder/skeg configuration or want a particular height of freeboard.

DESIGNER'S PREFERENCES. These may influence any aspect of the hull. Once the designer has calculated the physical dimensions of the boat, the shape of the hull sheerline, the stern, and many other details are left to his discretion. To get an idea of a designer's personal style and preferences, it is best to study some of his latest boats.

Figure 1.5 A typical IOR hull, intended to be efficient over the largest possible range of wind and sea conditions. Note how this shape is totally unlike that of the twelve-meter shown in figure 1.2, illustrating the critical impact of different rules on hull design. This hull has some distortions around the stern to gain a lower rating.

Thus it is easy to see why a number of equally good designs can look significantly different. If all boats were sailed in exactly the same waters, under the same expected wind and sea conditions, if there was only one rule used to rate all boats, if all owners wanted the same things and all builders used the same materials, then hulls would undoubtedly look very much alike. But for obvious reasons these many ifs will never apply. Consequently, racing design will always be affected by the numerous variables that make one boat potentially faster than the next.

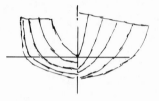

2 *What Kind of Keel?*

The shape of sailing yachts has changed dramatically over the years, and one of the areas of greatest change has been the keel. Fifty years ago, the keel was built as an integral part of the hull, and boats of that era usually had low ballast ratios. Herreshoff's *Ticonderoga,* for example, had a ballast ratio of 29 percent. Over time this long keel has evolved into the deep, narrow appendage of today, with resulting improvement in windward and light air performance. But as with almost anything else, higher performance in one area has tended to cause lower performance in another. With the reduction in keel lateral area has come less directional stability and more leeway. Overall, however, the gains outweigh the losses.

Now that the keel has become a pure appendage, aerodynamic data can be used to predict performance. (The similarity between a sailboat hull and an airplane is clearly illustrated in figure 2.1b.) Many technical papers have been written on this subject. For the information of the average sailor, this chapter discusses some ideas about the optimum shape for downwind and upwind keels, based on several of these studies and my own conclusions. It also describes some easy and inexpensive things an owner can do to improve the performance of his boat's present keel.

Determining Optimum Keel Shape

The ideal downwind shape is easy to determine, for a boat does not really require a keel when sailing downwind. All it needs is either

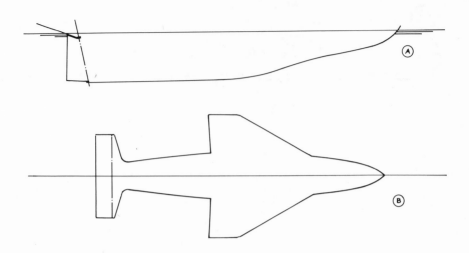

Figure 2.1a The underwater profile of an ocean racer of twenty years ago. *2.1b* A mirror image of the underbody of a modern ocean racer, showing the similarity between it and an aircraft design.

form stability or ballast to keep it upright, and a section shape that enables proper tracking with good helming.

The ideal upwind shape, however, is much more difficult to determine. There are many theories about what the best configuration is, and some are contradictory. Rather than review the thinking of different designers on this subject I'll express my own viewpoint here, encouraging the reader to explore other alternatives as well.

Figure 2.2   The terminology used to describe a modern keel. The various ratios are calculated as follows: taper ratio = tip chord/root chord; geometric aspect ratio = span/mid chord; area ratio = (lateral area)/*LWL*.

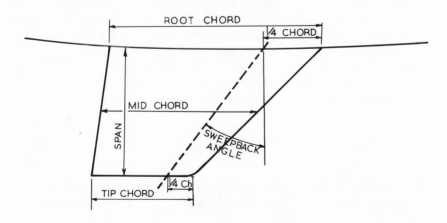

Let's start by considering what the keel does in the upwind condition.

1. It provides a side force which balances the heeling force of the rig.
2. It comprises 25 to 35 percent of the lateral plane of the boat and can therefore influence the position of the rig. (On dinghies this percentage is as high as 90 percent.)
3. It serves as a place to locate the ballast and, because the ballast comprises as much as 60 percent of the total weight of the boat, it can considerably influence trim.
4. It is also related to the size of the rig and the wind strength in which that rig is intended to be used.

The keel, then, is more than just a lump of lead. It serves important functions which must be carefully considered in its planning. All architects try to design keels that fulfill these functions well. But in actual fact, which keel shapes fulfill them best?

To help answer this question, I analyzed a number of profiles by different designers which had been published in various magazines. Since lateral area is one of the major factors in keel design,

Figure 2.3 Keel lateral area plotted against length on the waterline.

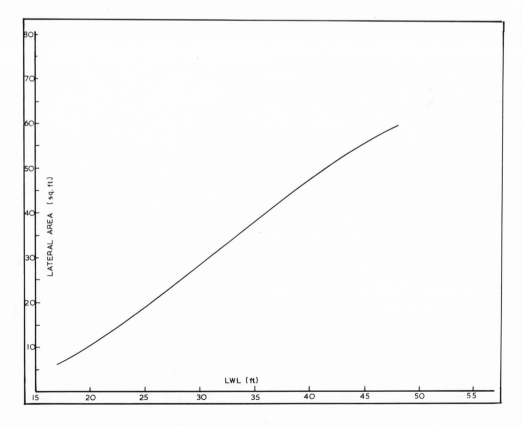

a good starting point was to scale off the areas from the profiles. I then plotted lateral area against *LWL* and drew a curve through those boats that were known to have good upwind performance. This gave me a graph that represented minimum lateral area for good windward performance over boats of varying length. It was immediately apparent that on larger boats, with generally lower sail area/displacement ratios, keels were proportionately smaller, causing the curve to level off at the top. (See figure 2.3.)

Having found the minimum lateral area, the next problem was to determine ideal shape. A graph of aspect ratios against sweepback angle yielded the straight, dashed line in figure 2.4. It was not conclusive. But when I plotted the points determined by P. DeSaix of the Stevens Institute (discussed in *SAIL*, May 1974), the results were more revealing. The solid line in figure 2.4 shows that most keels may have too much sweepback, perhaps because more sweepback looks so much faster when viewed in profile. (See figure 2.5.) I verified this line by a theoretical calculation that yielded very similar data.

Figure 2.4 Aspect ratio plotted against sweepback angle, showing the DeSaix line (solid) and a line extrapolated by the author from existing boats (dashed). The extrapolated line shows that many designers use too much sweepback, probably because it looks fast in profile.

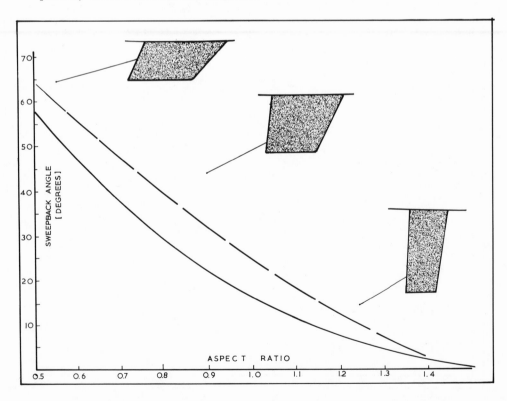

Figure 2.5 An example of a keel with probably too much sweepback for good windward performance.

Note that I have not yet taken into account taper ratio or aerofoil section. Taper ratio is a function of sweepback angle and as such can be graphed. The keel aerofoil section has long been the secret of each designer. I have deliberately chosen to neglect this factor, assuming that every architect designs for the optimum sectional shape.

Can this system be used to determine the optimum keel shape for a given boat? To test it, I decided to use a keel for a typical half-tonner and see how it compared with current designs. If the waterline length (*LWL*) of the boat is 23.0 feet, a keel lateral area of 16.4 square feet can be taken from figure 2.2. The IOR base draft (*DB*) is $(0.146 \times L) + 2$ ft. With an L of 25.68, this gives a draft for the keel and hull of 5.75 feet. If we then subtract the depth of the hull from the draft, we get the span of the keel.

$$\overbrace{5.75 \text{ ft.}}^{\text{draft}} - \overbrace{1.7 \text{ ft.}}^{\text{hull depth}} = \overbrace{4.05 \text{ ft.}}^{\text{span}}$$

And if the span is 4.05 feet, then

$$\frac{16.4}{4.05} = 4.05 = \text{midchord}$$

Thus, the aspect ratio is 1.0 (4.05 / 4.05).

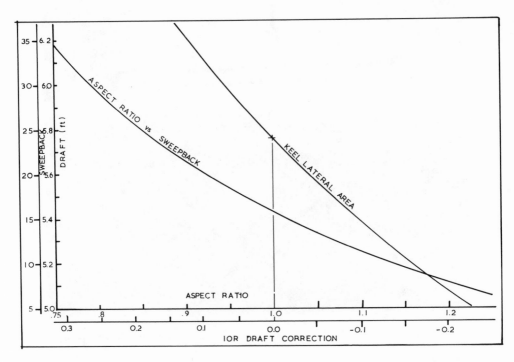

Figure 2.6   A graph that can be used to determine the optimum keel shape for a typical half-tonner.

By now going to figure 2.4, we can determine the sweepback angle for this aspect ratio. Because the lateral area is constant, any variation in draft will change the aspect ratio. This relationship between draft and aspect ratio can be plotted, as in figure 2.6. As the aspect ratio varies, a third axis measuring sweepback angle can be added to the graph. With the variation in base draft, there is also a variation in the IOR draft correction factor which will directly affect the rating. This is shown on a fourth axis in figure 2.6. If we desire a greater draft, say 6 feet, the draft correction factor increases to 0.075 feet. The sweepback angle increases to 19 degrees, and the aspect ratio is now .94.

Future studies no doubt will improve the accuracy with which keel performance can be predicted. But until that time, one can be reassured by the fact that most designers appear to be using similar profiles and section shapes. Figure 2.7 shows a typical profile for a two-tonner. There are, however, a few designs that do not conform to these general parameters. Unfortunately, short of investing in a new keel, there is not much an owner can do if he feels his present keel lacks enough lateral area or has too much sweepback.

Improving Your Keel's Performance

Other modifications, though, are simpler and less costly. Taken together, these measures can significantly improve the performance of an existing keel.

1. To reduce frictional drag, make sure your keel has no pits or bumps. Any pits or hollows should be carefully filled and rubbed fair with the surrounding area. Bumps should also be rubbed down smooth.
2. The trailing edge of the keel should be knife-sharp, provided that it is faired from about one-third of the way aft. Sharpening the last six inches is worse than leaving it blunt. If you cannot fair the keel to a sharp after-edge, then file a flat quarter-inch on it. (See chapter 10 on hydrodynamic drag.)
3. If you have a grounding shoe, make sure it is set into the keel fairly, with no hollows or bumps. The leading edge should have a slight radius, fairing parabolically into the section shape. Or better still, make the bottom of the keel perfectly flat for increased efficiency.
4. Check for cracks, chips, bumps and hollows at the hull/keel joint. They disturb the laminar flow and should be carefully faired, especially where the keel joins the hull at the leading edge.
5. While you are checking the keel, also check the keel bolts. All your diligent efforts to reduce frictional drag will be useless if the keel drops off because the bolts are corroded!

Figure 2.7 A keel shape commonly used on a modern two-tonner.

3 *IOR Sterns*

One of the greatest fallacies created by the International Offshore Rule is a belief in the "IOR stern." One finds reference to it everywhere. In articles and books by sailing journalists, in casual conversations at the yacht club, the comment "that boat has a typical IOR stern" is heard time and again. And so the myth is perpetuated.

That a single IOR stern does not exist is clear from the diversity of shapes seen on the racecourse. One need not be a naval architect to know that boats from different designers can have completely different stern sections and still be found at the head of the fleet. Nor is such diversity anything new. Boats designed to the old Royal Ocean Racing Club (RORC) rule, from which the IOR was partly derived, also had widely different sterns. Ironically, people twenty years ago talked about an RORC stern with as much conviction as they talk about an IOR stern today. It seems that some aspects of yacht racing don't change much at all.

Measuring a Stern under the IOR

Before looking at some contemporary sterns to see exactly how they differ, let's consider how a stern is measured under the IOR. To calculate the speed potential of a particular stern accurately, one should ideally obtain area measurements. But this is extremely difficult. Consequently, the IOR uses numerous point measurements instead. To a designer who is trying to design the fastest boat with the lowest rating possible, every measurement point (not only in the stern sections) becomes critical, and individual measurement points are given more or less emphasis, depending on their locations. This can lead to local distortions.

When the stern of an IOR boat is measured, two "chains" of predetermined length are placed around the section from sheerline to sheerline so that they bridge all hollows. Two measurement stations are established, both of which are a function of the beam of the boat. The After Girth Station (*AGS*) is located where the girth length is equal to 0.75 x *B* (rated beam), and the After Inner Girth Station (*AIGS*) is located where girth length equals 0.875 x *B*. (See figure 3.1.) Of course, the positioning of the aft girth stations is more difficult if there is a skeg or rudder in the way of the chain girth. If this happens, then the rule says that 4 percent and 15 percent of *B* buttock lines are to be utilized. Figures 3.2a and 3.2b show how.

From the two aft girth stations plus the two forward ones, various length measurements are taken. These are ultimately used to calculate the IOR Rated Length, known in the rule as *L*. A boat's rated

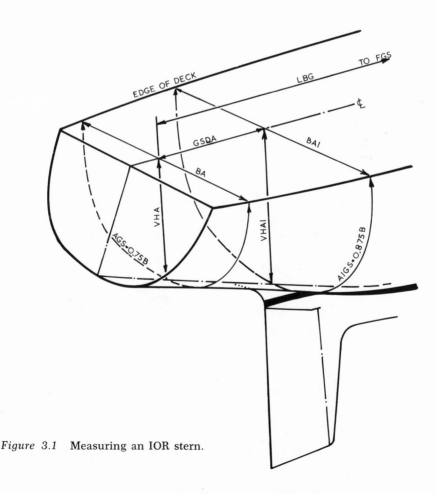

Figure 3.1 Measuring an IOR stern.

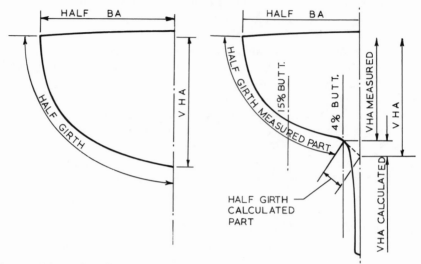

Figures 3.2a and 3.2b The measurement
points used when a skeg is in the way
of a girth station.

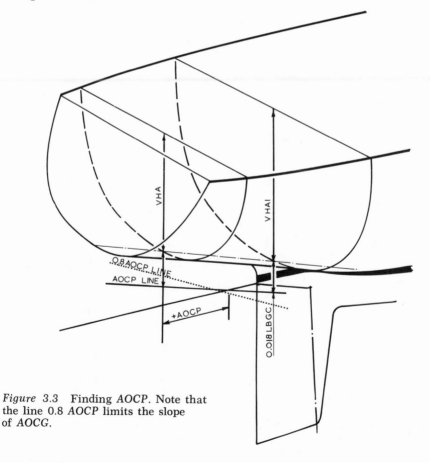

Figure 3.3 Finding *AOCP*. Note that
the line 0.8 *AOCP* limits the slope
of *AOCG*.

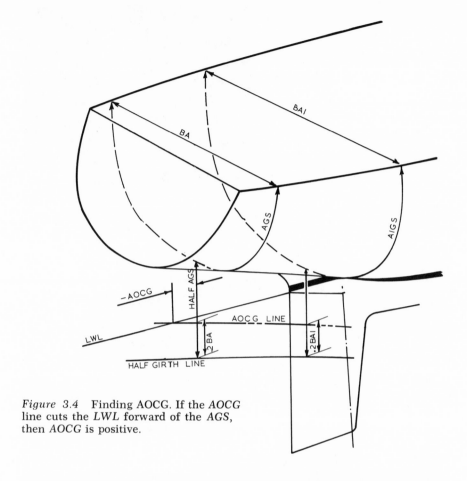

Figure 3.4   Finding AOCG. If the *AOCG*
line cuts the *LWL* forward of the *AGS*,
then *AOCG* is positive.

length is simply the distance between the forward and after girth
stations (*LBG*), minus a Forward Overhang Component (*FOC*),
minus an After Overhang Component Corrected (*AOCC*). *FOC* ap-
proximates how much further the Forward Girth Station (*FGS*) is
from the forward end of the rated length. Similarly, *AOCC* approxi-
mates how much further aft (or forward) *AGS* is from the after end
of *L*. Two factors, *AOCP* and *AOCG* (After Overhang Component
Profile and Girth), are averaged to arrive at the *AOC*. We will briefly
look at how each is determined.

   According to the rule, *AOCP* is intended to approximate the horizontal distance from *AGS* to a point where a line drawn at 0.018
LBGC (Length Between Girths Corrected) below the profile intersects
the waterline. Thus, as explained by figure 3.3, *AOCP* is a function
of the steepness of the stern profile and the length of *LBGC*.

   The second factor in the *AOC* is *AOCG*. It is intended to approximate the horizontal distance from *AGS* to a point where a line projected downward from the sheerline and equal in length to half the
girth station minus 20 percent of the beam intersects the waterline.
If you consider figure 3.4, it becomes clear that *AOCG* is simply a

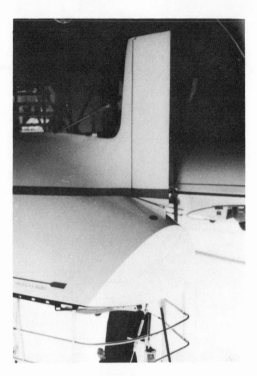

Figure 3.5
A clean-looking stern with
a fairly steep upward slope
of the buttocks.

function of the taper of the after end of the boat. Though *AOCG* may be readily apparent visually, the computer that calculates ratings has to be given this picture in the form of numbers. This requires fairly complex formulas which we can skip for the purposes of this discussion.

In recent years, designers have been getting lower ratings by making *AOCG* extremely step to reduce *L*. To stop this trend, the Offshore Racing Council has introduced limits on the closeness of a boat's girth stations and on the amount of slope that can be used.

Figure 3.6
The skeg on
this boat has
been carefully
positioned just
inside the 4
percent of
B buttock.

Figure 3.7
A dinghy-type stern
on *Circus Maximus*.

Figure 3.8
The sloping transom
on this boat helps
to push the
After Girth Station
further forward.

Figure 3.9
Planing boards help
extend this hull
without incurring
any penalty.

These limits take the form of *GLAI* (Girth Length Aft Inner) to govern distance between girth stations, and *AGSL* (Aft Girth Slope) and *APSL* (Aft Profile Slope) to govern slope. Briefly, *AOCG* cannot be more than 80 percent of *AOCP* without incurring a penalty.

Comparing IOR Sterns

Now let's look at some photos of sterns and describe how the IOR sees them. The boat in figure 3.5 has a fairly steep upward sweep of the buttocks aft—often a feature of heavy displacement boats. This increases the volume of the boat in the after sections and lowers the prismatic coefficient, thus giving greater speed potential at lower speed/length ratios. But this same steep rise aft also tends to create a high stern wave when the boat is moving at higher speed/length ratios ($V/\sqrt{L}$ more than 0.9), so that the boat tends to "lock" into a wave length equal to the sailing length. Theoretically, then, this stern is potentially faster in the light going, but has a definite maximum speed in heavy air.

The intersections of *AGS*, *AIGS*, and the 4-percent and 15-percent buttock lines are very sensitive points in the measurement of the After Overhang Component; this is clearly demonstrated in figure 3.6. Note how the skeg has been carefully sited just inside the 4-percent buttock.

Figure 3.7 shows a dinghy-type stern. The rule defines this stern as being one that makes the water "believe" the boat is longer than it actually is. Unlike the boat in figure 3.5, this boat will not be locked into any fixed wave length, and often it can surge or surf on large waves with great increases in speed.

A different approach is taken in figure 3.8. By definition the After Girth Station cannot cut the transom, and designers are using this requirement to help push the *AGS* further forward. The result is that *L* appears shorter, as clearly illustrated in the photo.

The stern of *Guia* is shown in figure 3.9. Here planing boards have been added to the transom to extend the waterline when the boat is moving at high speed. As long as these boards are within the limits defined by the rule, they are perfectly fair.

Different designers, then, have different ideas about what stern shape gives the greatest speed potential. The only generalizations that can be made are that most designers tend to look for good flow characteristics aft rather than rating rule distortions, although it does pay to observe the measurement points mentioned. Beyond this, there are no hard and fast rules. Consequently, there is no such thing as a single IOR stern.

4 *Efficient Deck Layout*

How often have you tried to sheet a sail on a fiberglass stock boat, only to find there was no track where you wanted it? Or how many times have you led a sheet to a stock boat winch, only to get an override as soon as you started winding? As many owners know, a standard deck layout is seldom as efficient as possible. Stock boat builders want to hold costs down, and in some cases this means a minimum of deck gear, and preference for less expensive fittings. Figure 4.1 shows how a stock boat with an extremely basic deck arrangement might look. Although workable, it leaves much to be desired.

Unfortunately, some stock boat owners resign themselves to similarly spartan layouts. They assume that significant improvements to a deck arrangement necessarily carry a high price tag in design and yard fees. This assumption, however, is mistaken. With a modest amount of knowledge and skill, an owner himself can install new track, add extra padeyes, or raise a winch to a more efficient height. Figure 4.2 shows the numerous improvements an owner might make to the rudimentary deck arrangement in figure 4.1. All of them are relatively easy.

In this chapter I'll review how to go about planning and carrying out alterations to your existing deck layout. The changes discussed are some of the ones most frequently required—adding extra tracks, padeyes, grabrails, cleats, and vents, and adjusting winch positions. Then I'll analyze some recent developments in custom racing decks to keep stock boat owners abreast of the latest go-fast ideas.

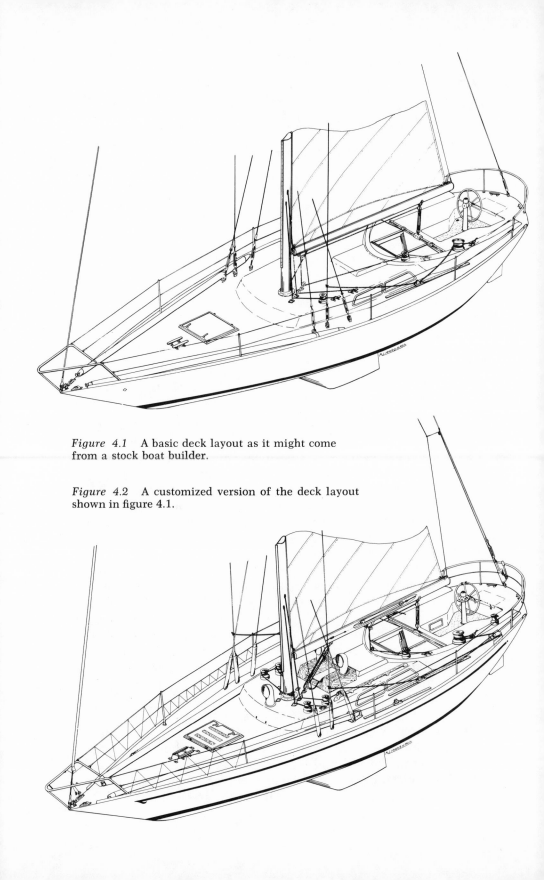

Figure 4.1 A basic deck layout as it might come from a stock boat builder.

Figure 4.2 A customized version of the deck layout shown in figure 4.1.

Improvements in Figure 4.2

- Headfoil added.
- Two pieces of shock cord added to slip over the tack horns and hold the sail tack.
- Pulpit bar and eyes for halyards added.
- Two types of sail nets added on the lifelines. (Note the starboard side is different from the port side.)
- Bow lights raised and integrated into the pulpit for better visibility.
- Deck lifeline added (shown on the starboard side).
- Spinnaker poles moved inside the shrouds for easier handling. (Note the guard on the aft end and the jaws turned down to prevent lines from catching.)
- Guards added on cleats.
- Hatch turned to face aft. (If a sea comes aboard it slams the hatch shut and little or no water goes below.)
- Nonslip added on hatch.
- Dorade vent added in front of mast. (This drains out of the forward side of the cabin top and is removed when racing. If not intended to be removed, it should have a guard.)
- Extra padeyes added.
- Extra winches added.
- Handrails added on the cabin top and inside the companionway hatch.
- Boots added on the shrouds. (These prevent sails from catching and and tearing and also streamline the turnbuckles.)
- Waterproof and watertight mast coat added.
- Vang added.
- Other Dorade vents added, as well as halyard tail box.
- Another heavy weather genoa track added.
- Mainsheet changed and the winch is now self-tailing. (The original cleat could be used for the genoa sheet.)
- Boom outhaul added, with a tackle inside the boom.
- Taglines used instead of stops on the mainsheet traveller, for easier and more precise positioning.
- Stanchion beside the coaming changed to allow it to hinge inboard ten degrees. (This will stop the spinnaker guy from bending it.)
- Genoa sheet footblock added. (The distance between the winch and the footblock should be at least eighteen inches, to allow any twists to come out.)
- Self-tailing spinnaker sheet winches added.
- Compass guard added.
- Small port in cockpit added. (This gives additional light in area of quarter berth.)

- Hydraulic backstay pump added.
- Shock cord taken up backstay to topping lift. (This holds topping lift off leech of mainsail and stops chafe.)
- Crown knot added on steering wheel at top center. (This indicates when the rudder is on centerline.)

Some Common Alterations

POSITIONING EXTRA SHEET TRACK. Before you can install extra sheet track, you must first decide where you want to put it. As illustrated in figure 4.3, most genoa tracks are placed on a line drawn at an angle to the centerline. This angle, which is taken at the tack of the genoa, varies from seven to twelve degrees, depending upon which sail is to be sheeted. For staysails the angle varies between six and nine degrees. Of course, you may want to remove your existing fore and aft track and install athwartship track instead. In this case, you must use on track for each sail of a different L.P. or foot length. Figure 4.4 shows how these tracks are laid out.

By using table a in figure 4.3, you can measure aft from the tack fitting and determine exactly where a new track should be located relative to the centerline. You may want to make some adjustment, however, to avoid placing the track over a coachroof or cabin top. This is especially important for genoa sheet track, since loads can be great enough to rip a track off a cabin top. Loads on a staysail sheet are not as high, so staysail track can be sited here. But be careful not to put it near a window, for if the cabin top lifts, the window frame may leak.

POSITIONING STAYSAIL TACK TRACK. It is often useful to install a piece of track for the staysail tack, but as with sheet tracks, its position must be carefully considered. For one thing, the position can vary, depending upon who your sail maker is, so check with him before drilling holes in the deck. In most cases the staysail is tacked at thirty-five to forty percent of J forward of the mast fitting. But if there is a hatch at this location, the track must be placed either fore or aft of it. Always be sure your staysail maker knows the track will not be sited exactly where it normally is, so that he can cut the sail accordingly. Figure 4.5 shows the most common positions for staysail tack tracks.

POSITIONING EXTRA PADEYES. Most stock boats do not come with extra padeyes near the mast, nor are there usually padeyes for runners, storm jibs, vangs, and so forth. These the owner must install himself. Figure 4.6 gives some of the places where padeyes might be needed.

Figure 4.3 Various genoa sheet track positions, showing the angles at which they are set. Table a gives the distances to measure from the centerline in order to obtain the required angle.

ANGLE θ	DISTANCE a	b
6°	1.25"	1.00
7°	1.46"	1.0'
8°	1.67"	1.0'
9°	1.88"	1.0'
10°	2.08"	1.0'
11°	2.29"	1.0'
12°	2.49"	1.0'

TABLE a

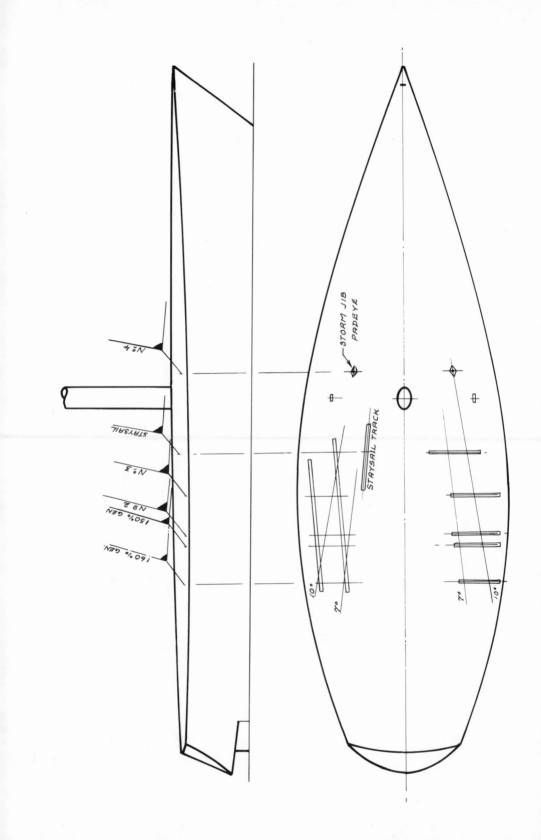

Figure 4.4 (facing page) When positioning genoa sheet tracks longitudinally, the spot where the sheet contacts the deck provides a good initial reference point. The track should then be carried both forward and aft of that point to allow the sail to be trimmed.

Figure 4.5 The staysail track can be located either on the centerline or athwartship. With an athwartship arrangement, the luff of the staysail can be moved to follow the movement of the spinnaker pole.

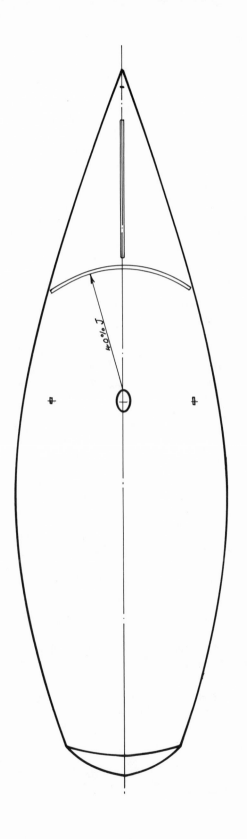

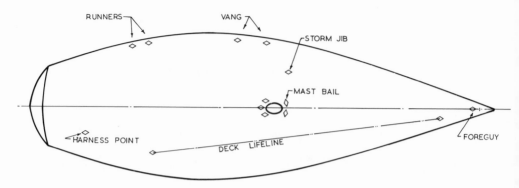

Figure 4.6 Some possible locations for extra padeyes.

POSITIONING EXTRA GRABRAILS. Grabrails are in short supply on many stock boats, and some boats come with no rails or handholds at all. If you want to add your own, carefully think through where they will be used most frequently. A multitude of ill-positioned rails is an eyesore and an annoyance. Figure 4.2 shows two of the most common positions—along the cabin top and inside the hatch. These have been found from experience to provide just the right grip at the right time. If interior grabrails are also called for, an easy solution is shown in figure 4.7.

BOLTING GEAR DOWN. On most stock boats, simply bolting a track, padeye, rail, or cleat to the deck is not enough. Almost all fiberglass decks are made of a balsa or foam core sandwiched between two layers of glass, and this material is not strong enough to fasten deck gear securely. Even if you don't crush the deck yourself when tightening the bolts, the upward pull on the fitting will probably do a good job of it for you. Consequently, some form of reinforcement is required.

There are many ways to reinforce a deck. One is to cut away the deck from underneath and fill the space with solid glass or a piece of hardwood, as illustrated in figure 4.8. Another is to insert a compression tube around each bolt; this technique is shown in figure 4.7. Whichever method you choose, remember to install local reinforcing plates or washers to help distribute the load over the surrounding material. Also remember to fill any holes or cracks with a waterproof sealant, to prevent moisture from getting into the balsa core and causing delamination.

ADDING EXTRA VENTS. Stock boats often have inadequate ventilation. If this is a problem on your boat, the only remedy is to add another vent or two. From my experience, a boat that will be sailed in very warm weather should have one six-inch vent per berth. This, of course, is a maximum. Every owner should consider where and when he intends to sail his boat in order to determine how much ventilation is necessary.

As to where to position vents, a word of warning: do not site them directly over a berth. A wash of water down the vent can drench a sleeping crewman, or at the very least it can make bedding too wet to be habitable. Be sure to consider heel angle, too. A vent that is not above a berth when the boat is upright may be directly overhead when the boat is heeled.

Vents come in many different styles, but the best known are probably the Dorade and Tannoy types. If you wish to install a Dorade vent, first purchase the cowl and then make the box to suit it. Figure 4.9 shows a section through a typical Dorade vent box. With proper

Figure 4.7   A handrail can be positioned both above and below deck. This reduces the number of bolts and holes in the deck.

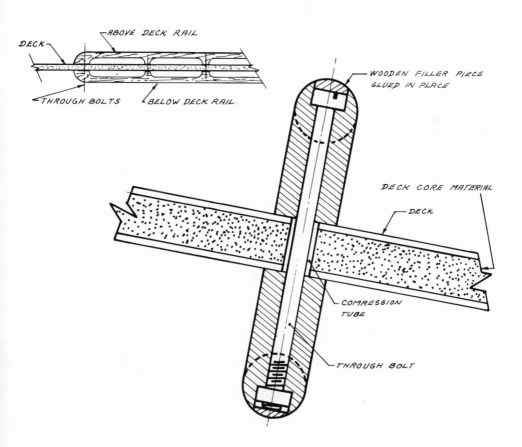

Figure 4.8   Methods of reinforcing the deck under a padeye.

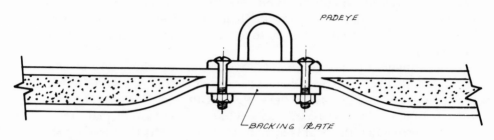

4.8*a* The core material has been removed entirely and more fiberglass has been laid in the recess. This is a good way to avoid having exposed bolts become "head-knockers."

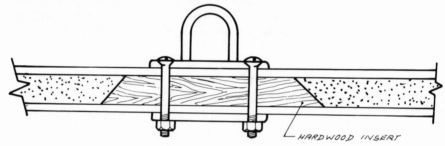

4.8*b* A piece of hardwood has been inserted in the core and glassed over.

Figure 4.9   Two cross-sections through a Dorade vent. The cowl may be extended down (dashed line). Also, a mesh or screen may be fitted over the deck hole to keep out insects.

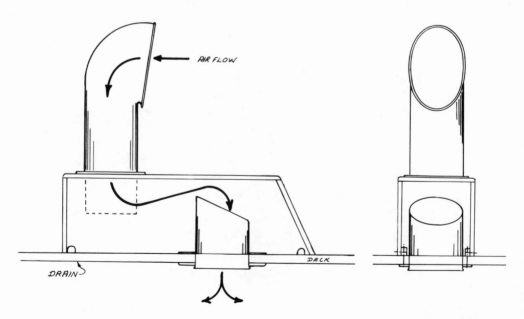

design, the side of the box can have a place for stowing winch handles, blocks, and other gear.

ADJUSTING WINCH HEIGHT OR ANGLE. Often a stock boat winch doesn't quite have a fair lead from a particular turning block, in which case the height or angle of the winch may need adjustment. To do so, first remove the winch drum and then the bolts holding the winch to the deck. Next, insert a piece of hardwood between the winch and the deck, to raise or tilt the winch as required. Figure 4.10 shows how. Of course, if the winch lead is fair in one situation but not in another, it probably makes more sense to remove and refit the appropriate turning block.

Analyzing Your Deck Layout

As you can see, many alterations can be made to an existing deck layout quite easily and inexpensively. All you need is a good eye for problem areas and some basic knowledge of how to get the job done.

Figure 4.10   Sheet lead a will almost certainly result in riding turns. Lead b is much better, but if it is not possible to obtain, then the winch may have to be repositioned, using a hardwood wedge, as shown in c. Drawing d shows the ideal angle for a sheet to approach a winch—aboupt 95 to 110 degrees.

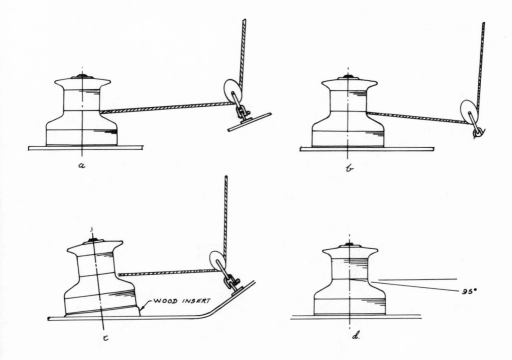

To begin analyzing the inefficiencies in your own deck arrangement, it may help to look back at figures 4.1 and 4.2 and compare the stripped-down version with the customized one. The improvements are summarized in the accompanying checklist. If any of them apply to your boat, you might consider some possible changes next season.

Another way to evaluate the deck layout of your stock boat is to compare it with some of the latest custom designs. To some extent, of course, this is an unfair comparison. A stock boat was never intended to be a grand prix racer. Still, some of the simpler features one sees on the decks of the best custom boats can be installed on a stock boat with less cost than one might expect. In the following pages I'll review some recent trends in custom deck layout. Depending upon his sailing needs and the limits of his pocketbook, each stock boat owner can decide for himself which, if any, might be suitable for his own boat.

State of the Art in Custom Design

In the last few years almost every major regatta has seen its share of innovations in deck and rig design. Even the casual observer notices the lighter spars, the new headstay foils, the increased use of hydraulics and linked winch systems. The experienced racing sailor, of course, notices much more. Improved headsail tacks, streamlined fittings attached to the mast, dinghy-type extensions on the tiller, larger-diameter steering wheels, the use of sheet stoppers, to name a few, are all part of today's racing scene. The deck, it seems, is an area of constant experimentation in the search for greater efficiency and improved boat speed.

WINCHES. When linked winch systems were the latest thing, designers sometimes linked together up to six winches, hoping to be able to apply up to six times the normal power to a single winch. Today, however, this quest for more and more muscle has been greatly curtailed. The reason is the efficiency loss inherent in an elaborate linked winch system. Each drive loses between 8 and 10 percent of its power at the bevel box, so the sixth winch in a six-winch linkage is doing little more than overcoming the efficiency losses of the other five! The latest designs, therefore, tend to limit linkages to two winches, often using a pedestal. Link boxes and chain drives are also becoming more efficient, as manufacturers seek ways to reduce losses with fewer and more efficient bevel drives.

Another efficiency-minded trend in winches is the use of self-tailing devices. Some modern racing boats use self-tailing winches extensively, but often with little thought about the position of the operator. On one boat, the spinnaker pole topping lift, foreguy, and afterguy, winches were all self-tailing, but a crewman would have needed eight-foot arms to operate any two simultaneously. This kind of design oversight unfortunately defeats the major purpose of self-tailing winches—to reduce the number of winch operators required. Thus, when self-tailing winches are used for the spinnaker topping lift, downhaul, and afterguy, all three winches should be placed within the operator's reach, as shown in figure 4.11.

Are sheet and halyard jammers gradually replacing some of the winches on top-class racing boats? This appears to be the current trend. But some riggers have reservations. Holding a sail only with a jammer or lockoff can be a dangerous practice, because the rope may slip. Also, jammers usually work on rope, not wire, so either a rope-to-wire splice or an all-rope halyard is required. Most sailors would agree that these alternatives are not very seamanlike or efficient.

Figure 4.11   A winch layout that places the topping lift, foreguy, and afterguy winches well within a single crewman's envelope of reach.

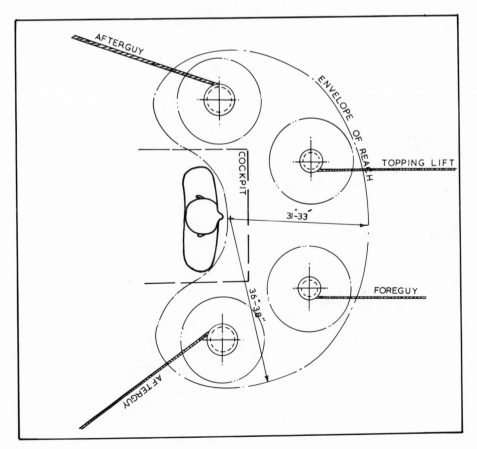

IN THE COCKPIT. One trend in deck layout is obvious to anyone who has observed racing boats over the years. Today's cockpit is no longer the place of shelter from the elements than the old, deep cockpit used to be. On most of the latest designs, cockpits are simply shallow pits used to position winches and other gear at the best height for operating efficiency.

Of course, cockpit size varies tremendously—from a mere foot-well to a space that appears to occupy half the boat. My own opinion is that cockpits on smaller offshore racers or ton cup boats should be no larger than absolutely necessary. A small cockpit gives more working area on deck and more interior space below. And with modern foul-weather gear, there is no longer a need for the cockpit to provide shelter for the crew on relatively short races. But on boats intended for the transatlantic or round-the-world races, a larger cockpit makes more sense. On a long ocean crossing, shelter from the elements can lessen fatigue, and a secure position for the men on watch is essential.

Other design changes have been going on within the cockpit. Take, for example, steering wheels and tillers. Gone are the small-diameter wheels of years past. In their place we see wheels of sixty to seventy inches in diameter recessed into the cockpit sole. The aim is to get the helmsman further outboard, where he can see the sails and seas. For the same reason, tillers now have long dinghy-style extensions, and large cockpits are fitted with footrests on which the helmsman sitting outboard can brace his feet.

In addition, the forward end of the cockpit is now becoming the control center of the boat. Sophisticated instrumentation, hydraulics, and other controls are all being sited there, mainly because this location offers easy crew access and good visibility. But when positioning instruments here, care must be taken so that the crewmen do not obstruct the helmsman's line of sight.

MASTS AND RIGGING. Most of the deck layout changes discussed so far have taken place rather gradually over the past several years. At the most recent regattas, however, masts and rigging seem to have undergone a sudden, dramatic change. Spars have become a lot thinner, and three and four spreaders are now being used to obtain the required stiffness. Instead of a fifth spreader at the level of the gooseneck, the more extreme of the new rigs have above-deck wires or alloy support tubes to absorb some of the vang and gooseneck compression loads. These supports may or may not be hydraulically operated.

Multiple-spreader rigs have several major advantages. The thinner, lighter mast tube reduces windage and weight aloft. And the mainsail is more efficient, both because there is less mast in front of it and because it is easier to bend the mast in a fore and aft direction. Still, multiple-spreader rigs also present some problems. For one

Figure 4.12 Lightness is in this year—even to the point of drilling holes in the boom. Note the above-deck mast strut and the hydraulic vang.

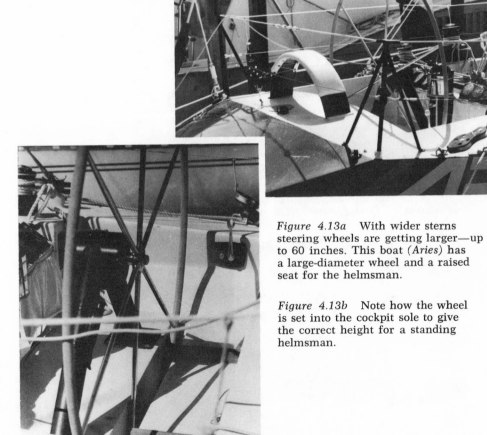

Figure 4.13a With wider sterns steering wheels are getting larger—up to 60 inches. This boat (Aries) has a large-diameter wheel and a raised seat for the helmsman.

Figure 4.13b Note how the wheel is set into the cockpit sole to give the correct height for a standing helmsman.

thing, they must be set up very carefully, with all shrouds under tension. Thus, while the aft lowers on a single spreader rig are often left a little slack to allow the mast to bend slightly, a multiple spreader rig bends so easily that any slackness in the shrouds may cause it to get out of column and collapse .

In the spring of 1978 the International Technical Committee (ITC) moved to restrict some of the latest extremes in rig design. The

Figure 4.14   Mr. Jumpa's cockpit is so wide that "footstools" have been used to help the helmsman maintain his balance when he is sitting out.

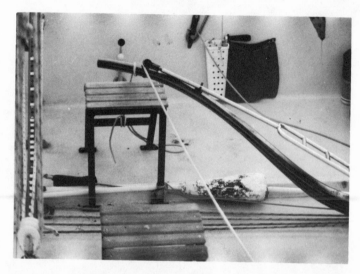

Figure 4.15   The spinnaker pole is stowed on the boom, dinghy style, on the light-weight *Mr. Jumpa.*

Figure 4.16 Light, small-diameter spars must be set up in tension. This is a triple-spreader rig set up for maximum bend, which gives a very flat mainsail.

Figure 4.17 Multiple sheet stoppers enable fewer winches to do more jobs. But each stopper should be clearly labeled.

rule now says that rigging cannot be attached to the mast below 25 percent of IOR Mast Height (I). (This is equal to the top of the spinnaker pole track.) It also says that no rigging other than the headstay and backstay can be attached to the mast in a fore and aft direction above 75 percent of *I*. With these changes to the rule, it is now very difficult for designers to create masts with more than three sets of spreaders.

In addition to innovations in the thickness and weight of spars and in the number of spreaders, mastheads, too, have undergone change. Usually, the two spinnaker halyards are now incorporated into the sheave box on each side of a single centerline genoa halyard. Either wing halyard can also be used for the genoa.

HYDRAULICS. By now hydraulics have become virtually essential equipment on modern racing boats. When rigs have multiple spreaders, hydraulics are the only way to make quick and easy adjustments under heavy load. But how far is enough in the use of hydraulics? One boat at the 1978, Southern Ocean Racing Circuit (SORC) had hydraulics on the headstay, the backstay, the vang, two babystays, two lateral mast support tubes, the daggerboard, and the mast partners. All that is needed now is a hydraulic reaching strut! Some people

Figure 4.18 Looking up a four-spreader rig with supports at the gooseneck (A), twin babystays (B), and double runners (C).

Figure 4.19 To lower windage, the shroud attachment points on *Evergreen* have been taken below deck.

Figure 4.20 The unusual transom of *Flying Goose*, Bob Derektor's new boat. Notice the exposed quadrant for ease of repairs and the sixteen-part backstay tackle.

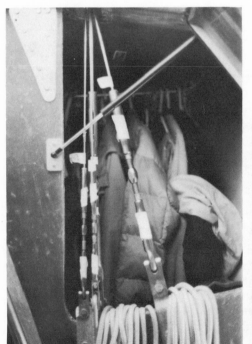

Figure 4.21 (above, left)   A four-spreader rig on *Bay Bea*. Note the relative size of the spreaders and their height. Compare this rig with the triple-spreader rig alongside.

Figure 4.22 (above right)   As masts become thinner and hydraulic vangs increase the loading at the gooseneck, mast struts are being used to counter the increased loads.

Figure 4.23   *Evergreen*'s hydraulic console.

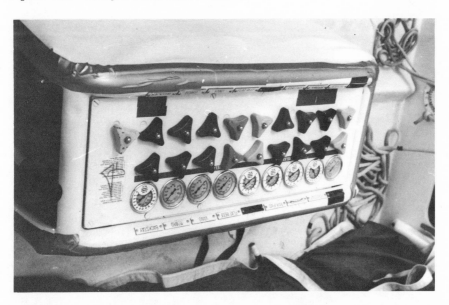

foresee a possible period of retrenchment, as designers seek to restore a balance between the use of hydraulics and the use of blocks and tackles. The ITC has tried to encourage such a move by ruling that the forestay must be fixed while racing, except on rigs with clearly swept-back spreaders (Bergstrom & Ridder rigs).

The Future

What will the next innovations in deck design be? As racing becomes more competitive, decks will inevitably become more efficient and lighter. So expect to see single pieces of gear fulfilling multiple functions, equipment that can be mounted quickly and less expensively, and increasingly efficient winches, perhaps even hydraulic ones.

5 *The Navigation Area*

Look at the interior plan of any boat and you'll probably find that the navigation area is merely a chart table and a seat. From these simple beginnings, the finished navigation area gradually develops—often in a piecemeal fashion. The builder adds a locker or two to hold instruments. The owner adds a small shelf for essential books. And the navigator, being adaptable, as most human are, accommodates himself to whatever ill-designed features his new home may have.

Most people would agree that this is not the best way to go about creating one of the most important areas in the interior of a racing boat, yet this is, in fact, how many of them are designed. I'll now look at two basic questions that must be considered when planning an efficient navigation area. The first is the matter of efficient use of space: how can the features essential to a navigator best be fitted in the limited room available? The second is the matter of ideal location: where in a boat is the most efficient place for a navigation area to be positioned? The following pages give some broad guidelines for answering both these questions. In the process, an owner may get some specific ideas for improving the navigation area on his present boat.

How Should Space Be Used?

The only way to begin to answer the question of efficient use of space is to list the essential features a navigation area should have. These are:

1. A place large enough to lay out charts and plot courses.

2. A place to keep charts not in use, preferably unrolled.
3. A place to stow pencils, protractors, dividers, and other small navigation tools where they can be easily located and reached.
4. A place to stow the sextant, signal flags, foghorn, and other larger
   navigation tools where they are easily accessible.
5. Places to position such instruments as the speedometer, log, echo
   sounder, loran, radio, radio telephone, and navigator's compass
   where they can easily be seen and used.
6. A place for the navigator to sit—or at least a place where he can
   hold himself securely in a rough seaway.

The next step, of course, is to consider how each of these needs can
best be met within the space limitations imposed by the particular
size of a boat.

A PLACE TO PLOT COURSES. Since charts of United States waters
vary in size to begin with, and since a navigator can usually work on
a folded chart, there is no "correct" size for a chart table. The guiding
factor is the amount of space available. Assuming that the average
chart is about twenty inches by forty inches, an acceptable chart table
on a boat of about thirty feet or less might be as small as twenty
inches by twenty inches. British Admiralty charts are all twenty-eight
inches deep and are folded so that they are twenty and a half inches
wide, no matter how wide the unfolded chart may be. Thus a table
twenty-two inches by thirty inches would suit both countries; twenty-
four by thirty-two is possible. A table of this size is easily within the
navigator's area of reach, as shown in figure 5.1. A maximum-sized
chart table is probably two and a half feet by four feet.

Figure 5.1 The
navigator's area
of reach.

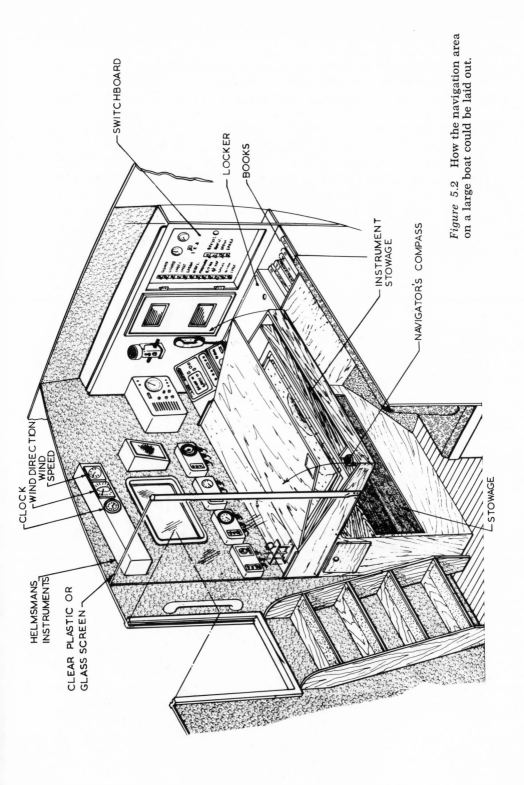

SWITCHBOARD

LOCKER

BOOKS

INSTRUMENT
STOWAGE

NAVIGATOR'S COMPASS

STOWAGE

CLOCK
WIND DIRECTION
WIND SPEED

HELMSMANS
INSTRUMENTS

CLEAR PLASTIC OR
GLASS SCREEN

Figure 5.2 How the navigation area
on a large boat could be laid out.

In addition to differences in feasible dimensions, the surface used for a chart table also varies depending upon the size of the boat. Compare, for example, figures 5.2 and 5.3. The first shows a large, fixed chart table which might be found on, say, a fifty-footer, while the second shows a more modest arrangement, suitable for a boat of under thirty feet. The main dining table also provides a work area for the navigator. And in extremely confined spaces, a portable navigator's box, like the one shown in figure 5.4, offers an adequate plotting surface. A chart can be taped to the inside of the plexiglass lid and a grease pencil used to lay off the course. This box has the advantage of being able to be used anywhere on the boat, including the cockpit. Whatever your space limitations, then, there is usually some way of providing the surface area needed to lay out a chart and plot a course.

Figure 5.3   How a navigation area might be fit into a boat under thirty feet.

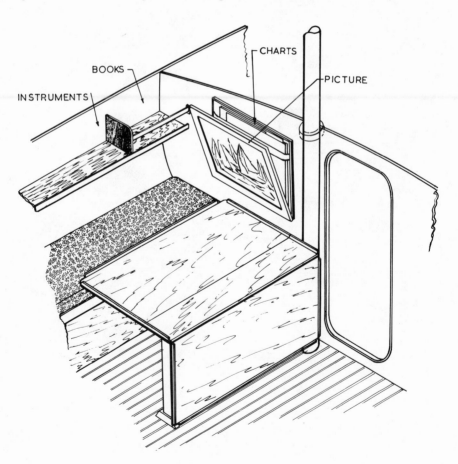

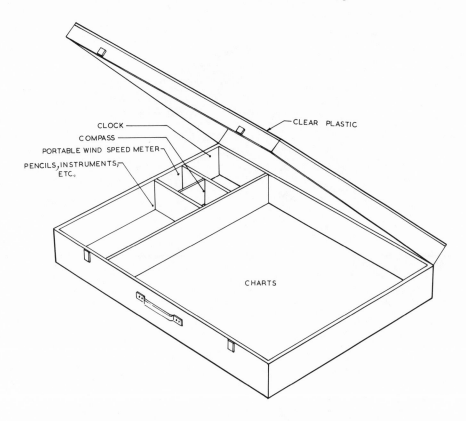

CLOCK
COMPASS
PORTABLE WIND SPEED METER
PENCILS, INSTRUMENTS, ETC.,
CLEAR PLASTIC
CHARTS

Figure 5.4 A portable "plotting box," designed by the author.

A PLACE TO STOW CHARTS. Usually a chart table is designed with a lifting top, like the one in figure 5.2. Charts are then stowed in the area inside the table, which is between three and six inches deep. If there simply is not enough space under the work top for this kind of arrangement, several alternatives are possible. Charts might be folded and stowed under a berth, or they might be kept in a hinged-panel compartment on a bulkhead, as illustrated in figure 5.3. Then too, they might be stowed rolled in a locker behind a berth, as in figure 5.5 The major drawback to this solution is that charts which have been rolled are different to keep flat when in use.

A rather good idea, often seen on Camper & Nicholson and Nautor boats, is to laminate the most frequently used chart onto the top of the table. All the navigator then needs when sailing in home waters is a grease pencil and a cloth for erasing his plots. This, however, does not eliminate the need for stowing less frequently used charts.

A PLACE TO STOW SMALL TOOLS. Pencils and dividers can usually be stowed in a wooden holder like the one in figure 5.6. This drawing

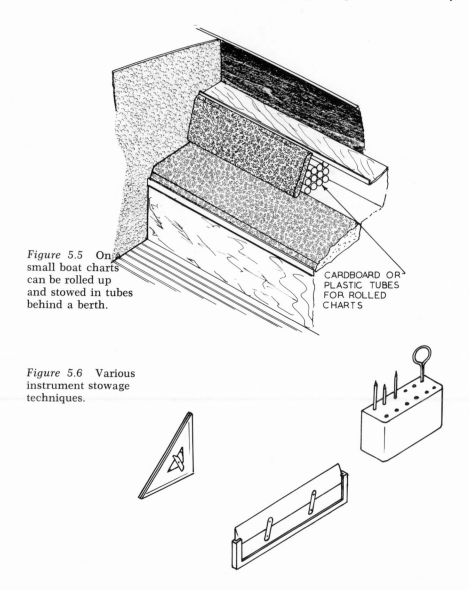

Figure 5.5   On a small boat charts can be rolled up and stowed in tubes behind a berth.

CARDBOARD OR PLASTIC TUBES FOR ROLLED CHARTS

Figure 5.6   Various instrument stowage techniques.

also shows ways to stow other small navigation tools on a bulkhead, when there is no suitable compartment under the lid of the chart table. When positioning such holders, though, it is extremely important to consider the navigator's area of reach. Speed and efficiency are obviously lost if a navigator must get out of his seat every time he simply wants a triangle or parallel rule.

PLACES TO STOW LARGER EQUIPMENT. The sextant poses special stowage problems since it must be kept in a place where it can be reached at a moment's notice and yet will not be easily damaged. On many boats, accessibility means inadequate security, and vice versa. The outboard locker in figure 5.2 is one place where a sextant might be stowed for both good access and good protection.

Other pieces of navigation gear, such as signal flags, the foghorn, and the radar reflector, are commonly stowed under the navigator's seat. But think how much better organized the navigation area would be if these had specially-designed stowage places of their own. In figure 5.2, for example, the the stowage compartment under the chart table might be fitted with holders for individual items.

PLACES TO SITE INSTRUMENTS. Most navigators seem to prefer that all electronic gear be clustered around the chart table. On larger boats, like the one in figure 5.2, such an arrangement is feasible. Virtually every instrument the navigator could want is directly in front of him. But a navigation area need not be crowded with electronics in order to be efficient. On smaller boats, where the navigator's space is more limited, only key instruments need be sited around the

Figure 5.7 The navigation area on an Admiral's Cup boat. Note how everything is within easy reach of the navigator—even his choice of reading matter.

Figure 5.8 The chart on this quarter-tonner has been taped to the hatch top to avoid having the navigator's weight below deck and in the wrong place.

chart table—and these can be positioned to one side if necessary. If the navigation area shown in figure 5.3, for example, the hull speed, wind speed, and wind angle indicators, and perhaps the depth sounder, might be located on the cockpit bulkhead to the navigator's right.

A SEAT FOR THE NAVIGATOR. A navigator spends a great deal of time at his chart table, so if at all possible he should be given a comfortable place to sit. On larger boats this is not difficult. The navigator almost always has a separate seat with a cushion, backrest, and its own safety harness. On smaller boats, however, the navigator may be forced to make do with the edge of a berth as he lays out his charts on the dining table. And in the tightest of accommodations he may even find himself plotting a course on the top of the ice chest, using the cook's harness for safety in rough weather. Obviously, the amount of comfort provided varies greatly with the size of the boat. But in all cases, every effort should be made to make the navigator's position as secure as possible, so that he will not have to spend half his energy simply holding himself steady.

Where Should the Navigation Area Be Sited?

After the question of how the navigator's space can be used most efficiently comes the question of where the entire navigation area should be sited. The ends of the boat, where motion can be quite violent, should definitely be avoided. The steadiest location is in the middle of the boat on the centerline.

Often, however, interior design considerations and personal preferences override the importance of achieving minimum motion and the navigation area is located elsewhere. On many fiberglass boats, for example, it is sited opposite the galley, which has several advantages. First, this arrangement allows the bulkheads on either side of the boat to be spaced symmetrically, thus offering greater structural strength; and second, it gives the cook an additional table top

Figure 5.9 The navigation area aboard a Swan 47. Note the switchboard's clear plastic door to keep out spray. There is plenty of storage space for books and instruments where the navigator can easily reach it. But the RFD compass would benefit if the earphones were stowed elsewhere.

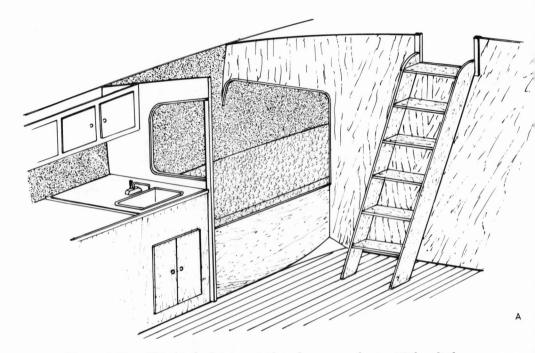

A

Figure 5.10a This kind of corner is found on many boats. With a little ingenuity, it can be turned into an adequate navigation area.

Figure 5.10b The same corner redesigned. A chart table has been added, supported by a stanchion, and a clear plexiglass panel separates the area from the companionway. The main purpose of this panel is to keep spray and rain off the chart table, but it can also serve as a place to mount instruments or tape the race instructions.

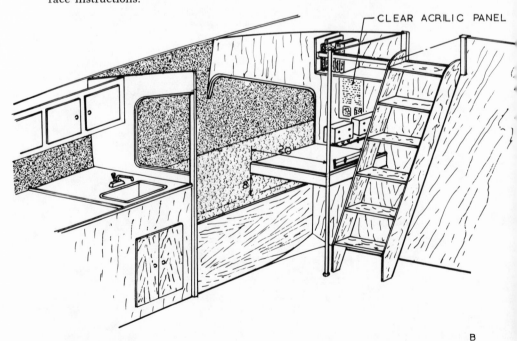

CLEAR ACRILIC PANEL

B

near the galley on which to work. Alternatively, on some motor sailers and large yachts with enclosed cockpits, the navigation area is sited directly in the cockpit. This layout, of course, has the advantage of allowing the helmsman also to plot courses.

Whichever site is eventually selected, an additional question must be answered. Should the chart table face outboard or in a fore or aft direction? Facing outboard has one major drawback: as the boat heels, the navigator often finds his charts and equipment either dropping into his lap or sliding away from him. For this reason, many navigators prefer to work on a table that faces fore or aft. Figure 5.2 shows an aft-facing arrangement. It has the added benefit of being

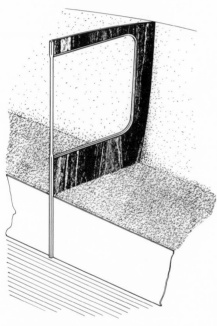

Figure 5.11a A long quarter berth is another possible site for a navigation area.

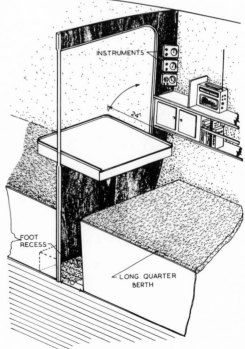

Figure 5.11b The finished conversion. The berth has been shortened and a foot well added. The chart table can swing up in a vertical position when not in use. If desired, a drop-in cushion could be used to restore the berth to its original length when the navigator is not working at the chart table.

located close enough to the companionway so that the navigator can easily communicate with the helmsman.

From a series of sometimes large, sometimes small decisions, a navigation area is gradually built up. An owner's preferences naturally play a large part in this decision-making process. But personal preference alone is not always a sufficient guide to achieving an efficient layout. Some knowledge of the principles of good design is also needed. By carefully considering fundamental design questions before construction begins, an owner may be able to avoid some of the many common errors that make the job of the navigator more frustrating than it need be.

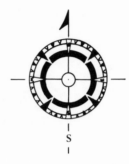

6 *Galley Design*

When man first went to sea, mealtime must have been a rather dull affair. Having no means of cooking aboard, seamen had to be content with dried food, or perhaps some raw fish—not much more. The addition of a brazier carried in the forepeak must have been considered an impressive invention, for a crew could now prepare meals, however modest, over an open fire. This simple arrangement endured for many centuries, but as men began venturing farther and farther from shore, building themselves larger and more sophisticated ships, galleys, too, began to grow more elaborate. By the eighteenth and nineteenth centuries, European war ships had monstrous iron stoves on which the crew's meals were prepared. Granted, means of storage were still very limited, and food could grow moldy on especially long voyages. But all in all, the sea-going gourmand had come a long way.

The twentieth-century galley has come even further. All-electric, microwave ovens have replaced cumbersome iron stoves; well-stocked freezers have been substituted for the traditional barrel of salted beef. But because of the many conveniences often demanded by today's cooks, galley design has become increasingly difficult. More and more features and appliances must be packed into a small area, without compromising the efficiency of the work space. In this chapter we will review some of the factors that must be considered in planning the galley on a modern boat, as well as some of the possible solutions to basic galley design problems.

Fundamental Considerations in Galley Design

The first thing a designer must consider before beginning to plan a galley is obviously the size of the boat. The features that can be incorporated into the galley of an eighty-footer are almost unlimited, while those that can be fitted into a quarter-tonner are restricted. Over the middle range of sizes, however, say thirty to forty-five feet, galley design possibilities are fairly similar, and intelligent planning can make the most of them.

After size, the purposes for which the boat will be used are the next morst critical factors affecting galley layout. One important question is whether the boat is intended strictly for racing, strictly for cruising, or some of both. Different answers mean different solutions to certain basic design problems, such as where to locate the galley and how much space to allot to it.

On a strictly racing boat, for example, the hull shape, sail plan, and deck arrangement take priority over the interior layout, and within the interior itself, the navigator's area, the sail stowage bins, the berths, and the gear lockers all take precedence over the galley. Consequently, the galley on a racing boat is often a conglomeration of odd corners with very little work space. On a strictly cruising boat, in contrast, the interior layout often has a higher priority than any other aspect of the boat, and below deck the galley is second in importance only to the dining and social areas. The result is a generous-sized, fully-equipped work space with numerous special features. In between these two extremes, of course, is the galley on the boat intended for both racing and cruising. It may not be as cramped and spartan as its counterpart on the ocean racer, but it is also not as large and well fitted out as the galley on the pleasure-oriented cruiser. This, in fact, is the kind of compromise arrangement that the majority of boat owners face.

In addition to the basic issue of whether the owner intends to race or cruise, there are other questions regarding the purposes for which a boat will be used, which can also potentially affect galley design. How long, for instance, will the boat usually be at sea? It is meant primarily for day sailing, for weekend excursions, or for longer trips? And will it usually be sailed by a full complement of crewmen, or mostly by a skeleton crew? Clearly the designer must know the answers to all such questions before he finalizes his general plans for the galley layout.

Solving the Work Flow Problem

With these basic considerations in mind, the next step in galley design is planning the overall arrangement. Where, for example, will the

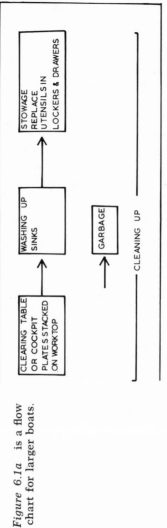

Figure 6.1a is a flow chart for larger boats.

Figure 6.1 Efficient movement of food toward the table for serving and back to the galley for washing up is critical to good galley design.

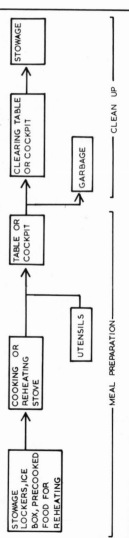

Figure 6.1b is a flow chart for a typical quarter-tonner.

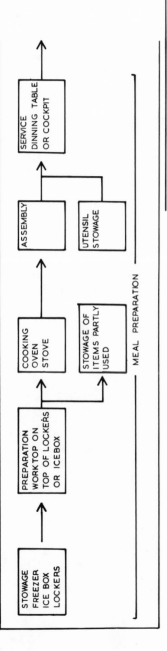

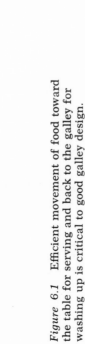

stove be in relation to the sink, or the sink in relation to the icebox? These are essentially problems of designing for good work flow. To solve them, one must take a look at the sequences in which food will be prepared, served, and cleared.

The flow chart in figure 6.1a summarizes these stages as they can typically be handled on most middle-sized boats, those between thirty and forty-five feet. If the galley layout is efficient, food will reach the table hot. This means that the work top where food is put in serving dishes should be next to the dining table. Efficient galley arrangement also requires that the cook be able to prepare food with a minimum amount of wasted effort. Consequently, the ice chest, utensil storage lockers, sink, stove, and counter tops must all be laid out in a way that eliminates extra walking or reaching back and forth. And finally, a good galley must be efficient at cleanup time as well. When the meal is over, it should be possible to stack the dirty dishes, dispose of the garbage, wash up, and put things away with relative ease.

How does the galley on your boat measure up to these standards of efficiency? The answer depends, for one thing, on the basic shape of your galley area. The straight galley, which runs down one side of the boat, is clearly the most inefficient. The L-shaped galley is better, but it too requires a fair amount of walking while preparing food. The best of all galley shapes is undoubtedly the U, in which the cook's movements are reduced to a minimum because everything is within reach and there is no through-traffic, as there is in the straight galley, and possibly even the L-shaped one. The U-shaped galley arrangement in figure 6.2 takes into consideration the work flow sequences in figure 6.1a. The food moves smoothly from the icebox all the way to the table, and almost everything needed is within easy reach of one person.

On a smaller boat, of course, say a quarter-tonner, this type of arrangement would not be possible. That does not mean, however, that the galley of a smaller boat must therefore be inefficient. It simply means that one's expectations are slightly different because of the reduced space the galley occupies. Figure 6.1b maps the work flow in the galley of a quarter-tonner. Of necessity, the stages here are somewhat simplified when compared with those in figure 6.1a. But the incorporation of work flow requirements into the galley arrangement

Figure 6.2 (facing page)   A U-shaped galley on a fairly large boat. Note how the layout takes into account the meal preparation and clean-up sequences in diagram A above. Other good features are the nonslip steps on the ladder (the nonslip mat in the galley is not shown), the drainage grating below the ladder, the protective bar in front of the stove, and the removable fiddles.
Key: A: ice box; B: work top; C: locker; D: assembly work top; E: cutlery drawer; F: garbage can; G: table.

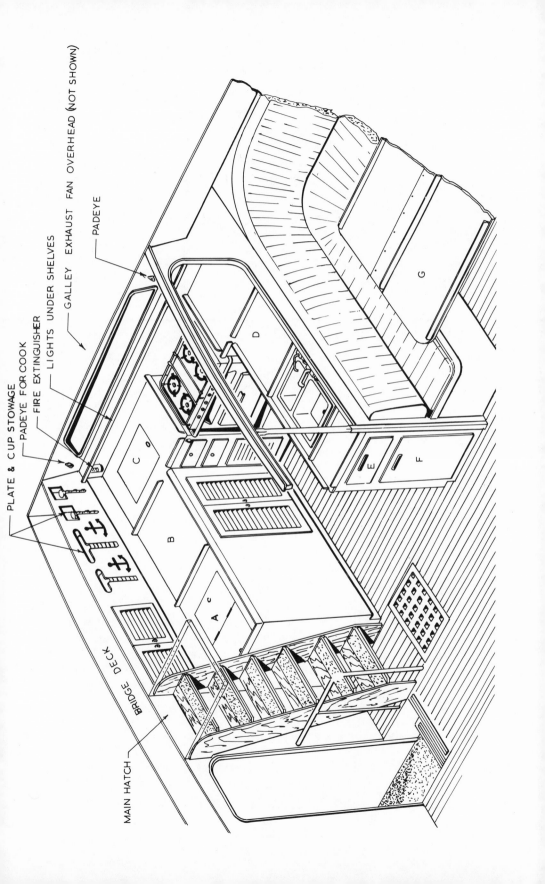

PLATE & CUP STOWAGE

PADEYE FOR COOK

FIRE EXTINGUISHER

LIGHTS UNDER SHELVES

GALLEY EXHAUST FAN OVERHEAD (NOT SHOWN)

PADEYE

MAIN HATCH

BRIDGE DECK

A

B

C

D

E

F

G

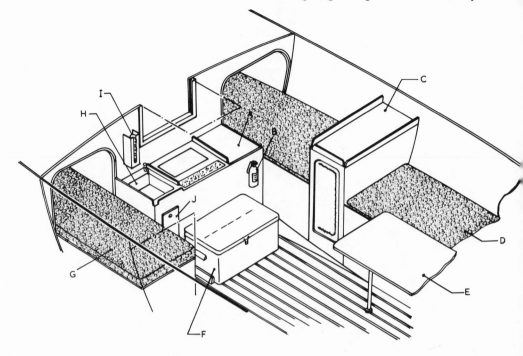

Figure 6.3 The galley layout on a quarter-tonner (twenty-six feet overall).
Key: A: cover over single-burner stove; B: fire extinguisher; C: hanging locker;
D: berth; E: table; F: portable ice box; G: quarter berth port and starboard;
H: sink; I: cup rack; J: trash can.

is exactly the same on a smaller boat as on a larger one. Figure 6.3
is an example of a quarter-ton galley that allows for efficient handling
of food preparation and food serving, as well as cleanup.

Paying Attention to Details

But the best overall layout possible is not enough to make a truly
well-designed galley. Good galley design involves more than simply
solving the problems of work flow and relative placement of different
items. It also involves attention to details—details related to appliances such as the stove or the refrigerator, to work tops and storage
lockers, to lighting and ventilation, and to a number of other special
features, particularly those dealing with safety. Such attention to detail ultimately enables the sea-going cook to function as efficiently as
possible.

Beginning with appliances, consider the stove first. It should be
gimballed, of course, with a damping mechanism, fiddles, and some
arrangement for securely holding pots. It should also have a valve for

shutting off the fuel line. The fuel tanks for the stove should not be located in the galley, but rather in some area accessible from the deck, and they should be vented over the side.

Iceboxes and refrigerators are another important concern. They should have access from the top instead of the side, in order to help maintain coolness. They should also have shelves or racks inside, although these should not extend full width, and perhaps a few lengths of shock cord down one side to help secure large items. Insulation should be from four to six inches thick, and a good drain is needed, leading to its own sump tank or to the bilge. For an icebox, always consider whether or not you can fit a twenty-five-pound block of ice inside. And for a refrigerator, aways note how long it takes to fully cool by running the engine; excessive cooling time may mean too little insulation. If a boat is too small for an icebox to be fitted, perhaps on a quarter-tonner, a portable ice chest can be used instead. Its location can be carefully selected to allow it to serve additional functions—as a seat for the navigator or the cook, for example.

A deep twin sink is very useful on a sailing boat, for washing up as well as simply for putting things in. A sink should be positioned as near to the centerline as possible, to avoid reverse filling when the boat is heeled. If a pressure freshwater system is fitted, it is a good idea to have an emergency hand pump. The economy-minded might want a seawater hand pump as well, which can be used to draw washing water into the sink, thus saving fresh water for drinking and cooking.

The design of counter tops in the galley is also extremely important. All surfaces should be easy to clean and are therefore usually made of stainless steel or formica. Crevices in rear corners can trap and collect food, so these corners should be curved or filled as shown in figure 6.4. Good, deep fiddles should be fitted, leaving a gap at the counter corners so that crumbs can be brushed off. (See figure 6.5.)

Figure 6.4 When food collects in a sharp corner (a) it can cause rot. A rounded corner (b) is much better.

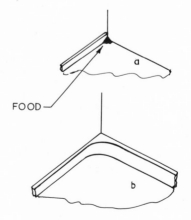

FOOD

Figure 6.5 Some
features that should be
incorporated into a good
galley.
Key: A: rounded corners;
B: trash can; C: no
corner fiddle so that
crumbs can be easily
swept away; D: lift and
pull drawers; E: a toe
recess so the cook can
stand close to the work
top.

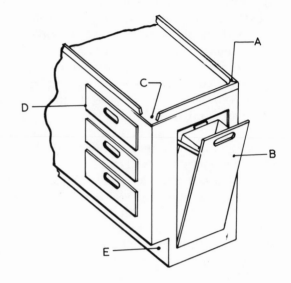

A small toe recess under the counter allows the cook to stand closer
to the work top, and this should add to both comfort and safety. And
finally, to increase the total amount of counter space in the galley,
a formica sink top that matches the surrounding counter is always
helpful, as are slide-out work tops.

Storage space is always in short supply on a boat, and the galley
is no exception. Care should be taken to design lockers, storage bins,
and receptacles as efficiently as possible. One idea for holding plates
and cups is a simple recessed rack. For stowing cans and bottles, a
fiberglass bin can often be shaped to suit the space available under
the cabin sole. Access to the bin is through a lift-out lid in the sole.
The garbage container, which is usually located under a counter, can
be stainless steel or plastic with a watertight cover to shut out smells
and prevent leakage when the boat is heeled. It should be able to hold
standard size garbage bags. An often overlooked point about the
garbage container is that it should have a handle and be completely
removable for emptying and cleaning.

Good lighting is another essential feature of a well-designed galley. Exposed lights, however, are generally a bad idea, because they
can be broken so easily. Hidden lights, fitted under a locker, for example, are far better. Always be careful, too, that galley lighting is not
excessively bright, or it might disturb the sleep of the off-watch crew.

In addition to good lighting, galleys must also have good ventilation. Opening ports provide both ventilation and natural light, but it
is not always possible to fit them, nor is it always possible to leave
them open, particularly in heavy seas. Consequently, cowls or Dorade

vents are a typical feature of most boats. There should be at least one such vent for the galley. On many boats, too, fans are used to draw and circulate the air, and to be effective, these should have an output of at least 150 cubic feet per minute.

Galley stoves often pose special ventilation problems. On many larger boats, the stove has a stainless steel overhead hood leading to a vent, with a fan fitted as an integral part of the hood. There is usually a filter in the system, which should be removable for cleaning. When a hood is not fitted, it is a good idea to position a fan directly above the stove.

And finally we come to the question of safety. What features should be incorporated into a galley arrangement in order to help avoid injury to either the cook or the the boat? For fire safety, a galley fire extinguisher should be positioned in easy reach, and all woodwork close to the stove should be insulated with asbestos or sheathed with stainless steel. For the cook's safety in rough seas, the galley floor should either be nonslip, or (preferably) covered with a cork mat which can easily be removed and cleaned. In addition, strong points for a safety harness should be located in and around the galley, and there should also be overhead grab rails. A protective bar should be fitted in front of the stove to prevent the cook from falling onto a burner, and there is less possibility of injury in a fall if the counter corners are rounded rather than square. Good, secure latches on lockers—not magnetic latches—are also needed to keep dishes, utensils, and food from flying out when the boat hits a large wave. If all these simple safety features are included in the galley design, the end result may still not be ideal, but at least you will no longer find the cook sliding around the galley trying to catch pots and pants as they fly off a wildly swinging stove!

7 / Safety Features

In this modern world it seems that for every activity, no matter how insignificant, there are guidelines for safety. Boating is no exception. Yacht racing especially appears to have a proliferation of committees concerned with safety.

Don't get me wrong. I'm not belittling safety committees. I would gladly create ten more committees if I thought one of them would save a life. What I'm asking, though, is which of the various organizations concerned with safety should sailors take notice of? Does the racing man defer to the Coast Guard edict of no legs over the side? Not in my experience. Does the person who sails on a lake in a sloop rating twenty-one feet use the Offshore Racing Council (ORC) regulations for the one overnight race his club holds per season? Whose safety rules do we adhere to when? And how safe is safe enough?

In the space of this chapter, it would be impossible to describe and evaluate all the safety regulations of different sailing organizations. Therefore, I would like to limit this discussion to the safety rules of the ORC, and hope that all sailors, not only racing men, will take heed of these minimum standards. Ultimately the responsibility for safety rests squarely with you.

Hatches, Companionways, and Ports

The ORC special regulations say that hatches, companionways, and ports must be watertight. But how many really are? I suspect that many boats would be disqualified from racing if the rules pertaining to hatches alone were strictly enforced. One hatch I saw at a recent regatta consisted of a sheet of plexiglass fixed between two pieces of alloy angle. Other poorly designed hatches are shown in figures 7.1a and 7.1 b.

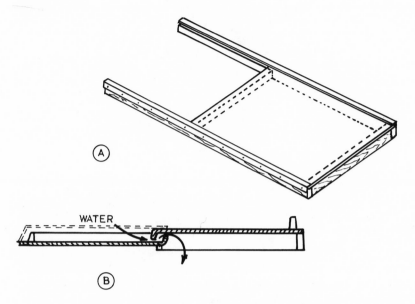

Figure 7.1a This hatch consists of two pieces of alloy angle holding a piece of clear plastic in place. It has no hand grips and would probably fall apart on the first race. *7.1b* This hatch may look at first glance as if it is well made, but water can get in where indicated. The remedy is to fit a cover (shown with a dashed line) over the entire unit.

What makes a hatch truly watertight? The answers differ somewhat, depending upon whether you are talking about a lifting or a sliding hatch. Because lifting hatches are usually located forward, where sea can break over them, they must be particularly leak-proof. Fortunately, there are many good mass-produced alloy lifting hatches on the market, but some people prefer the look of a solid wooden forehatch. Figure 7.2 shows a well-made wooden lifting hatch and a section through it. Note the tightly-fitting inner lip lined with sponge sealer. The water trapped in the interior groove escapes through a small drainage hole. Also note the dodger groove, which extends around the hatch. Like all good lifting hatches, this one should open aft, so that green water breaking over the bow will slam it shut rather than washing below. A good lifting hatch, too, should be able to be opened and locked from both inside and out.

On a sliding hatch, the most critical component is the slide, which must work smoothly and efficiently but without leaking. Figure

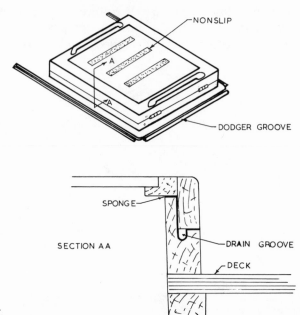

Figure 7.2   A lifting
forehatch and section.

7.3 is a section through a wooden hatch slide, like the kind that might
be found on a custom-built boat. On a GRP boat, the hatch cover
would probably be a one-piece molding. Note, in figure 7.3, the good
fit between the slide mechanism and the hatch. This is an important
feature to look for. Also check that the ends of a sliding hatch close
tightly, allowing water to run off onto the deck rather than into the interior. (This is a problem with the hatch in figure 7.1b, for example.)
And finally, make sure that the cover has drain holes. With design
and construction elements such as these, a sliding hatch should be
reasonably watertight. I have yet, however, to meet an absolutely leak-
proof one.

   Problems of leakage, however, are not due to structural flaws
alone. They can also be caused by poor positioning. One common mis-

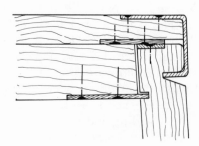

Figure 7.3   A section through
a hatch slide.

take is placing the bottom edge of a companionway hatch too near to the cockpit sole. Figure 7.4 is an example of one such installation. What happen when the cockpit fills? The water goes below faster than it goes out the drains. A companionway hatch should be at least nine inches above the cockpit sole—preferably more. Unfortunately, the ORC does not specify a minimum height-above-sole dimension for companionways, so some manufacturers simply make them level with the sole. The ORC does, however, require that, on boats with cockpits opening aft to the sea, the lower edge of the companionway must not be below the main deck level.

In bad weather, protection against leaking companionways is particularly important. The ORC regulations state that during a storm a boat must have some way of blocking off a companionway to the level of the main deck at the sheerline abreast of the hatch. This is usually done with swash boards. But be careful of the type you use. The hinged kind, shown in figure 7.5a, is not very effective, since it bangs every time the board pitches. The only remedy is to fasten the board tightly with a lock. But who wants to be locked below deck in rough weather? A better solution is illustrated in figure 7.5b. Here two swash boards simply slide in on top of one another, leaving a gap for ventilation above the main deck level.

Figure 7.4   If this cockpit fills, the water will go below before it can drain off.

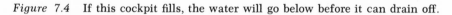

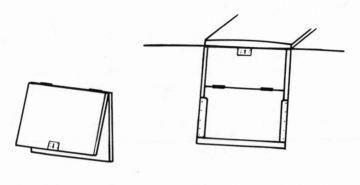

Figure 7.5a A hinged
swash board. If not
locked when closed it
will continually bang
as the boat pitches.

7.5b Swash boards that
simply slide in place,
leaving a gap above for
ventilation.

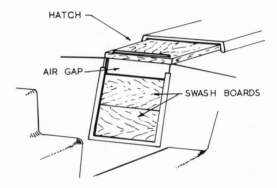

In addition to the danger of water washing below through the
companionway in rough weather, there is also the danger of hatch
windows and ports breaking. This is a possibility no matter what material the windows are made of. Consequently, the ORC requires that
boats carry storm boards for all hatches and ports over two square
feet in area. It is good practice, however, to carry coverings from all
ports. A thin sheet of plywood, with screw holes drilled at intervals, is
best. It can be fastened securely and is easily stowed under a berth
when not in use. Also, label the boards to indicate to which port they
belong, and try them on for fit at the beginning of each season. Remember, you won't be putting a board in place on a warm sunny afternoon. It will more likely be in the middle of a full gale when the boat
is pitching violently.

Although not specified in the ORC regulations, several other
features contribute to making a hatch as safe as possible. One is its
structural strength. A good hatch should obviously be strong enough
to hold the weight of even the heaviest crewman without danger of
breaking. A hatch should also provide the minimum number of obstacles to crew activity. Handles, for example, should be as flush as
possible so as not to snag sheets. And finally, potentially slippery
hatch windows should have nonslip applied to them. The 3 M tape

works well, but there are many other good brands on the market. One-inch-wide strips at six-inch intervals should be adequate.

Of course, when laying nonslip, don't stop with hatches alone. If your boat is fiberglass, as most are these days, you may have many other slippery places. Why not take a look around and apply nonslip where needed. How about a little on the top of the cockpit coaming or around the mast? Think about where you stand when the boat is heeled—one foot in the angle between the side of the coachroof and the deck. How often have you slipped when your foot was there? Remember, you spend more time in the cockpit, so be sure to safeguard the most heavily trafficked areas there. Also, what about the molded, nonslip part of your fiberglass deck? Is it really skid-proof? Why not paint it with a good nonslip deck paint before your next sail?

Cockpits

The ORC requires that a cockpit be a structurally sound, permanent part of the hull which is watertight up to the main deck level. Bow wells, mid-deck crew pits, and stern wells are all considered cockpits, in addition to main cockpits. The ORC specifies maximum cockpit volume below the lowest coaming. If you want to work out the maximum volume for any of the cockpits on your boat, the formula is 6 percent of L x B x FA for boats competing in category 1 events (long races far from shore, such as the Bermuda or the Fastnet, and 9 percent of L x B x FA for all others. The numbers are taken straight off your rating certificate. The ORC also puts a limit on cockpit depth. For all boats, regardless of the type of race in which they sail, the cockpit sole must be at least 2 percent of L above the LWL.

A very important safety requirement is that cockpits be quickly self-draining at all angles of heel. This means that drains must be of adequate size. The ORC regulations state that on newer boats rating twenty-one feet and over, the combined area of cockpit drains must be no less than the equivalent of four drains three-quarter inch in diameter. On boats rating under twenty-one feet (and on larger boats built before 1977 which sail only in short races in protected waters, or on any boat built before 1972), the combined drain area must be at least equal to two drains one inch in diameter.

To see how your cockpit drains measure up, try this simple and often instructive experiment. Turn off the sea cocks and fill the cockpit with water. Note how deep the boat sinks in the water, adding extra for a full crew. Then time the emptying of the cockpit. The results might surprise you. Rod Stephens allows three minutes as the maximum time allowable. Unfortunately, many cockpit drains do not perform this well.

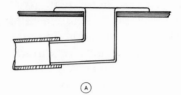

Figure 7.6a Through-hull fittings
like this one will slow water flow.

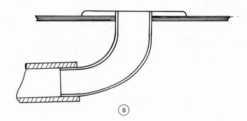

7.6b A better design
for cockpit drains.

Sometimes it is only a sharp bend in the drain that slows emptying. Try to make sure your cockpit drain pipes flow smoothly to the
through-hull fitting, as shown in figure 7.6. And regarding through-
hull fittings, or sea cocks, here are a few things to check. Do you carry
spare hose clips? Do you ever check your hose clips and fastenings?
Do you carry softwood plugs to fill the hole left if sea cock bolts corroded and the sea cock fell out? Don't rely on the odds that these problems won't happen to you.

Lifelines, Stanchions, and Pulpits

For maximum security, taut double lifelines, with the top line no less
than two feet above the deck, should be fitted on boats rating over
twenty-one feet. Boats rating under twenty-one feet only require a

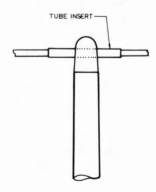

Figure 7.7 A steel tube insert in the
plastic head of a stanchion stops
chafe.

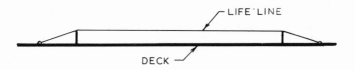

Figure 7.8 Supporting a safety harness lifeline on two posts keeps it clear of the deck.

single line, eighteen inches above deck. All lines, double or single, must be supported by stanchions at intervals not less than seven feet. It has been my experience that the plastic-topped stanchions are sometimes chafed and cut by the lifeline wire. A steel tube insert solves this problem, as shown in figure 7.7. But better still is the stanchion where the wire actually passes through a steel eye. All stanchions should be through-bolted or welded to the deck. If you ever fell heavily against a stanchion, you were probably glad it was securely bolted. In addition, the ORC requires that all boats have a through-bolted or securely welded bow pulpit, as well as a fixed stern pulpit, unless the lifelines around the stern are arranged in a way that adequately substitutes for a pulpit.

One lifeline not mentioned in the ORC regulations is the one that runs along the deck and is fastened securely to a padeye at either end. To my mind, this is ideal for attaching a personal harness to. If it is laid out properly, a crewman can move fore and aft without having to unclip his harness every few feet. A method used on older boats, but not seen often today, is to support the lifeline on two small posts where it is clear of the deck. Figure 7.8 shows how.

Other Equipment

What about some of the other equipment you should have on board to ensure that your boat meets adequate safety standards? The number of bilge pumps required varies depending upon how far from shore a boat will be sailing. Boats competing in longer races should have at least two manually operated pumps, one of which is capable of being worked when all hatches, companionways, cockpit seats, and lockers are closed. On boats entering short races in protected waters, one bilge pump will usually suffice. Remember, too, that bilge pump handles should be kept where they can be easily found. Other equipment that should be handy is a foghorn, a radar reflector, a set of code flags with a code book, and essential navigation gear. Larger boats should have two anchors, both with sufficient cable.

Emergency navigation lights, emergency steering gear, and adequate storm sails are also important, as are tools and spare parts, a radio receiver, and for boats sailing far offshore, a marine radio transmitter. Although some of these items are not usually considered safety equipment per se, each in its own way adds some measure of safety to the boat, and under the right circumstances can help save lives.

The equipment most directly responsible for saving lives, of course, includes such things as horseshoes, man-overboard poles, life jackets, and life rafts. The requirements regarding these items are as important as any set of rules in racing. Although most of this gear may never be used, its proper maintenance and positioning on the boat can literally make the difference between life and death when a serious emergency strikes.

All boats should have at least one horseshoe-type life ring with a light and drogue, positioned within easy reach of the helmsman. Boats entering longer races should also have a second horseshoe aboard, with a whistle, a dye marker, a drogue, a self-igniting high-intensity water light, and a pole with a flag attached. The flag must be able to fly at least eight feet above the water, and the pole must be fastened to the horseshoe with twenty-five feet of floating line.

Figure 7.9   The liferings on this boat are stowed in a handy recessed compartment, where they are easily accessible to the helmsman, yet create little windage.

Because man-overboard poles are so unwieldy, stowing them can pose a problem. Often they are taped to the liferail, where they can easily be knocked off, so many people end up adding more and more tape, until the pole is virtually unremovable. This was the case when I fell off a boat during a race. The boat was 150 yards away before the pole and life ring hit the water. I think a better way to secure the pole is to tie it to the backstay with stopping cotton, or to put it in a plastic tube which can be taped to a lifeline or screwed down to the deck.

One additional point. Do you ever hold a man-overboard drill? In his preseason workup, a skipper would be wise to throw a life ring over the side when the crew is least expecting it and shout man overboard. If anyone grumbles, just let him know that next time it could be he in the water. Man-overboard drills had not been practiced on the boat from which I fell off, and it took the crew a full twenty minutes to come back for me. (They claimed the delay was because they had to vote on whether to turn around and collect me!)

A man overboard is just one type of accident that can happen at sea. In the event that an entire crew must abandon ship, a well-maintained and fully equipped life raft may be their only chance of survival. The ORC specifies that a life raft must be stowed directly on deck, or in a special, easily accessible compartment opening to the deck and containing only the life raft. To meet ORC regulations, a life raft must be able to carry the entire crew even when one buoyancy compartment is empty. It must also be supplied with a variety of equipment, including a sea anchor, an air pump, a signaling light, flares, a repair kit, a baler, two paddles, and a knife. By regulation, life rafts must be inspected every two years, either by the manufacturer or by some competent authority. Also, one should periodically check the gear on board a life raft, such as the flares and signaling light, to make sure they are properly working. As a life raft maker's representative once said: "We seldom get complaints about the ones that don't work!"

To many who are highly concerned with safety, the precautions one can take are almost unlimited. To others, endless rules and regulations can restrict sailing so much that it's no longer fun. There is no reason, however, for safety and pleasure to be incompatible. When sailors observe the rules of good seamanship, safety becomes and integral part of sailing, to the benefit of all concerned.

⑧ Designing Boats for Courses

Designing boats to suit particular courses is nothing new in yacht racing. For years America's Cup boats have been carefully designed to perform well in the expected wind and sea conditions off Newport in September. In offshore racing, however, this kind of approach is not often taken. Granted, through cumulative successes and failures, boats suited to particular courses have gradually evolved. But the kind of systematic analysis of prevailing conditions that precedes the development of twelve meters is seldom done for IOR boats.

Given this situation, several questions naturally arise. If a thorough study of wind and sea conditions were done for an IOR series, what would the "ideal" boat look like? And how similar are existing boats to this optimum design? Are the boats that are closest to it consistently at the head of the fleet? To answer these questions, I analyzed the conditions that generally prevail for the Admiral's Cup series to see what type of boat would be best suited to them. The method outlined here, of course, is not limited to Admiral's cuppers. It can be applied to any boat racing in any area and any series—from boats competing in the SORC off Florida to those competing in the Southern Cross in the waters around Sydney.

Analyzing the Conditions

Prior to the start of the racing season, I collected wind and wave data for the English Channel area. Wave surveys for the Owers Light-

84

ship (a mark of the course for the Channel race), the Varne Lightship, the Lands End (a mark of the course for the Fastest race) were available through the National Institute of Oceanography, Surrey, England. Wind surveys for the Solent conducted at the Calshot meteorological station were available through the Southampton Weather Centre, Hampshire, England. (I felt that these were applicable over the Channel area as well.) The Owners Lightship was near enough to the Calshot station to allow comparisons of wind and wave data.

THE WIND DATA. The wind surveys I obtained were broken down according to the average number of hours per month that the wind blew from any given direction and at any given speed. The data spanned the ten-year period from 1960 through 1969. Using the figures for the months of May to August, the English racing season, I calculated two things: (1) the percentage of time that the wind

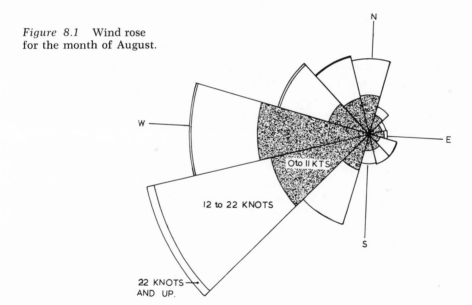

Figure 8.1   Wind rose for the month of August.

Table 8.1   Percentage of hours the wind blew at any given speed.

WIND SPEED	MAY	JUNE	JULY	AUGUST	AVERAGE
0-3	9.6	9.2	8.3	8.6	8.9
4-10	41.9	45.9	49.4	47.9	46.3
11 21	46.6	42.9	41.1	41.8	43.1
22 33	1.9	2.0	1.1	1.6	1.7
34 & OVER	0.1	0.0	0.0	0.0	0.025

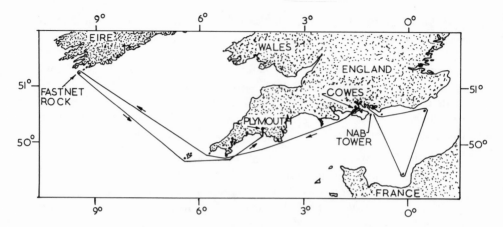

Figure 8.2 The courses. The Fastnet is a 650-mile race around Fastnet Rock off Ireland. The Channel race goes around the Royal Sovereign light tower and either the Cherbourg or Le Havre buoy.

blew from particular directions, and (2) the percentage of time that the wind blew at particular speeds. The first of these I summarized using wind roses, like the one shown in figure 8.1. The second is summarized, for the purpose of this article, in table 8.1. All I needed now was a summary of the courses sailed during the season. This I plotted in the form of course roses.

To illustrate how this various wind and course information can be analyzed, consider the month of August. Figure 8.1 and table 8.1 indicate the most likely wind conditions during this month, while figure 8.2 traces the courses sailed on the Channel and Fastnet races held in August. These course vectors are plotted in the course rose in figure 8.3. The wind and course roses (figures 8.1 and 8.3) can be

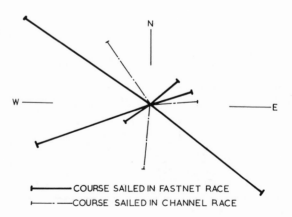

Figure 8.3 Course rose for the Fastnet and Channel races.

superimposed to determine the probability of obtaining a particular wind direction on any given leg of a course.

Notice that the predominant wind direction is from the southwest, with due west being the second most frequent direction. This means that the Fastnet race would usually be a beat to Lands End. A more detailed breakdown of the wind speed data suggests that the wind would most likely be over ten knots but less than eighteen. The greatest possibility of a gale would come from the southwest. Continuing the analysis of predicted sailing angles, from Lands End to the Fastnet and back to the Scilly Islands would probably be a reach with a run for the final leg to Plymouth. Given the predominant wind direction, the Channel race, interestingly enough, would be a reach around the course (which it was in 1973 and 1975), with wind strengths of about ten knots or slightly over. The possibility of the wind becoming more westerly would only serve to ensure a reach. But if the wind backed to southerly (the third highest possibility), the leg across the Channel would be a beat, as happened in 1971. By performing this kind of wind and course analysis for all races held during the four months of the season, I could get a good idea of the various conditions an Admiral's Cup boat would be likely to encounter.

THE WAVE DATA. The next step was to consider the effects of accompanying sea states. Briefly, I used the wind data collected to find significant wave heights from a sea state chart. I then calculated a wave spectrum and compared it with the wave spectrum obtained directly from wave surveys. The two coincided quite closely.

Determining the Best Type of Boat

I was now ready to begin outlining the type of boat most likely to perform well in an Admiral's Cup series. From the wave spectra I had, I determined the added resistance of a boat in a typically encountered seaway. Then, by adding this increased resistance for expected wave conditions to the stillwater resistance, I obtained a total hull resistance. Already knowing the probable wind strength, next used various coefficients to calculate the sail area needed to drive that hull at maximum speed.

As for the ideal size of an Admiral's Cup boat, the smaller boats seem to be best. For one thing, the predicted winds for the English Channel area are fairly light during the racing season, so rig size must increase disproportionately as hull size increases. This and other factors led me to the conclusion that a boat rating between thirty-one and thirty-three feet stands the greatest chance of sailing in conditions that suit her best.

Part IIII

Preparing
for Racing

Introduction

Good preparation is essential to success in any sport, and yacht racing is no exception. Like the football coach who neglects to develop a game plan, the racing skipper who fails to plan ahead can seldom hope to win. To be truly effective, preparation must always be complete. Overlooking one important detail can cost the entire race. A classic example is the owner who spends thousands on new sails but doesn't bother to remove hundreds of pounds of unnecessary gear before the start. The result? A drop in boat speed due to excess weight that could be equivalent to towing a small dinghy!

The following chapters are all concerned with some form of prerace preparation. From reducing drag to tuning a rig, from developing polar curves to getting a crew in shape—all are ultimately reflected in a boat's performance.

9 Preparing for Your First Race

For the boat owner who has never raced before, the initial venture into competitive sailing can be traumatic. The novice racer is almost always certain that his boat is destined to finish at the bottom of the fleet—if not dead last. Sometimes, of course, this gloomy forecast becomes a self-fulfilling prophecy. But the outcome of a first race need not be this discouraging. With careful preparation, even the most inexperienced racing man can approach the starting line with a minimum of trepidation, and perhaps even with enough self-confidence to go on and win.

How prepared are you for your first race? If you've never raced before, you probably don't know the answer to this question, and may even be resigned to letting the race results be your primary guide. Hopefully, this chapter can help you avoid such a trial-and-error approach. In it, I've outlined some of the basic things you can do to get yourself, your boat, and your crew ready for their first major competition.

Several Weeks before the Race

You can hardly begin preparing for a race too early. A number of matters demand your attention at least several weeks in advance. For one thing, you should familiarize yourself with any special race

91

requirements. For instance, the ORC Special Regulations usually apply to races run under the IOR. They cover such items as cockpit and hatch size and construction, lifeline positioning, type and number of bilge pumps, design and stowage of horseshoes and life rafts, essential navigation equipment, and numerous other safety features. The ORC imposes slightly different regulations depending upon the category of race in which a boat competes. Category I events are long races, far offshore, such as the Newport to Bermuda race; category 2 events are also long races, but never far from coastlines, such as the Vineyard or Fastnet races; in category 3 are races inshore or on coastal waters, such as those on Long Island Sound or the Solent; and finally, category 4 consists of short races on lakes or very sheltered waters. You should make certain what category of race you are entering, so that you can fit your boat out accordingly. Even if you are not competing in an IOR event, it is wise for any boat that will be raced regularly to meet these minimum safety standards. In addition to the ORC Special Regulations, the level-rating classes (quarter, half, one, and two ton) have rules governing size of crew, number of sails, and various other factors. Still other regulations may be specified in the race circular, so be sure to obtain a copy early, if possible.

This is also the time to make certain that your boat's equipment is in good repair. Check that your sails are in good condition, and that all deck gear is in top working order. Also see that you have all the sheets, guys, and spinnaker gear you need. If the race is to be overnight, make sure that the ship's lights are functioning, and that you have a sufficient number of properly operating flashlights.

Now that you're checking the condition of your boat, you might consider having a competent designer or sailmaker look over your rating certificate. Sometimes a minor adjustment in some feature can reduce your rating significantly at very little cost. This can only improve your boat's competitive performance.

Finally, don't neglect early planning for crewmen, since they are the people who will ultimately make the difference between winning, just losing, or losing miserably. Compile your list of crew carefully, and double-check that everyone will be available. If you have never raced before on any boat, try to find at least one crewman who has. Also try to locate a good navigator with racing experience. If you are going to navigate yourself, be sure to have up-to-date charts for the areas in which you will be sailing, plus all the necessary tidal information. For a long race, you may also want to read up on weather forecasting. And if you plan to be on the helm at the start, you should read up on the racing rules, too, so that you'll be certain who has the right of way in different situations. No one wants to be disqualified for a rule infringement right at the start of a race.

A Few Days before the Race

As race day approaches, other preparations can be made. First, have the boat hauled out of the water and scrub the bottom of the hull clean. It is surprising how often this seemingly small reduction in hydrodynamic drag can make a difference in close competition. Next, make arrangements to deliver the boat to a marina in the area where the race will be held. If the trip is a long one, you might want to take your full crew along. This offers an excellent opportunity for everyone to learn his way around the boat and for you to try out different sails and settings. Not only will the group have practice working together as a team, they will also have a chance to assess one another's strengths and weaknesses, so that crew duties can be assigned accordingly.

At the Start

After all the effort spent in getting the boat, crew, and yourself ready, make sure you leave for the start with plenty of time to spare. On the way, hold a quick prerace briefing to inform the crew about the course, the expected weather conditions, the watch system, and so forth. If some of the crew are still unfamiliar with the boat, now is your last chance to execute a few trial drills before the race. It is essential that everyone know where the gear is and how it operates, as well as what one another's sailing techniques are, before you hit the race course. And even if you have sailed with one another before, it's a good idea to take this time to practice again.

First sail closehauled, then bear away and set a spinnaker. Gybe a few times and then change back to a genoa. While sailing closehauled check the mast bend and sail shape, making any necessary adjustments. Look at the sheet leads on the genoa. Do they need changing inboard or outboard? Forward or aft? Can you lay the course closehauled? Also check the angle through which you can tack and make a note of it. If you are sailing near a headland, check for windshifts, gusts, and lulls. Advance knowledge of wind patterns in the area may be a big help later.

Next bear away. If this brings you down onto the course, check to see if a reacher or spinnaker will give you more speed. Be sure to try these sails out. If you don't, you could end up making the wrong decision on the racecourse. Sail for a while on the approximate heading for each leg, setting the sails to suit. Provided the wind doesn't change too greatly between now and the race, this practice may give you the kind of slight advantage over your opponents that can put you in the lead.

Now sail to the starting line, arriving about half an hour before your start. If you can, take a bearing on the line and check which end, if any, is favored. Make sure the navigator checks the wind speed and wind angle every few minutes, so that any changes or fluctuations will be noted. Also, watch how the boats in the classes in front of you are starting. Above all, keep clear of the line until it is your time to start, but don't make the mistake of straying too far away. By now, you should have some idea of how you intend to start. So tell the crew! If your start is to be a good one, everyone must be aware of what the strategy will be.

When the class directly ahead of you is away, begin timing your approach to the line. Sail once across the line, and then back to the point from which you intend to start. Sail for the line a second time, seeing how your time compares with your first trial. Again sail back, and if you have time make a third trial approach. If not, try to position your boat exactly where you want it to be when you want it to be there. Now go for the line. If you have done everything right, you should hit the line at maximum speed a split second after the gun goes off.

Of course, all this is easier said than done. One of the most common mistakes is approaching the line too early. But this is easy to correct. Simply ease out the genoa or main and slow the boat. If, on the other hand, you approach the line too late, you can only hope that the race will be long enough to allow you to make up the time. Other difficulties at the start, besides problems of timing, are the obstacles introduced by other boats. Here it is a clear case of knowing the rules. If you're sure you have the right of way, shout loud and hard at the offender. It will psychologically help you and hinder him, and possibly cause him to hesitate just long enough to let you through.

On the Racecourse

You've finally started. Presumably you have no protest flags flying against you, and you're free and away. Now settle down as quickly as possible and concentrate on gaining boat speed. If you are at the helm, let the tactician, not yourself, take a look around to make sure you are clear of any wind shadow from another boat and that you have room to tack if necessary. Tactically, of course, every race is different, so it is virtually impossible to give much more advice in a brief space, but the checklist which follows should help. Just be sure to work your strategy out carefully and do whatever you can to maintain boat speed. A race is seldom won or lost until you cross the finish line.

CHECKLIST

Obtain all necessary information
- the ORC special regulations, if required
- the rules for level-rating classes, if required
- the race circular and other available race information
- the latest copy of the racing rules
- up-to-date navigation charts and tidal information

On the boat, check to see that
- the mast and rig are set up properly
- all running rigging is in good condition
- you have all the sails you need in good repair
- all deck gear and deck lights function properly
- instruments and electronic equipment are in good working order
- all life-saving equipment is in good condition and properly stowed
- no minor adjustments can be made in your rating

Make sure all your crew is available, especially
- the skipper
- the tactician
- the navigator
- the foredeck chief
- the helmsmen
- the cook

Check the following things
- that the bottom of the boat is scrubbed clean
- that you have sent in your entry form, if necessary
- that you have obtained a berth near the race location
- that you have spares aboard for a long race (ripstop, winch pawls, etc.)
- that there is enough engine and cooking fuel aboard
- that the oil levels in the engine are adequate
- that the electrolyte in the battery is OK
- that sufficient grease is on the stern shaft and rudder bearings
- that you know the long-range weather forecast

Make sure that
- all the crew are aboard by counting heads

- all food and gear is aboard
- the bilge is pumped
- the batteries are fully charged
- you have up-to-date weather and sea condition information
- there is enough water and fuel aboard
- the sails are packed properly
- the sheets, guys, winch handles, and blocks are laid out
- everyone who needs them has taken seasickness pills

AT THE START

Do the following

- check the correct course
- check the wind angle and wind speed continually
- run the line and check its angle to the wind
- check the tide from buoys and lobster pots
- get sails up and sail on the first leg of the course, checking sheet leads and sail trim
- make several tacks, holding the boat momentarily into the wind to check the wind angle; these tacks also serve to get crew positions organized
- check the compass heading on each tack and work out the tacking angle
- listen for the gun signals
- observe which boats are doing best in the classes that have already started
- work out your own starting strategy and tell the crew
- make sure all lines are inboard and securely fastened
- try to hit the line at maximum speed

10 *Are You Towing a Dinghy?*

After finishing a race, have you ever launched the inflatable dinghy as you come into the mooring? If so, you know first hand the considerable drag which it exerts on its painter or towrope. Did you ever stop to think that you may also be towing a dinghy around the race course? Not literally, of course. But you may have so much extra gear on board that you have increased your boat's wetted surface by an amount equal to the wetted surface of a dinghy. Although some people may think this highly unlikely, in fact it isn't unlikely at all. In this chapter I'll discuss how a boat's resistance can be substantially reduced, first, by removing excess weight, and second, by keeping the hull fair and smooth.

Reducing Weight and Wetted Surface

Let's consider a typical two-tonner, the owner of which both races and cruises. When the boat is racing, the owner carries a full crew of eight, plus all their personal effects and enough food and sails to cover every contingency. When the boat is cruising, he may carry an outboard barbeque which bolts on the transom, a water hose for marinas that don't have one, awnings, hammocks, and an extra-heavy-duty battery, so that he doesn't have to run his portable generator often. The problem is, he seldom bothers to remove this cruising gear when he races. No wonder he is often heard complaining about his consistent losing streak.

Our hypothetical owner may still insist that each of these items does not weigh very much—and taken separately, he may be right. But let's add them up and see what the total is:

Hibachi or portable grill	4 pounds
Charcoal	10 pounds
Hose pipe	8 pounds
Awning and supports	6 pounds
Hammocks	6 pounds
Spare battery	44 pounds
Generator (portable)	32 pounds
Fuel and funnel for generator	14 pounds
	124 pounds

In addition to this miscellaneous cruising gear, the boat also carries a full complement of sails, including a spare cruising mainsail and number two genoa, a number four jib, and a storm spinnaker. And just to be sure, the owner may also have a starcut that can double as a storm spinnaker. (Wise skippers of rival boats have listened to the weather forecast and left their number four jibs and spinnakers ashore.) Then, too, there are various pieces of spare deck gear not needed for racing.

So let's add all this up:

Spare mainsail	50 pounds
Spare Number two genoa	40 pounds
Number four jib	36 pounds
Storm spinnaker	18 pounds
Spare gear	22 pounds
	166 pounds

The total so far is 290 pounds. Now our owner is getting the idea, and he searches for a few more items to eliminate. He comes up with this:

Spare charts (keeping only those for the area sailed)	8 pounds
Books	22 pounds
Heavy-duty anchor and warp (he still has the ones required by the rules and another light kedge)	48 pounds
Chart table, useless odds and ends	4 pounds
Junk he should have thrown out long ago but kept	9 pounds
22 tins of canned food (he is going on a day race)	18 pounds
Torn staysail (he was going to send it to a sailmaker but never found time)	14 pounds
	266 pounds

The grand total is 556 pounds. Now let's see how far that will sink this boat, which has a *LWL* of 36′ 6″ and a *BWL* of 10′ 6″. From figure 10.1 we find that 1,250 pounds will sink the boat one inch, so we have $\dfrac{556}{1250}$ = 0.45 inches of sinkage. Now if *LWL* is 32.5 then

32.5 × 2 (both sides) × $\dfrac{0.45}{12}$ feet × 110 percent (allowance for

curvature of boat) = 2.65 square feet of extra wetter area, or about one-third the surface area of an average-size dinghy! This means that our owner is losing about one-third the power needed to haul a dinghy behind his boat. No wonder he is at a competitive disadvantage.

That disadvantage increases as a boat becomes smaller. If you apply the same excess weight to a half-tonner, you will find the sink-

age is $\dfrac{556}{640}$ = 0.87 inches, or almost twice as deep. The extra wetted

area is 3.57 square feet, which represents a much higher percentage of total wetted area.

Of course, some critics are going to argue that removing gear reduces the self-efficiency of the boat and increases the chances of not having the right sail or equipment for the job. My answer is to remove *only* the gear that is not essential for the course on which you are racing. For example, if all the marine weather stations forecast light to medium winds and you are going to sail a twenty-mile course

Figure 10.1 A pounds-per-inch immersion chart. Find your boat's *LWL* and *BWL*, join with a straight line, and read off the pounds per inch immersion.

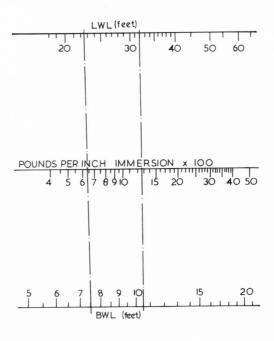

in easy reach of the port, I would leave certain sails ashore. (Many rules, however, require stormsails to be on board when racing.) Furthermore, there is no reason to carry all kinds of cruising gear when you are going to return to your home port after every race.

Then too, not all the potential weight reduction need come from removing gear. Another way to reduce wetted surface is to remove the inside ballast, often fitted to increase stability. A simple calculation will tell you how many foot pounds of righting moment you are losing by removing the ballast. By calculating the moments, a smaller and lighter amount of lead can often be fitted on the bottom of the keel to give you greater stability for less weight; if you do decide to do this, however, your boat must be reinclined under current IOR regulations.

With all these suggestions for reducing wetted surface in mind, you might wonder why all boats aren't stripped-out, lightweight machines. In the upper reaches of competition, this is precisely what they are (although both the IOR and, lately, the IOR Mark IIIa, do compensate the heavier boats by giving them lower ratings). Yet removing weight from a boat is not always entirely advantageous. One reason is the effect it may have on fore-and-aft trim. Bow-down trim is often useful, especially for boats racing under IOR. Of course, whatever rule you race under, the boat must be level in racing condition to achieve its designed performance.

Fairing the Hull

Removing weight, which reduces wetted surface, is one method of lowering resistance. Another is to make sure your hull is smooth and free of weed or slime. This means either obtaining the services of a diver or periodically regularly having a haulout. If your boat is hauled out and the yard allows you to work on the bottom, you can do the job yourself. First, make sure the hull is smooth and fair (no hollows or bumps). If there are hollows, scrape off the antifouling and fill them. Then rub down and antifoul, remembering to rub the antifoul down before the boat goes back into the water. Bumps can be simply rubbed down. Be particularly careful that areas around the hull and keel joint and around the rudder are smooth and fair. Plastic fairing strips can be fitted around the rudder stock to help water flow and decrease resistance. (See figure 10.2.)

To rub down the bottom, use wet-and-dry emery on a board and rub with strong strokes, working from forward to aft. One useful aid is to add some liquid soap to the water you are using, to moisten the wet and dry. It will serve as a lubricant and help stop the emery cloth

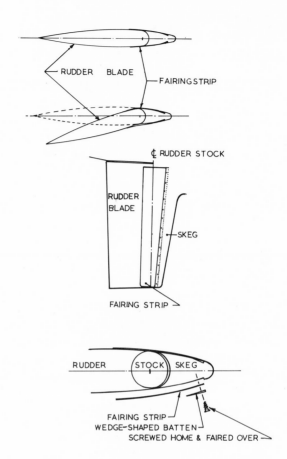

Figure 10.2 Plastic fairing strips can be put around the rudder stock to improve water flow and decrease resistance.

from clogging. The bottom will be at its smoothest when water "sticks" to it instead of forming beads and running off.

If you are interested in achieving maximum boat speed, your overall aim is lower resistance. You get this by reducing on-board weight (and wetted surface) and by keeping your hull smooth and fair. Always remember that resistance is highest when a boat is sailing slowly. So the next time you are tempted to say "it only weighs a few ounces," or "my hull is smooth enough," think of the last time you were drifting along and wishing you could go faster.

11| Reducing Aerodynamic Drag

So important is a clean, smooth hull to top performance that a large percentage of haulout time each winter is devoted to scrubbing and sanding the bottom. Considering the amount of effort spent trying to reduce hull friction, it is surprising that so many owners spend comparatively little time worrying about resistance above the waterline. Yet this kind of drag can do just as much to slow a boat sailing to windward as a fouled underside can. How much effort do you invest in trying to reduce windage, or aerodynamic drag, as it is technically called? If you are looking to improve on past performance next season, a review of some of the factors that contribute to aerodynamic drag is a good place to start.

Causes of Drag

The shape of an object clearly affects its wind resistance. This is known as form drag. Because of its streamlined shape, lenticular rod rigging usually creates less form drag than a round rod—provided, of course, that it is fitted at the best angle to the wind. Figure 11.1 shows various rigging shapes at different wind angles. Obviously, one would not want to face lenticular rod rigging ninety degrees to the wind (as shown in drawing) or else its advantage would be completely lost. Considerations such as this influence not only rigging but also mast profiles and sections. The shape of deck gear, too, affects wind resistance. A square vent box, for instance, could be designed as in figure 11.2 to help reduce form drag.

Another type of aerodynamic drag is induced drag, which is caused by eddies of air flowing around the top and bottom of the sails. The magnitude of induced drag depends, for one thing, upon apparent wind speed: the greater the wind speed, the greater the drag. It also depends upon the shape of the sail and its distance from the deck. The greater the aspect ratio of the sail, the less drag there will be; and the lower the sail to the deck, the lower the drag.

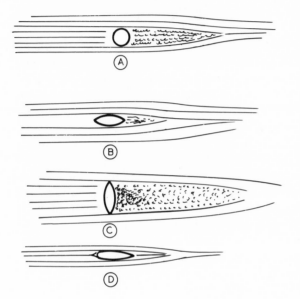

Figure 11.1a
A round-rod shroud has the same drag from all wind angles.

11.1b   A lenticular rod has low drag when facing into the wind.

11.1c   Lenticular rod at ninety degrees to the wind creates more drag than round-rod rigging.

11.1d   An aerofoil shape has the lowest drag of all.

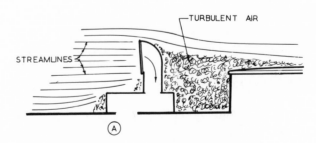

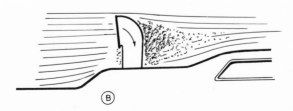

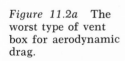
Figure 11.2a   The worst type of vent box for aerodynamic drag.

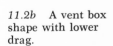
11.2b   A vent box shape with lower drag.

Friction is a third cause of aerodynamic drag. It is also responsible for the hydrodynamic drag you are trying to reduce when you spend so much time polishing the bottom of your boat. If the surface of the hull is rough, or if it has particles of dirt or organic matter attached to it, water molecules flowing past will be slowed down, and so will the boat itself. The same principle applies to air flowing past the above-water parts of the boat. Thus the secret to maximum speed is to have everything on the boat as smooth as possible. This requires some effort. The rigging or mast should be worked on, cleaning and polishing as required. The sails should be folded carefully after each use to preserve a uniform flat surface where possible. Even the hull above the waterline could be rubbed down to help reduce windage.

A final cause of increased aerodynamic drag is the series of extra objects on deck that needn't be there at all, or at the very least, needn't take up as much space as they do. People are sometimes the biggest offenders in this category—the crewman who stands when he could be sitting, for example.

Each of these factors, then, contributes to total aerodynamic different areas of the boat, making the job of reducing excess windage one of attending to a large number of small details. This is why it is a mistake to discount the drag one particular item creates simply because it seems so minor. It is not the drag from each individual item, taken by itself, that is important, but rather their combined effects. Total excess drag can be significant, and the difference between eliminating or ignoring it can certainly make the difference between winning and losing.

Reducing Drag

What are some of the things to look for when trying to reduce total windage? To answer this question, let's review the entire boat, starting at the masthead. Are there any old fittings at the top of the mast that could be removed? Can the masthead backstay crane be shortened? Are there any tang bolts sticking out that could be filed down to the nut and centerpopped, to stop them from coming unscrewed? Look for spare flag halyards, flag halyard cheek blocks, and loose tape ends.

Just below the masthead are the upper shroud tangs. If these are external, can they be replaced with internal tangs next winter? On the way down the mast, look at the topping lift and staysail boxes. Can these fittings be streamlined at all? And, of course, any protruding bolts on this area of the mast should be filed back.

At the spreaders, check the inboard end. No doubt it looks something like figure 11.3. The addition of a simple sleeve will consider-

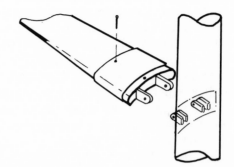

Figure 11.3 A
streamlined sleeve which
can slide over the tang
pins and reduce drag.

ably streamline the air flow around this portion of the mast. And
while at the spreaders, also check the spreader ends. Is there enough
padding to reduce chafe but not so much that you have a large blob
acting like a brake high up above the deck?

Under the spreaders are the shroud tangs. Can these, too, be
replaced by internal tangs. Progressing down the mast, you come to
the spinnaker pole track. Can it be cleaned up in any way, or even
recessed into the mast? Do you have winches and cleats on the
mast. It would reduce windage significantly if these items were on
the deck, especially if your crew is prone to coiling a halyard and
looping it over the winch for safekeeping. And while speaking of halyards, can any be replaced by a messenger in order to reduce the
frontal area just a little bit more?

The aspects of the mast we have been considering so far are
mainly those parts that might be reduced in size, thus decreasing
windage. But there is also the factor of friction drag to take into account. The essential question in this case is obviously whether or not
the mast and rigging are as clean and highly polished as possible,
allowing air to flow smoothly around them.

After the mast, the next area of the boat to consider is the boom.
How much does its positioning contribute to aerodynamic drag?
Lowering the boom will gain sail area for only little increase in rating,
and it will also gain more effective air flow over the sail due to the
end-plate effect. If you do not want to lower the gooseneck, however,
ask your sailmaker to incorporate a "droop" into the foot of the mainsail. This gives you no increase in rated sail area, yet better light air
performance.

In addition to adjusting the position of the boom, consider
whether the boom can be streamlined in any way. The reefing lines
can be made internal, if they are not already. And instead of having
a six-part mainsheet hoisted into the breeze, why not use a wire
strop and keep the length of the six-part tackle to a minimum?

And finally we come to the role of deck gear in increasing aerodynamic drag. First, while near the mast, take a look at the turn-buckles. Are they rough-edged, with frayed tape sticking high into the airflow? If so, a highly polished boot will reduce both form drag and friction drag. Next, at the bow, can the pulpit be cleaned up, re-duced in size, or simply polished? Do you really need that heavy sail netting? Can it be replaced with a smaller diameter line? Can those parallel-sided stanchions, one inch in diameter, be replaced with smaller, tapered ones? Do you remove the Dorade vents and the guards when racing? What about the dodger that you use when cruis-ing. Will it come off? The horseshoes fastened to the stern pulpit probably cause more windage than two crewmen. Can they be fast-ened inside the cockpit, to the transom, or low down on the after deck, where they are still within easy reach but cause no windage at all?

The items discussed here are only a few of the things that can contribute to increased aerodynamic drag. Clearly, it would be im-possible to list every item on every boat that might be removed, re-duced in profile, polished, or streamlined in order to lower windage. However, it is simply a knowledge of the principle, of the basic fac-tors involved in aerodynamic drag, that really matters. From there, it is up to each owner to decide how much of an effort he is willing to make toward reducing wind resistance. If a large number of seem-ingly minor measures is taken, the collective effect will undoubtedly help to get your boat around the course just a little bit faster. And that, after all, is what wins races.

12 Setting Up and Tuning a Masthead Rig

Why does a fast design with good sails and a competent crew end up lagging behind similar boats in the fleet? Almost every owner has wondered about this concerning his own boat at some time. Although there can be many reasons for poor performance under racing conditions, one possibility is an improperly tuned rig. The job of setting up and tuning a modern masthead rig is, of course, a fairly time-consuming one which requires some degree of expertise. But when done correctly, it can increase speed significantly and also make a boat easier to handle. Quite obviously, improvements such as these can make a big difference on the racecourse.

Several basic factors are involved in setting up and tuning a rig. First is the positioning and wedging of the mast. Almost all modern through-deck rigs are designed for the mast to be wedged at the partners. Wedging shortens the unsupported span of the mast and allows for a smaller mast inertia. At this stage of setting up, the masthead should be positioned squarely on the centerline.

Once the mast has been wedged, the next factor to consider is lateral tuning—the degree of athwartship bend in the spar. Smaller, nonmasthead designs, such as dinghies, may get more speed if the top of the mast is allowed to fall off to leeward. This reduces heel angle and weather helm, widens the slot between the genoa and the mainsail, and reduces backwinding. But with the masthead rigs on larger boats, lateral bend may quickly get out of control as wind speed increases. Consequently, most masthead designs are tuned for a laterally straight spar.

107

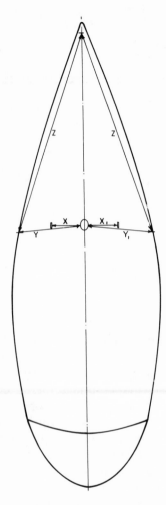

Figure 12.1   Check that X and X_1 are
equal. If not, measure Z from tack to
toerail and check distances Y and Y_1.
If they are equal, the mast collar is in
the middle of the boat.

And finally, after lateral tuning, there is the factor of fore and
aft tuning. This really consists of two separate adjustments—mast
rake and mast bend. Rake refers to the fore or aft lean of the mast;
the spar remains straight along its length but is tilted at the foot.
Fore or aft rake causes a corresponding movement in the center of
effort of the sails. Thus, to reduce weather helm, the mast is raked
forward, while to increase helm, it is raked aft; the actual amount
varies with the particular boat and the expected wind conditions.
Mast bend, in contrast, refers to the fore or aft curve of the spar
along its entire length, and is used to control the fullness or flatness
of the mainsail, and unlike the other factors just listed, it is often
adjusted during a race.

Positioning and Wedging

The fundamental aim when positioning and wedging a mast is to get the spar to rise straight from the centerline and be firmly fixed at the deck. While the mast is still on the dock, check to make sure that the mast collar is on the centerline, as illustrated in figure 12.1. First, measure from the top of the collar to the toerail on either side of the mast, and note any difference between the two sides. Then, measure the distance on either side from the stemhead to the chainplate. Again, these measurements should be the same on the two sides of the boat. If they are not, measure an equal distance on either side from the stemhead to the toerail, approximately opposite the aft lower chainplate. Mark the toerail at these points, one on each side of the boat. At this stage, too, check that all the chain-plates have rounded corners and that the holes are not elongated.

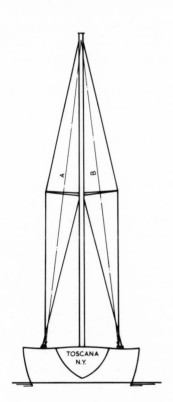

Figure 12.2   When *A* equals *B*, the masthead is on the centerline.

Figure 12.3   If the masthead is on center and the mast is bent as shown, tighten the starboard diagonal and ease the port diagonal to get the mast to stand straight.

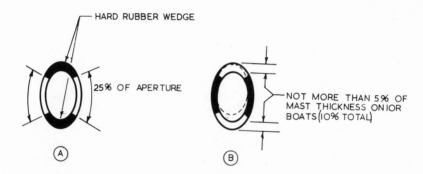

Figure 12.4a Fore and aft mast wedging. The "wedges" are parallel-sided rectangular pieces of hard rubber. *12.4b* Lateral mast wedging. The mast is able to move forward in the partners as the spar is bent.

Now the mast can be lowered into the boat. Connect the shrouds and stays and make them hand-tight, plus two or three turns. Next, hoist a tape measure to the masthead (on the main halyard sheave if it is on the centerline) and measure down, either to the aft lower chainplates, or to the marks you made earlier on the toerail. Adjust the shrouds until the measurements are the same on both sides of the boat, as shown in figure 12.2. This ensures that the masthead is on the centerline. By sighting up the mast (the mainsail track is the easiest place), the spar can be checked for sideways bend and the shrouds adjusted until it is laterally straight. (See figure 12.3) At this stage, also look for fore and aft bend and adjust the headstay, backstay, and double lowers, if fitted, accordingly. And finally, make another check to see that the masthead is still on the centerline.

If everything is done properly, the spar should be perfectly straight with the masthead on center. The next step is to insert wedges at the partners. For a fiberglass boat, use parallel-sided pieces of hard rubber. (The term "wedge" comes from the days of wooden masts, when tapered wooden wedges were used.) The rubber should be about 25 percent larger than the space to be filled. (See figure 12.4.) Fit a bridle to the mast, as shown in figure 12.5, so that the mast can be pulled forward, allowing the rubber to be slipped in. (Note that this is fore and aft wedging; later, when discussing rake, we will consider lateral wedging.) When in place, the rubber should fit firmly.

That was the easy part. Now the bridle must be turned 180 degrees, and the mast pulled aft until the second piece of rubber can be inserted. Finally, with both wedges in place, fasten a long hose clamp tightly around them to hold them securely to the mast.

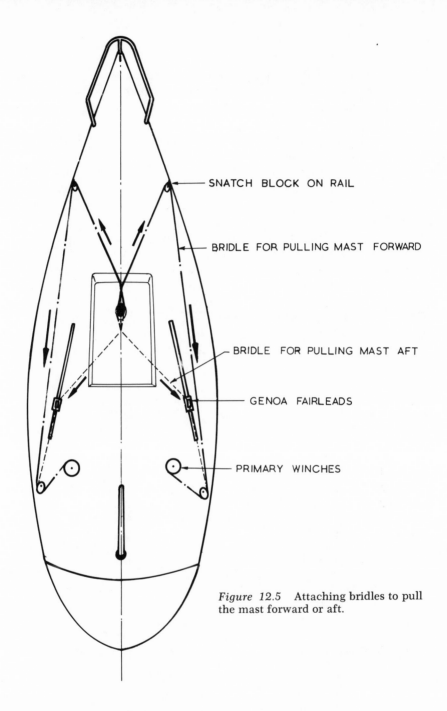

SNATCH BLOCK ON RAIL

BRIDLE FOR PULLING MAST FORWARD

BRIDLE FOR PULLING MAST AFT

GENOA FAIRLEADS

PRIMARY WINCHES

Figure 12.5 Attaching bridles to pull the mast forward or aft.

Athwartship or Lateral Tuning

With the mast now set up straight, the next problem is to tension the shrouds correctly, so that the mast remains laterally straight even when the boat is heeled. This is done in two ways. One is to heel the boat at the dock and tighten the upper shrouds on the lower side with each heel. The other is to tune the shrouds on alternate tacks when the boat is sailing to windward. In actual practice, both of these methods are typically used in conjunction with one another. The first rough tunes the rig, while the second enables the final adjustments to be made.

To tune the rig laterally at the dock, lead the spinnaker halyard to an adjacent dock and take up on it. This will heel the boat. Do not use any lines other than the spinnaker halyard, because the sideways loading can ruin them.

First, consider the tuning of a single-spreader rig, since the procedure is so easy. (See figure 12.6.) With the boat heeled to about fifteen degrees, tighten the upper shroud (V_1-D_2) on the lower side, until there is neither slackness nor tension in it. Then heel the boat in the other direction and tighten the upper shroud on the opposite side. When the boat is returned to vertical, measure again to center the masthead. Finally, make sure the mast is perfectly straight from top to bottom, with no bend in the middle. If there is any mid-spar bend

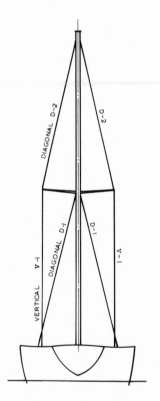

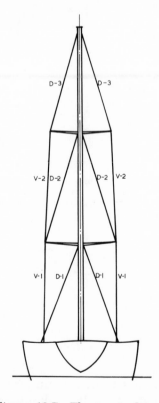

Figure 12.6   The terminology used for a single-spreader rig.

Figure 12.7   The terminology used for a double-spreader rig.

to one side or the other, it can be removed by tightening the lowers (D_1). But be sure, on a boat with double lowers, to tighten the forward one first, making it slightly more taut than the aft one.

A double-spreader rig is far more difficult to tune. (See figure 12.7) The general technique is to center the masthead by adjusting the V_1-V_2-D_3 on either side, leaving the D_2's fairly slack. Then tighten the D_1's and D_2's to eliminate any bend in the middle of the mast. Again, the basic tuning can be done at the dock. An important point to remember is to avoid overtightening the D_2's. As shown in figure 12.8, this can make the masthead appear as if it were falling off to one side, when in actual fact it is the middle of the mast that has been pulled off-center. Last, check to see that the spreaders are tilted up, not drooping below the horizontal, and that there is the same amount of tilt on both sides of the rig.

If you intend to tune the shrouds while sailing, pick a day when the wind is blowing a steady twelve to fifteen knots. While sailing on one tack, remove the cotter pins on the lee side and tighten the shrouds hand-tight. Then replace the cotter pins and go about onto the other tack. Once settled on the new tack, again remove the cotter pins from the lee side and tighten the shrouds. Check up the mast

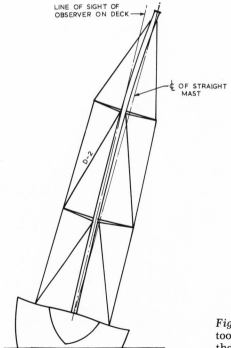

LINE OF SIGHT OF
OBSERVER ON DECK

℄ OF STRAIGHT
MAST

D-2

Figure 12.8 The D-2 (indicated) is too tight, and to an observer on deck, the top of the mast may look as if it is falling off to leeward.

groove for straightness. By tacking back and forth and sighting up the mast after each tack, you can achieve a fine degree of athwart-ship tuning. Finally, when the mast is laterally straight, bend the cotter pins over and tape them.

Fore and Aft Tuning

MAST RAKE. How much rake a mast should have is governed by the amount of helm experienced when the boat is sailing. If the boat is new, you can often get a fairly accurate suggested rake angle from the builder or designer. If not, it is best to set the rig of a new boat up with the mast vertical fore and aft. This can be done by using a plumb bob, as illustrated in figure 12.9. Then, after you have had a chance to sail the boat under varying wind conditions, the rake can be adjusted. When there is no means of altering rake while the boat is underway, the mast should be set up so that there is little or no helm in light winds and some helm in medium weather. (The amount of helm in heavy air is not that relevant to mast rake, since

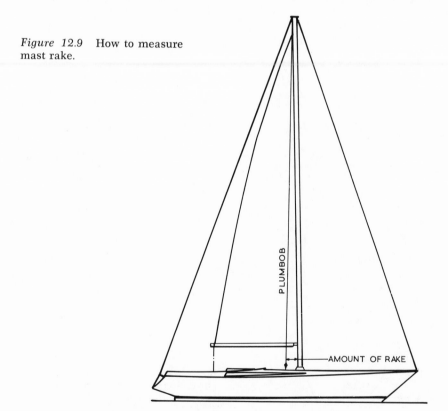

Figure 12.9 How to measure mast rake.

in heavy winds the sails would be changed or reefed to reduce weather helm.) Generally speaking, if you find that there is too much lee helm, you should rake the mast aft; if, on the other hand, you find there is too much weather helm, you should rake forward.

On some designs, mast rake must be adjusted at at the dock. If this is the case, the headstay will probably be fitted with either a turnbuckle, linkplates, or a series of toggles, and the backstay with a turnbuckle or a tackle. Turnbuckles on both the headstay and backstay allow for the most precise adjustment.

To alter the rake of a mast with headstay and backstay adjusters of this type, first determine the existing degree of rake. This can be done by hoisting a plumb bob up to the masthead on the main halyard and measuring from the aft side of the mast to the plumb bob at the deck. Next, take the boat out for a sail in ten to fifteen knots of apparent wind, perhaps at the same time you fine-tune the rig laterally. When sailing close-hauled, observe how the helm feels. There should be about three to five degrees of weather helm. If you have too much weather helm, rake the mast forward when you return to the dock, easing the backstay and tightening the headstay. If, on the other hand, you experience lee helm, rake the mast aft and adjust the headstay and backstay accordingly. By trial and error you will eventually arrive at an angle of rake that affords a good helm position for most wind strengths.

This at-the-dock method of adjustment is no longer necessary with the development of hydraulics. With hydraulic headstay and backstay adjusters, it is possible to rake the rig while the boat is underway. This allows a constant helm angle to be maintained in varying wind conditions. Consequently, boat speed is increased, quite often dramatically.

There are three schools of thought about mast rake when hydraulic headstay and backstay adjusters are used. One holds that the mast should lean from the foot, with the partners wedged laterally; another argues that the mast should pivot at the partners, leaving the foot free to move; and the third claims that the mast should be deck-stepped and pivot at the foot. Figure 12.10 shows these different methods of raking the mast. Of the three, the first is presently allowed under the IOR, but the maximum rake is limited to 10 percent of the longitudinal thickness of the spar; the second is banned under the IOR; and the third is now restricted, because one Admiral's Cup boat that used it could rake the rig as much as seven and a half feet at the masthead.

Regardless of where the mast pivots when it is raked, the procedure for tuning is similar on all boats that use hydraulics. The rig should first be set up with the mast raked in an average position and the hydraulic adjusters fully extended, so that there is neither slack

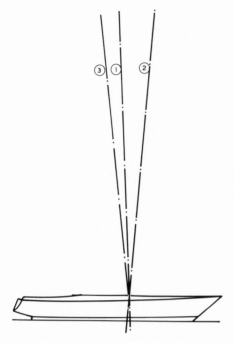

Figure 12.10 The various ways to rake a mast. 1. The mast is pivoted at the foot. Under the IOR this method has the most restricted range. 2. The mast is pivoted at the partners. The range in this case is restricted only by the extent to which the foot can move, although the IOR has penalized this type of mast pivoting. 3. The mast is stepped on deck. This allows the largest range of movement.

nor tension on the stays. Given this arrangement, maximum load on the system should occur when both cylinders are pumped half-way down. Now measure the degree of rake, using a plumb bob, and record the figure for later reference. When the boat is out sailing, the mast can be raked further forward to decrease weather helm, by letting off the backstay adjuster and pumping down the headstay adjuster, and vice versa. In this manner, the same tension is maintained on the rig, but the angle of the mast is altered. Remember, when adjusting rake, that the positions of the genoa sheet and halyard and the main sheet must also be moved accordingly. And when fitting out the boat, remember that the best type of hydraulic headstay and backstay adjusters are those with a locking device, the jaws of which can be wound down manually if the system fails.

MAST BEND. So far we have talked about setting up and raking a straight mast. Much of the time on the race course, however, a straight mast is not desirable, for it makes the mainsail efficient over a very narrow wind band. Aft mast bend is used to made the mainsail flatter, and thus more effective, as wind strength increases. Forward bend, on the other hand, makes the main fuller and consequently more effective in lighter winds. In general, mast bend has the greatest effect on the top half of the sail, where the outhaul, cunningham, main sheet, and vang do not exert as large an influence as they do on the lower half of the sail. The differences between mast rake and mast bend are summarized in figure 12.11.

Mast bend is usually achieved in one of three basic ways, depending upon where pressure is applied. The most obvious method is to exert tension on the headstay or backstay while the mast is wedged firmly at the partners and held at the foot. Another technique, used on twelve meters, is to push the mast at the partners while the masthead and foot remain fixed. And a final means, of course, is to hold the spar stationary at the masthead and partners, and move the foot.

Most ocean racers use headstay and backstay tension to bend

Figure 12.11   The difference between mast rake and mast bend is that the mast stays straight when it is raked. The drawing at the left shows three methods of raking a mast. All involve movement at two points. In A the mast is raked aft by moving the head and the partners; in B the mast is raked by moving the foot forward and the head aft; and in C the foot and the partners move while the head stays in the same position. Of these three methods, A is the most common. To bend a mast, in contrast, only one point is moved, as illustrated in the drawing to the right. In X, the head is moved aft; in Y the partners are moved; and in Z the foot is moved to get bend low down. Of these three techniques, X is the most common, and Z is the most difficult, due to the high compression loading on the spar.

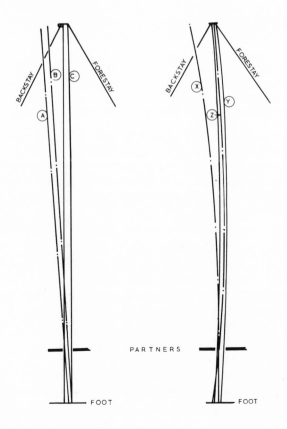

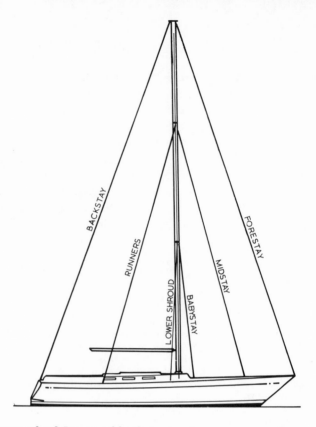

Figure 12.12   What moves what? Increased backstay tension compresses the mast, pulls the head aft, and tightens the forestay. The runners oppose the midstay load and stop the mast from pumping in a seaway. The runners are also used to straighten or reverse the bend in the top third of the mast; this increases mainsail fullness and gives greater drive in light winds. The midstay is used to increase forward mast bend in the top third of the spar and to oppose the runner loads. The babystay serves a similar function to the midstay but it bends the mast in the bottom third. When double lowers are fitted, mast control is somewhat more difficult. The forward lowers should be set up a little tighter than the aft lowers, and as the backstay is tensioned the forward lowers will pull the mast forward, inducing bend.

the mast, plus a midstay, runners, and a babystay or double lowers to control the bend. Figure 12.12 shows the effects that each of these has on mast bend.

Quite obviously, no one set of procedures can be followed to achieve optimum mast bend on all boats, but certain general guidelines are useful. First get the spar sitting up straight in the boat so that the helm is well balanced in light airs. Then slacken the shrouds as well as the headstay and backstay, and move the foot of the mast back as far as an inch or so, depending on the size of the boat. The mast will now be leaning slightly forward. Tighten the headstay, backstay, and shrouds back to their original positions and you will have introduced some amount of bend.

When sailing, the bend can be increased by pumping the backstay adjuster fully down; if more is required, it can be achieved by tensioning the babystay. But beware of too much mast bend. Most sparmakers and designers allow for a mast deflection of only about 50 percent of the diameter in the middle of the spar. If in doubt about the maximum bend for your boat's mast, check with your builder or designer.

Maximum mast bend, however, does have its usefulness when a tight headstay and flat mainsail are required—say, at the top end of the wind range for the heavy number one genoa. At the lower end of the heavy number one range, in contrast, a straight headstay and a full main are often required for pointing ability and power. This means a straight mast with a substantial loading on the runners. The benefits of this tuning technique were clearly illustrated by John Marshall of North Sails during a race on Long Island Sound last season. When John tensioned the runners, almost to the point of reverse bend, the top third of the mainsail became visibly deeper and more drive was added aloft, where it matters. Of course, in this case a sail-maker was tuning the rig and sails until they matched perfectly. But there is no reason why the average sailor cannot take note of the amplified speed dial on his speedometer when adjusting his own rig.

HEADSTAY SAG. In any discussion of fore and aft tuning, the topic of headstay sag inevitably arises. The tension in the headstay, as most sailors know, governs the pointing ability of the boat. Unfortunately, it is impossible to get an absolutely straight stay, so sailmakers cut sails with some hollow in the luff to allow for the sag. Tensioning the stay removes some of this hollow and flattens the sail. This is done as the wind increases, usually by pumping down the backstay, since tension on the headstay and backstay are effectively the same. Conversely, easing the backstay increases headstay sag, makes the genoa fuller, and gives more power in lighter winds, although the boat must be sailed a little more freely. When hydraulic headstay and backstay adjusters are used, however, it is better to ease the headstay off first, which will also allow the rig to rake aft for light air windward work.

Now you have it. A general rule is that in lighter winds the rig should be raked aft, with more sag in the headstay, which gives you a fuller sail. As the wind picks up, tighten the headstay and rake the rig forward, thus reducing weather helm and increasing pointing ability.

But what about the backstay? How much tension should be applied to it? About one-third of the breaking load is the maximum, so if you are not sure what the breaking load for your boat is, ask your rigger.

One final word of caution. If you have beefed up the rigging in any way, check with the designer about what loads can safely be applied. If you do not have hydraulics and want to check your own rigging loads, you may be able to borrow a rigging dynamometer and mark the position of maximum load that can be put on the system.

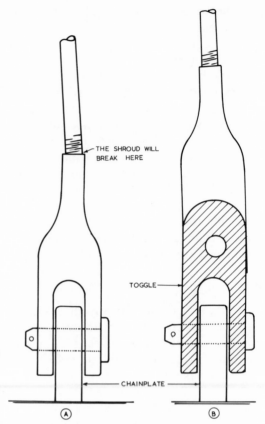

THE SHROUD WILL
BREAK HERE

TOGGLE

CHAINPLATE

Ⓐ   Ⓑ

Figure 12.13a If no toggle is fitted, the shroud will eventually break at the point indicated. *12.13b* Using a toggle is a better arrangement.

Other Practical Tips

In addition to the general techniques for tuning a rig, several other related points are worth noting. One is the use of toggles. Often, chainplates are not exactly aligned with the shroud, or there is restricted movement of the shroud across the chainplate, as shown in figure 12.13. Both these conditions can lead to breakage when the shroud is tensioned. To reduce the risk of failure, toggles should be fitted between all chainplates and turnbuckles. Toggles also help if the mast tangs are slightly out of true. But remember to lubricate the turnbuckles and toggles a little to aid turning and to help stop corrosion.

Finally, check that all cotter pins are fitted, cut to length, and bent open as desired. All pins should be inserted from outboard toward the mast, in order to avoid the chance of tearing the sail. Then, with the pins in place, the turnbuckles should be taped lightly to cover the exposed pin and reduce the risk of anything catching.

13 *Understanding Hydraulics*

As racing boats become more sophisticated, so too does their equipment. Not many years ago, most backstays were tensioned by a turnbuckle with handles or by blocks and tackles. The hydraulic adjuster was a rarity. Today, however, almost all top boats have some form of hydraulic tensioner on the backstay at least. And the latest racing boats, of course, have much more.

There are several reasons for this switch to hydraulics. One is the precision of control they allow. With hydraulics, the load on a stay can be viewed on a pressure gauge and adjusted with great accuracy. Another reason is efficiency: hydraulics enable high loads to be moved short distances without first having to release the load. Also, adjustments can be made from a centrally-located control panel, saving crew time and movement. And because hydraulic leads usually go under the deck, complicated systems of deck hardware are eliminated. For these basic reasons, then, hydraulics provide the perfect answer where the load is high and the stroke short.

The Uses of Hydraulics

Hydraulic adjusters can be used in many different areas. The most common are on the backstay and headstay, the babystay, and the boom vang. More esoteric uses are on the mast partners, the boom outhaul, the spreaders, the cunningham, and the daggerboard tackle. Since this chapter is not intended to turn the average sailor into an expert on hydraulics, we'll focus primarily on the more typical functions, discussing each one in some detail.

THE HEADSTAY/BACKSTAY ADJUSTER. The best type of hydraulic ram for a headstay or backstay is the single-acting kind, with a mechanical locking device. The locking mechanism reduces wear on the system, and if the hydraulics fail, the ram can still be operated by hand—an important safety feature when racing offshore.

Until recently, many racing boats had both headstay and backstay adjusters, but the IOR has restricted this practice. Under the amended rule, the headstay must be fixed while racing unless the boat has swept-back spreaders, in which case the backstay must be fixed. This change is intended to eliminate the high cost of multi-hydraulic systems and the extreme masthead movements they could achieve. So what does the hot-shot racer do now? One alternative is to install link plates on the headstay and adjust them before the start to suit the expected wind conditions. Figure 13.1 shows a pair of link plates.

With today's hydraulic systems, the backstay tension is adjusted almost as often as sheet and halyard tension, to control headstay sag

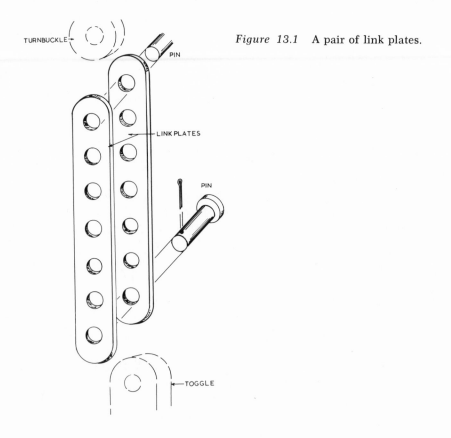

Figure 13.1   A pair of link plates.

and alter the amount and position of draft in the genoa. In light winds, it is best to ease the backstay slightly, which also eases the headstay. This moves the draft in the genoa aft and increases its fullness and potential power. As the wind strength rises, the tension on the backstay should be increased. This pulls the masthead aft, tightens the headstay, flattens the genoa, and moves the draft forward. The result is better boat speed and pointing ability. But how does one know when the backstay has been tightened enough? A good rule of thumb is not to use more pressure in pounds than one-third the breaking strain of the stay. Tables 13.1a and b give breaking strains and the limit of backstay pressure for stainless steel wire of various sizes.

THE BABYSTAY OR MIDSTAY ADJUSTER. As for a hydraulic backstay, a single-acting ram is most efficient for a babystay. A babystay adjuster helps to control fore and aft mast bend when used in conjunction with the backstay adjuster. In heavier winds, tensioning the babystay produces greater mast bend, which in turn eases the leech of the mainsail, flattens the sail, and increases its drive. In light winds, on the other hand, easing the babystay tightens the mainsail leech, makes the sail fuller, and increases its potential power. Note, however, that when easing off the babystay, you may also want to ease the mainsheet slightly. This will help maintain an open leech.

THE BOOM VANG ADJUSTER. The hydraulic adjuster on the boom vang has a slightly different job to perform than the adjuster on the backstay or babystay. A hydraulic boom vang must be able to support the boom at an initial position and lower it as required. The system must also be designed so as to allow the mainsheet to be trimmed without breaking either the boom or the vang. A single-acting ram can be used here, although it must have a compression rod to take the weight of the boom when the hydraulic pressure is off. Also, the single-acting ram does not have an up stroke, so it can only lower the boom, not raise it as well. The double-acting ram, with its separate up and down strokes, has the advantage of being able both to lower and raise the boom. But if the mainsheet is tensioned while the vang is pushing up, either the vang or the boom may be damaged. Consequently, the best type of hydraulic ram for a boom vang is probably the single-acting spring-loaded kind, or the kind with a compressed air chamber. When the vang is tensioned, the spring loads or the air in the chamber compresses. Then, when the tension is removed, the ram extends and returns the boom to its original position.

As a device for tensioning the mainsail leech, the hydraulic vang almost totally replaces the mainsheet. On smaller boats, too, the vang adjuster can be used to help bend the mast or the boom, and thus flatten the mainsail. But before you rush out and buy a hydraulic vang, check with a naval architect to make sure that the boom on your boat is strong enough to accommodate one.

What should one look for when adjusting a hydraulic vang? When using the vang to lower the boom, watch the leech of the main-

Table 13.1a   U.K. Rigging

Diameter	H. R. Spencer's 1 x 19 wire	Maximum backstay pressure	South Coast Rod Rigging	Maximum backstay pressure
1/8	1,590 lbs.	530 lbs.	1,790 lbs. (4BA)	600 lbs.
3/16	4,410	1,470	3,230 (2BA)	1,080
1/4	6,350	2,116	5,980	2,000
5/16	10,200	3,400	9,640	3,200
3/8	12,900	4,300	14,450	4,800
7/16	—	—	20,000	6,666
1/2	—	—	26,500	8,833
9/16	31,300	10,433	—	—
5/8	41,000	13,666	34,925	11,641

SOURCES: H. R. Spencer's Catalogue.
South Coast Rod Rigging Catalogue.

Table 13.1b   U.S. Rigging

Diameter	Stainless steel 1 x 19 wire	Maximum backstay pressure	McWhyte rod rigging	Maximum backstay pressure
1/8	2,100 lbs.	700 lbs.	1,891 lbs.	700 lbs.
3/16	4,700	1,600	4,278	1,426
1/4	8,200	2,750	7,595	2,531
5/16	12,500	4,200	11,688	4,000
3/8	17,600	5,800	17,112	5,700
7/16	23,400	7,800	23,296	7,700
1/2	29,700	9,900	30,426	10,100
9/16	37,000	12,300	38,517	11,555
5/8	46,800	15,600	47,554	15,851
3/4	59,700	19,900	68,463	22,821

SOURCE: McWhyte Catalogue.

sail to see that it is not too tight; a tight leech can stall the airflow out of the sail and slow the boat. Also make sure you are not working against the topping lift. If you have a bendy boom, which is unlikely on an offshore boat, tighten the vang enough to remove mainsail fullness. But don't fall into the trap of making the sail too flat.

OTHER HYDRAULIC ADJUSTERS. Adjusting the backstay or headstay, the babystay, and the boom vang are the most common uses of hydraulics, but others are also found. Hydraulic boom outhauls can be used to tension the foot of the mainsail. When this is done, the black band is put on the adjuster, and not on the boom end, where it would move with the spar. Hydraulic boom outhauls were used on some of the latest twelve meters, as were hydraulic mast partners. In offshore competition, hydraulic mast partners first appeared in 1974 on *Siren Song* (now *Tempest*). The IOR, however, has currently restricted mast movement to 10 percent of the fore and aft diameter of the spar, making hydraulic mast partners too powerful for the job. And it has also ruled out mechanical bending of the spar, which hydraulic mast partners constitute.

Installing a Hydraulic System

Almost all modern hydraulic systems with multiple rams operate from a central console in the cockpit. It is only when a boat is fitted with just one adjuster—for instance, on the backstay—that the pump and the adjuster are combined. Several different consoles are shown in figure 13.2. Each has a single pump with separate release and locking valves controlling the flow of hydraulic fluid to the various systems. The loads on the adjusters are shown on separate dials. Each system also has a central reservoir, from which fluid can be drawn to allow all the rams to be fully extended at any given time.

The location of the control panel should be very carefully considered. There are several key factors to keep in mind.

1. *Visibility.* The panel should be sited so that crewmen can easily see it, and so that a man working at the console can easily see whatever ram he needs to adjust.
2. *Crew movement.* The panel should be placed in a spot where it can be reached with a minimum of crew movement.
3. *Maintenance.* The panel should be positioned so that the reservoir is higher than the pump but can still be easily topped up. There should also be easy access to the back of the panel for cleaning and trouble-shooting; this means that it is usually somewhere near the forward end of the cockpit.

Figure 13.3a shows one site that takes these three factors into consideration.

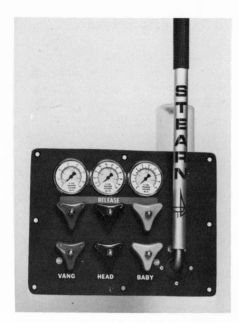

Figure 13.2a A Stern three-function, three-gauge hydraulic control panel. *13.2b* A David Carne hydraulc panel which can move the masthead forward or aft without removing the load.

Trouble-Shooting

Usually a hydraulic system is installed by a boatyard, so many owners do not know enough about how the system is put together to solve common problems. If any of the following troubles occur on the race course, here are some steps to take.

PRESSURE LOSS. If there is any pressure loss in a hydraulic system the first thing to do is to make sure that all the valves are

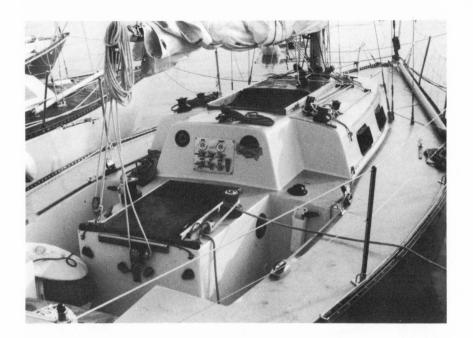

Figure 13.3a   A good position for a hydraulic console. The dials are easily visible and all the rams and their effects can be seen when operating the controls. *13.3b* This is not a good position for a hydraulic panel because a crewman must face aft to operate the equipment.

closed. This prevents the remaining pressure from draining away, leaving the rig slack. Then check out these possibilities:

1. Inspect for leaks anywhere in the system. Check the hose fittings for seeping fluid. Also check the cylinder seals. A cylinder with a faulty seal will show fluid where the piston rod emerges. Be sure to check the pump end of the system as well. It may be that the pump itself is leaking, which calls for new pump seals.

2. If there is no visible sign of a leak, the pump valve may be obstructed by dirt. You may not want to try to clean it thoroughly on the race course, but a temporary solution is to open the valve as far as possible and pump, hoping that the fluid will remove the obstruction. If this fails, the pump must be disassembled as soon as possible and cleaned.

CYLINDERS THAT CANNOT BE PUMPED OR DO NOT HOLD THEIR PRESSURE. If this is your problem, there is probably air in the system and the whole thing must be bled. Loosen the hose connection at the end of one cylinder and allow any air to escape. Pull the cylinder out until it is fully extended and pump until fluid flows from the loosened fitting. Then tighten the connection and repeat the procedure with the other adjusters. Remember to fill the fluid reservoir after working on each cylinder, or you may end up simply pumping more air around the system!

THE PUMP WON'T WORK. First check that the valves are open. Then check for materials caught in the valves. Next, make sure there are no damaged components. If it still doesn't work, replacement of the entire pump is the only cure.

Routine Maintenance

Attending to hydraulics only when they break down is not enough. Like everything else on a boat, the system requires routine maintenance to stay in tip-top condition. Again, here are a few general guidelines.

After every race. Wipe the cylinders and rods clean.

Once a month. Check the oil level. Check for signs of leakage. Check the tightness of the fittings.

Once a year. Flush out the entire system and refill it with fresh oil. Check the hoses and fittings for wear and chafe.

Once every two years. Return all cylinders and pumps to the manufacturer for new seals and a complete checkup.

14 *Polar Curves*

You are racing hard and it's 3:30 A.M. on the midnight to 4:00 A.M. watch. The wind, which has been light all evening, has just shifted ten degrees, and you have retrimmed the sails. What would you do now?

1. Go back to your half-awake state, waiting for the next watch and listening to the jokes emanating from the cockpit?
2. See how the wind shift affects boat speed and course?
3. See if another sail would give better boat speed?

If you think you should do the first, you were lucky even to have noticed the recent wind shift, and there's little chance you'll do much more toward winning this race for the rest of the watch. On the other hand, if you think that the second is your most likely course of action, you're on the right track, although you haven't gone quite far enough. Unless you do both two *and* three, you're not getting the best boat speed possible.

But how, in the dark and when you're tired, can you determine if the boat is sailing at its maximum potential and if it needs another sail? The answer is to make a polar diagram—and not just one diagram, but two or three. There are four types of polar charts: a true wind polar curve, an apparent wind polar curve, what I call a sail potential chart, and a sail change chart. In this chapter I'll discuss how to make each type, what it costs, and how to use it.

True Wind Polars

True wind polar curves are probably best known for their use aboard America's Cup boats. Their cost, like almost everything associated with twelve meters, is high. To plot true wind polars, one begins by taking literally hundreds of readings of apparent wind angle (β), apparent wind speed (Va), and boat speed (Vs), as well as numerous calculations of leeway angle (λ). These figures are recorded for each possible sail combination—always when the boat is sailing at its maximum potential.

How are these various factors measured? Apparent wind angle, apparent wind speed, and boat speed are obtained from instrument readings. Several recording methods are possible. A crewman can simply check the instruments at predetermined intervals and keep a log of the readings, pen recording devices can be used, or the data can be collected on magnetic tape for processing directly into a computer. The leeway angle can be estimated, or it can be calculated by sailing between two fixed points, as shown in figure 14.1. This latter method, however, has big disadvantages if the wind is at all variable or if there is any current. Another method of determining leeway angle is to tow a high-resistance object, say a length of chain, on a low-resistance line or wire that is long enough to avoid wake effects. Then take bearings along the wire, while somebody else takes bearings along the ship's centerline. (If this method is not accurate enough due to compass variation, make up a scale of degrees and put it along the transom.)

Having compiled all this data, the next step is to tabulate it and then to use a formula to resolve the apparent wind angle into the true wind. This final calculation is rather complex because certain corrections must be made for heel angle, instrument fluctuations, and increased leeway due to the effects of rough waters. To simplify, we will not get into mathematics here, but instead just show the solution graphically in figure 14.2. Because of the large amounts of data involved, it is customary to use a computer at this stage, which tends to push up the cost.

Figure 14.1 A way to calculate leeway angle by sailing between two points.

Figure 14.2   A diagram of forces to obtain true wind.

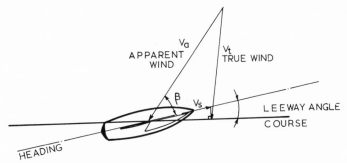

Another way to get the data needed to plot true wind polar curves is by tank testing. All the variables are known or can be calculated by using sail coefficients every time the boat is towed down the tank. But again, this method is extremely expensive because of both the tank time and computer time required, and it is not really cost-effective for an existing design.

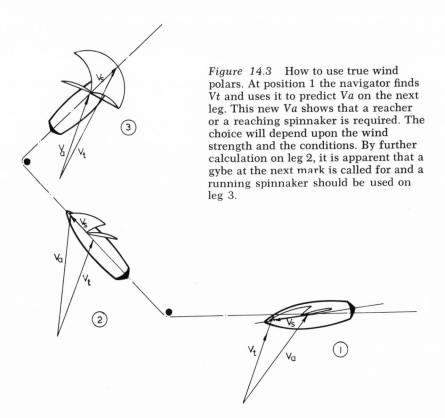

Figure 14.3   How to use true wind polars. At position 1 the navigator finds Vt and uses it to predict Va on the next leg. This new Va shows that a reacher or a reaching spinnaker is required. The choice will depend upon the wind strength and the conditions. By further calculation on leg 2, it is apparent that a gybe at the next mark is called for and a running spinnaker should be used on leg 3.

There are many uses for true wind polar curves. For instance, to find apparent wind strength and direction on the next leg of the course, the navigator reads the ship's speed, apparent wind direction, and apparent wind speed off the instruments, and having already decided the leeway angle, he then calculates true wind angle. Knowing the true wind angle and the course of the next leg, he can work backward to obtain the apparent wind angle and speed for that leg. From these he can recommend the best choice of sails. Figure 14.3 illustrates the solution.

Apparent Wind Polars

Apparent wind polar curves are made in a similar fashion to true wind polars, except that the data is plotted graphically without resolving it for leeway and true wind. Figure 14.4 shows a typical set of true wind and apparent wind polars. Note how they differ in shape. They also differ in how they can be used. True wind polars are used for a variety of purposes, but the apparent wind/true wind triangle must always be solved. Apparent wind polars simply indicate the speed at which the boat should be going with respect to the force and direction of the apparent wind.

Sail Potential and Sail Change Charts

Individual owners must decide if they want to invest both the money and the effort required to plot true wind or apparent wind polars. Sail potential and sail change charts are much cheaper. They cost only your own time and the food your crew eats while sailing to collect data. But sail potential and sail change charts also have somewhat different purposes than true wind or apparent wind polars. A sail potential chart serves as a check on your sails in that it tells you the speed you should get out of the boat when you use a particular sail. If, for example, a sail has been blown out, a sail potential curve will indicate a loss in speed before that loss becomes otherwise apparent. A sail change chart, on the other hand, shows what sails to use in what wind strength and when to change sails.

Here is how to collect the data for both these charts. Assume that over the winter you buy new sails for your boat. But you're not quite sure which sail will do what, so you decide to gather some information before you go racing. First, get your instruments accurately calibrated. If there are uncorrectable errors, make sure you know what they are. For example, a log may read 2 knots when the boat is mov-

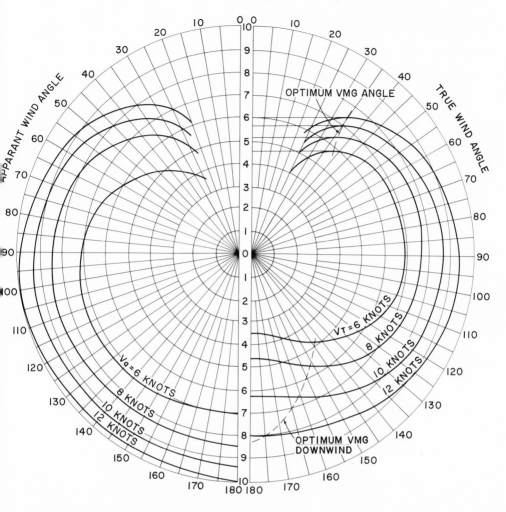

Figure 14.4 True and apparent wind polars.

ing at 2 knots over a measured mile, but 6.3 knots when the boat is moving 6 knots. A graph can be plotted for such an error and appropriate corrections made later. Figure 14.5 shows part of a typical log correction plot. Once the errors are calculated, don't touch the instruments until all the readings have been taken.

Now take the boat out in your local waters and, weather permitting, set the number one genoa and trim for maximum upwind speed. (It is important to sail in the local waters in which you'll be racing because sea conditions do affect the drive you can get from a particular sail, especially going to windward.) As you sail the boat to

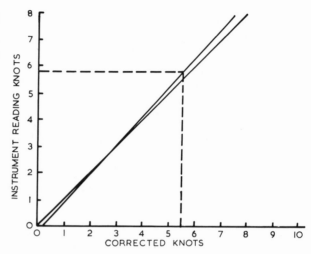

Figure 14.5 A typical log correction chart. The readings would be entered from the left to obtain the corrected readings from the baseline.

windward with the number one genoa and a full main, record wind angle, wind speed, boat speed, heel angle, and sea state. Figure 14.6 is a typical sheet for recording these numbers. Sail to windward for at least twenty minutes, taking readings about once every minute.

Your next step is to sail off at, say, thirty-five degrees apparent for twenty minutes, then at forty degrees apparent for the same amount of time, and so on, taking the required readings at regular intervals. Follow this procedure for wind angles up to about fifty

Figure 14.6 A typical plotting sheet.

BOAT NAME _____	SHEET POSITIONS
DATE _____	MAIN _____
RACE _____	GENOA _____
SAIL _____	OUTHAUL _____
SEA STATE _____	CUNNINGHAM_____
	TRAVELLER _____

BOAT SPEED V	APPARENT WIND SPEED V	APPARENT WIND ANGLE β	HEEL ANGLE ϕ	REMARKS

degrees. Then set the staysail inside the number one genoa and go through the same drill. Repeat for all sails and possible sail combinations, until you have exhausted your inventory. It is quickest and most accurate to take readings at five-degree intervals for upwind headsails and the starcut, and at fifteen- or twenty-degree intervals for spinnakers.

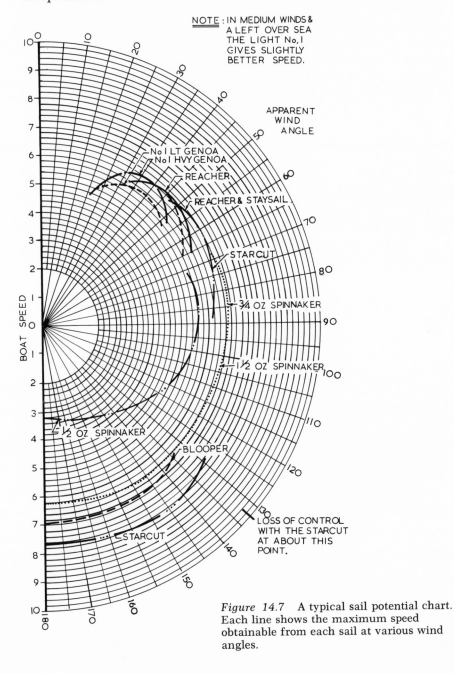

NOTE: IN MEDIUM WINDS &
A LEFT OVER SEA
THE LIGHT No.1
GIVES SLIGHTLY
BETTER SPEED.

APPARENT WIND ANGLE

No 1 LT GENOA
No 1 HVY GENOA
REACHER
REACHER & STAYSAIL
STARCUT
¾ OZ SPINNAKER
1½ OZ SPINNAKER
1½ OZ SPINNAKER
BLOOPER
STARCUT

LOSS OF CONTROL
WITH THE STARCUT
AT ABOUT THIS
POINT.

BOAT SPEED

Figure 14.7 A typical sail potential chart. Each line shows the maximum speed obtainable from each sail at various wind angles.

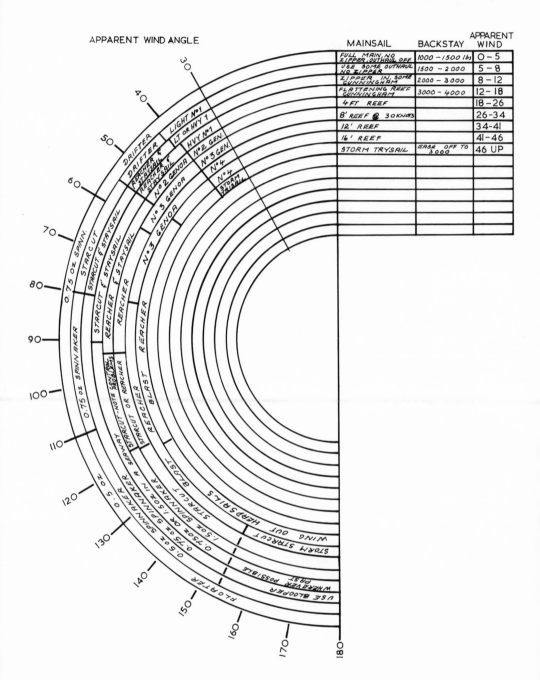

Figure 14.8   A typical sail change chart.

The entire data-gathering stage could take a fairly long time, even when the wind is favorable. For even better results, you might try taking readings when racing, since you will undoubtedly be sailing the boat harder and faster. But be prepared for the task to take more time. And remember that after several days at sea a crew tends to tire and their performance drops off slightly, so try to make as many plots as possible on the first day of a long race or on short races. Remember also that readings for new or recut sails should be taken at the earliest opportunity, and periodic checks of old sails should be made to determine if any are losing power with age.

With the data in hand, you're now ready to work up a sail potential chart. Take all the readings for the number one genoa and plot a chart of boat speed against wind angle for a constant wind speed. It will become clear that as the wind angle changes, boat speed will increase and then fall, until you arrive at a point where the reacher gives greater speed (at the crossover point A in figure 14.7). You will also arrive at a point of increased boat speed when the reaching staysail is added. Keep plotting the graph for all the sails, and a polar plot like the one in figure 14.7 will emerge. Make notes at the side regarding such things as the use of sails in different sea conditions.

A sail potential chart can show where the weaknesses are in your sail wardrobe. For instance, if all the sails are working their best, the extreme outer edge of the polar plot will be almost a fair curve, as in figure 14.4. Any gap or hollow shows where you lack a sail. And a sudden bump means that one sail is working better than the others, so you might want to purchase two more sails to fair the curve on either side of the bump.

In addition, you may want to construct a sail change chart, like the one in figure 14.8. The crossover points in your sail potential curve indicate when sails should be changed. The data logged from sailing trials give you the wind limits for the various sails if these limits are not supplied by the sail makers. Make notes in the margin or have a separate column to show where the traveler and jib leads are set, and so forth.

With a sail potential chart and a sail change chart, it is easy for the skipper to call sail changes and to know what kind of speed each sail should give, thus removing the questions of which sail, when, and will it give more speed? Let's hope that these plots will mean a few more trophies gracing the skipper's shelf at the end of the season, fewer bad sail calls from the back end, and a lot less grumbling from the sharp end.

15 *Crew Fitness*

Every weekend thousands of yachtsmen eagerly take to the race-course. Many of these people consider themselves to be highly active sportsmen, but what exactly does sailing do for physical fitness? The exercise it offers is sporadic. The level of tension is high. The nutritional value of the food can be terrible. And the sleeping patterns on a long race can be insane. If the contributions of sports to personal health were rated on a scale of one to ten, yacht racing would languish in the near-zero range.

Yet paradoxically, to survive this abuse without negative effects on performance, one should ideally be in top physical condition. How many of us really are? Statistics show that the overwhelming majority of adults are significantly out of shape—many dangerously so. This includes most sailors, who in their other lives are merely sedentary, overworked, stress-ridden businessmen. Fortunately, however, flab is not inevitable. Modern research indicates that a simple program of proper diet, regular exercise, and adequate rest and relaxation can reverse even the worst case of physical neglect. The results are a marked improvement in mental and physical performance, not to mention the years such a program can add to your life. So if you truly want to get back into shape and enhance your sailing pleasure, now is the time to start.

What Is Fitness?

One of the problems many people have with getting into shape is their lack of knowledge about what fitness really is. We tend to equate fitness with weight control. As long as we are not grossly overweight, we consider ourselves in reasonably good shape. But true fitness is much more than that. Although all overweight people may be unfit, it does not follow that all people of normal weight are automatically in good physical condition. Fitness involves a combination of three important elements—stamina, strength, and suppleness. Without all three, one cannot consider oneself in top shape.

Stamina is the capacity to keep going—to run long distances, for example, without feeling breathless or on the verge of collapse. In physiological terms, stamina is a measure of the body's efficiency in transporting the oxygen needed to expend energy. This means good development of the lungs, heart, and blood vessels. For yachtsmen, poor stamina usually shows up in chronic fatigue on the racecourse. The crewman who has difficulty staying alert throughout his watch, who begins to feel exhausted if required to make a number of rapid sail changes, and who gets winded after a few turns of the winch handle has inadequate stamina.

Strength is a second component of physical fitness, and the one many people think of when they picture the well-trained athlete. Simply put, strength is the ability to overcome resistance when lifting, pulling, climbing, and so forth. The yachtsman requires strength for a number of reasons: to pull halyards and sheets, grind winches, and haul heavy sail bags, are examples. But when developing strength, don't concentrate on the arms and shoulders alone. Complete fitness means good muscle tone throughout the body, including the back, stomach, and legs.

Suppleness, the third element of fitness, is the ability of muscles, tendons, and ligaments to allow the joints of the body to move freely and easily. It is suppleness that enables a crewman to move quickly during a sail change, to get in and out of a trapeze without difficulty, and to pull a spinnaker in quickly. Sailors who lack suppleness are stiff in their movements and often appear clumsy. Suppleness, of course, is not an all-or-nothing affair. Most people are reasonably supple in joints (shoulders and elbows, for example) but not in others (back and knees). Again, complete fitness requires that all areas of the body be lithe and flexible.

Exercise: Where to Begin?

Many people who know they should start an exercise program aren't sure where to begin. What kind of exercise should they engage in and how often? Some make the mistake of trying to do too much at once. They may set a goal of running three miles every morning, plus doing a half hour of calisthenics every night. Such people are almost certain to become discouraged with their grueling regime and quit. An ambitious program will do you no good if you can't stay with it, so plan something that is achievable. Also plan something that offers a good balance between developing stamina, strength, and suppleness. An hour a day of weight-lifting is not ideal for physical fitness, but half an hour every other day of running or swimming, supplemented by proper warm-up exercises, is.

AEROBIC EXERCISE. The most important form of exercise for general good health is the kind that develops the lungs, heart, and circulatory system. In other words, exercise that builds stamina. Kenneth Cooper, a physician whose research findings have become world famous, coined the expression aerobic exercise for stamina training. Aerobic means "with oxygen," signifying that exercise of this type improves the transport of oxygen throughout the body. In particular, aerobic exercise increases the amount of air breathed in and expelled by the lungs, facilitating the exchange of oxygen and carbon dioxide; it increases the oxygen-carrying capacity of the blood and expands the capillary network of the blood vessels; and it encourages the heart to pump more efficiently, thus putting less strain on it.

The best sports for stamina training are running, cycling, and swimming, but several others are nearly as beneficial. Handball, racquet ball, tennis, rope skipping, cross-country skiing, and even brisk walking are among the many possible forms of exercise that offer aerobic value. The most important thing is to look for a sport that requires sustained and rhythmic movements, rather than sporadic ones. But remember that interest level is important too. Don't force yourself to engage in a form of exercise that you hate. If you choose a sport you enjoy, you'll stand a far better chance of sticking with it.

The amount of aerobic exercise you get each week is critical to the pace of your physical improvement. Many experts suggest between fifteen and thirty minutes every other day as a beneficial and achievable goal. How you spend that time will vary greatly, depending upon your present condition. Always start out slowly and increase the rate of your workouts gradually. If you are starting a running schedule, for example, spend your first session alternating between walking and jogging. Never overexert. Exhaustion does not contribute to fitness and it can be dangerous. As you get back into shape, you'll find that you can steadily increase the proportion of your time running, as well as your speed. A man age thirty-five might set himself an ultimate goal of running two miles in under eighteen minutes four times a week. The goals one sets, of course, always vary with age. But in any case, the only way to optimum fitness is through slow, incremental progress.

These are very general guidelines. For more information on how to plan an aerobic program, you might start by investing in a copy of Kenneth Cooper's book, *The Aerobics Way*. And as he and other experts suggest, a complete physical examination and your doctor's advice are essential before you begin training.

SUPPLEMENTAL EXERCISES. Aerobic activities should always be preceded by warm-up exercises aimed at enhancing suppleness and reducing the risk of injury. Any good fitness book will give you a series of stretching and bending exercises to follow. Remember, though, that calisthenics should stretch the muscles, tendons, and ligaments gently. Forcing more movement in a joint than you are capable of can cause harm. There are also several popular warm-up exercises that can place undue stress on certain joints. Leg-lifts while lying down, for example, can be stressful to the lower back. So consult a doctor or competent manual rather than inventing your own warm-up regime.

In most cases, increased muscle strength is a natural byproduct of aerobic activities. But if you want to develop certain muscle groups more fully—perhaps your arm muscles for lifting power, or your stomach muscles for hiking out on a trapeze—you can easily incorporate a few resistive exercises into your warm-up program. Push-ups, pull-ups, or the use of simple weights and pulleys, all are good for this purpose. Again, consult a fitness handbook for the specific exercises that suit your needs. Isometrics can also achieve the goal of greater muscle strength, but some experts say that they have the drawback of inhibiting blood flow more than resistive exercises, and that their results are in some ways less effective.

Diet and Fitness

Complete fitness cannot be achieved through exercise alone. Good diet is also essential. If you are overweight, you are probably always on the lookout for a way to shed pounds rapidly. There have been many diet fads over the years. Some of these can actually be dangerous to your health and none is more effective in the long run than a simple change in your eating habits to reduce your calorie intake while maintaining balanced nutrition. Studies show that people who lose weight by some crash method nearly always gain it back within a year or two. In contrast, those who follow a sensible diet plan, plus regular exercise, go for years without weight fluctuations of more than a pound or two.

Most health books have tables listing the calorie content of various foods. You should read over such a list before beginning a weight-loss diet. Often some innocuous-seeming food turn out to be much higher in calories than you expect. And in the early stages of a diet, you should also keep a written record of your calorie intake each day. Many people greatly underestimate the number of calories those extra helpings and between-meal snacks add up to. Of course, the total calories you can consume and still lose weight will depend upon your size and level of physical activity. Any doctor or a good diet and exercise book can help you set a reasonable goal.

The composition of the foods you eat is also important for fitness. For example, diets low in protein and high in sugar and caffeine can exacerbate the condition known as hypoglycemia or low blood sugar. Paradoxically, a high intake of sugar stimulates the pancreas to over-produce insulin, a hormone which burns sugar. The result is a drop in blood sugar below normal levels, accompanied by a feeling of chronic fatigue. This is not to say that one should eliminate carbo-hydrates from the diet completely; in moderation they are as essential to good health as are proteins. And fats in moderation are also essen-tial. A diet that promotes optimum fitness is one that is properly balanced.

What constitutes a well-balanced diet? Dr. Kenneth Cooper defines a balanced weight-reduction diet in the following manner:

1. It should be low in carbohydrates (perhaps 50 to 60 grams a day), but not completely lacking in them. (To get some idea of what this means, two slices of rye bread contain about 25 grams of carbohy-drates, and so does the average bowl of breakfast cereal, a medium-sized baked potato, or a glass of apple cider.)
2. It should be high in protein, without large amounts of cholesterol-rich foods such as eggs, animal fat, shellfish, whole milk, and cheese. (Some doctors recommend an intake of no more than 300 milligrams of cholesterol daily, and even less if possible. When you realize that a single egg contains about 235 milligrams, you realize how easy it is to exceed this maximum.)
3. It should allow some fats, but only of the polyunsaturated type, and only one to three teaspoons per day.
4. It should include plenty of liquids.
5. It should include a good multiple vitamin and mineral supplement.
6. It should eliminate the empty calories of refined sugar found in candy, pies, cakes, and soft drinks.

A good nutrition book can help you plan meals that meet these goals and also satisfy your hunger.

Combatting Stress

One should not leave the topic of fitness without a word on one of the biggest obstacles to complete physical well-being—stress. The more scientists have learned about stress, the more they have become aware of its implication in many illnesses, including chronic head-aches, backaches, ulcers, and heart problems. Some doctors have gone so far as to suggest that stress may contribute to the onset of almost any disease, including cancer.

In today's world, stress seems almost unavoidable. Prolonged tasks, exacting demands, unclear or remote goals, and general frus-tration of any kind can all cause stress. It is hard to imagine getting through an average work day without encountering one or another of these conditions. Still, certain steps can help reduce stress.

First, exercise. One byproduct of regular aerobic training is a significant reduction in tension. The rhythmic, sustained activity burns up the adrenal hormones produced in stressful situations, thus allowing the entire body to release built-up tension.

Second, relaxation. With special instruction, one can learn to relax at will all the major muscle groups of the body. If you are chron-ically tense, your doctor should be able to recommend a professional program of relaxation training. The average person, however, can practice relaxation himself simply by becoming more aware of muscle tension in stressful circumstances. Tension in the neck and shoulders is particularly common. In a race, for example, a helmsman might make a conscious effort to periodically roll his head from side to side, loosening that strained feeling. You may be surprised at what a dif-ference such a small thing can make to performance. Also, muscle relaxation before sleep is especially beneficial to proper rest.

Fitness and Sailing

Physical fitness is clearly important for its own sake. It not only im-proves your chances of living a long and healthy life, it can also con-tribute greatly to your performance at work and your enjoyment of leisure time. This includes your performance and enjoyment on the race course. Regattas and long offshore races take a far smaller toll of you mentally and physically when you are in top condition.

Getting started, of course, is usually the most difficult part of establishing a fitness program. One way to overcome the inertia is to make fitness training a group project. If a number of crewmen on your boat live near one another, you might begin jogging together. Or you might collectively join a fitness program at a local YMCA. Exercise tends to be more fun when it is social, thus increasing the likelihood that you'll stick with it. Moreover, a group fitness program can build a sense of camaraderie among the crewmen who participate. This will naturally extend to the race course, making for a more congenial and hopefully a more efficient team.

16 Running Your Boat Like a Business

What does a boat have in common with a business? Not much, many people would answer. A business is related to work, they'd say, a boat to relaxation. The goal of business is to earn a profit, the goal of boating simply to enjoy oneself. This is a perfectly understandable attitude to have toward sailing. Many people work hard all week long and want no part of more work on the weekend. But these same people who seek a pleasant pastime should not complain when they trail the fleet on the race course. To win consistently in offshore racing, a person must be as serious about campaigning for his boat as he is about campaigning for a new product. In fact, some direct analogies can be drawn between running a successful racing boat and running a successful business.

Selecting and Organizing a Crew

Consider first your method of crew selection. How many times have you picked up a few extra crewmen in the yacht club bar before a race? And how many times have you agreed to take your nephew and brother-in-law along, even though their sailing experience is limited to a sunfish or a sailboard? If such practices sound familiar, think of the consequences if they were applied to a business. No company could expect to be successful if it assembled its staff in such a casual fashion, often putting social considerations above professional qualifications. The same is true of selecting a racing crew. But how does one go about finding and screening potential candidates? The answer is, in much the same way as one goes about hiring a new business employee.

RECRUITING NEW CREWMEN. The first step in crew recruitment may be the hardest—locating good, experienced sailors who want to join your boat. As in business, word of mouth often turns up some of the best candidates. Ask sailing friends, sail makers, designers, and boatyard operators for recommendations and compile a list of possible choices. Often, however, there are good sailors available who are not well known to the racing establishment. You might try to locate these people by advertising in sailing magazines. But always be sure to specify where your boat will be racing. Otherwise you might have applicants from two or three hundred miles away!

Once you have compiled your list of potential crewmen, begin by calling the most qualified ones first. If you are not completely sure about a person's past racing experience, don't hesitate to ask him. And don't hesitate to try a person out on a trial basis to begin with—either in a minor race or before the season starts. This will give you a chance to see how well he sails and how hard he is willing to work before you sign him up on a permanent basis.

Personality, of course, is also important; a new crewman must be able to get along with everyone else on the boat. But don't make the mistake of considering amiability before all else. That humorless guy who never laughs at your jokes may still be the best helmsman you can find. As long as a person's personality is not disruptive to your crew, you should consider him for the job, just as you would in a business.

Finally, when it comes to making the decision about who does and who doesn't join the crew, you may want to make the choice yourself, or you may want to ask the advice of a few key crewmen whose opinions you value. Alternatively, if you are very democratic, you may want to put the decision to a vote of the entire crew. Either way, everyone involved should understand what the most important criteria for selection are and choose accordingly.

DELEGATING RESPONSIBILITY. A number of men, no matter how experienced, do not in themselves make a crew. For this you need organization. Organizing the crew and delegating responsibilities are among the most important decisions to the success of an offshore racer. First, you'll want to select the very best watch captains you can—people you can trust to run the boat as well as, if not better than you can yourself. As in business, don't select a manager on the basis of friendship, select him on the basis of skill.

And once you've decided to put a particular person in charge as watch captain, make sure you give him the freedom to do his job.

One of the most common mistakes a manager can make in business is to try to do everything himself, no matter how many other qualified people are on hand. So don't stand at the helm shouting out orders for hours on end. If you want something done, tell the watch captains and let them tell the rest of the crew in their own ways.

Assigning people to the jobs that are best for them is also critical to a racing boat's success. When making crew assignments, be sure to take into account the principle of comparative advantage. Just because you have a hot-shot crewman aboard, don't try to get him to charge around the boat attempting to get his hand into everything. This is a sure way to guarantee he'll end up doing nothing well. Instead, decide what task is the most valuable for that man to perform. If he's an excellent helmsman, for example, and you have few other good helmsmen on board, don't hesitate to keep him occupied at the wheel, in spite of the fact that he can also wind a winch twice as fast as any of the other men. The helmsman's job is far more important to your success. For the same reason, you wouldn't put your best sales manager part-time in the typing pool simply because he can also type twice as fast as any of the secretaries. Always assign your top hands where they can do the most to help win the race.

But don't forget that your more inexperienced crewmen should also be given a chance to learn new skills. From time to time, let your less experienced men try out new jobs—perhaps on minor races. You may discover some hidden talent somewhere. And you'll probably help some of them to become better all-around sailors, which can only work to your advantage in the long run.

Improving Your Equipment

Just as a business cannot turn out a first-rate product with poor equipment, even the best crew cannot win races if the boat and its gear are in disrepair. If you sincerely want to win, now's the time to take a complete inventory of your boat. Ask yourself first, "Is this the most efficient piece of gear for the job? Can it be improved in any way?" If you are quite honest in making your evaluations, you will probably find that there are many pieces of equipment on the boat that could be made to work better. Take sails, for example. A proper set of racing sails must be perfect. Don't tolerate that hooked leech or the wrinkle around the batten pocket. They both reduce boat speed and make it more difficult to stay at the head of the fleet. Similarly, make sure that your rig is tuned just right, that your winch layout is as efficient as possible, that windage is held to a minimum, and so on. Attention to such details can greatly increase your performance on the racecourse.

The second question to ask yourself is "Do I need this item on board? What does it contribute to winning?" Again, if you are completely honest, you will undoubtedly find many things on the boat that can just as well be left ashore during a race. What about those cans of paint you have stowed in the bilge? What about that barbeque, that inflatable dinghy, and that dockside water hose? Each of these items may not weigh much in itself, but together they add up to a substantial amount of excess baggage. Leaving them behind will make your boat that much lighter, and therefore that much faster.

Planning and Executing Your Strategy

No business could survive without a carefully worked out strategy. So too in yacht racing. Planning is all-important, and must begin well before the race. If you are your own navigator, be sure to plot the course before arriving on the boat. Estimate your speed for different wind conditions and calculate the tidal currents accordingly. Also, be sure to check the weather forecast regularly. Then, on race day, brief the crew on what to expect—the course they'll be sailing, the marks to observe and on what side to pass them, and the predicted weather and sea conditions. Poor communication can cost money to a business. Don't let it cost you the race.

Of course, part of a good strategy is being properly prepared to carry it out. So once your race plan is formulated, make sure your crew is practiced enough to execute it flawlessly. Get the men together early in the season or between races and drill them in sail changes, tacking, and gybing. You may be surprised at the amount of increased efficiency that results on the race course. The performance of even the best sailors can usually improve when they learn to work together as a well-organized team. And there is no way to accomplish this but to practice.

These, then, are essentially the steps to take if you want to run your boat like a business. Some people would say that this approach is likely to make racing a rather grim occasion, with no fun left in it at all. But others would argue just the opposite. Some of the most successful firms are also the most enjoyable places to work. The pleasure comes from being part of a winning team. The same holds true for racing. For many sailors who truly want to win, knowing that they're sailing on one of the best boats in the fleet is the greatest pleasure of all.

Improving Performance on the Racecourse

Introduction

Much of today's racing gear is highly sophisticated. Anyone who doubts this need only take a look around the deck of a modern ocean racer. Lift off the drum of a three-speed linked winch and you'll find a complex mesh of gears, pawls, and bearings. Look at the rigging on the latest designs and you'll see extensive use of hydraulic adjusters. Compare such innovations to the state of the art only a dozen years ago, when most winches were single speed and rigging could be adjusted only before the start of a race.

Given these strides in sailing technology, crewmen today have a good deal more to learn about the sport of ocean racing. Constant practice, of course, is still one of the ingredients of successful crew work. But having the required skills is also essential. This section deals with some of the many techniques that can improve performance on the racecourse. Methods of tacking, spinnaker handling, foredeck work, and mainsail control are a few of the practical topics included here.

17/ *Tack Fast*

How often do you tack during a race? Too many times, would probably be the winch grinder's answer. And when you do tack, do you look upon it as an easy drill, and then perhaps don't do it properly? Or is it an operation you view with dread because it loses you so much time?

As with most things, tacking becomes easier and consequently faster when you are skilled in the right techniques. A good tack, where the winch grinder, tailer, helmsman, and mainsail trimmer are co-ordinated, can save twenty to thirty seconds over a sloppily executed tack. So if you go about fifteen times on an upwind leg, that's more than seven minutes saved on one leg of the course. Think how many times that would have put you in first place last season! To improve your crew's tacking techniques, let's review what each man does and how he does it.

Winching during a Tack

THE WINCH GRINDER'S JOB. People often think that winding a winch is the least skilled job on a boat—it appears to require a great deal of brute strength but not much know-how. Consequently, on the race course, the biggest crewman with the least sailing experience often ends up on the powering end of a winch handle. What can go wrong, you reason, as long as he does what he's told? Unfortunately, a lot can go wrong.

Let's observe the scene as the boat tacks. First, the novice winchman carefully places himself in the tailer's way, so he's moved to a less obstructive position. Now he finds himself braced high on the weather side, handle in the winch, waiting for his order to wind. The boat tacks, and he is immediately off balance because the lifeline he was using to keep himself upright on the high side is now on the low side and he is almost horizontal. So precious time is wasted while he readjusts his position. Finally, he begins to wind. But the tailer shouts "More turns! More turns!" and the novice winchman lets go of the handle and leaves it in the winch while he waits for the tailer to put more turns on. Meanwhile, the boat slams into a sea and the novice falls into the cockpit onto the tailer, who by this time has three turns around the winch and two around the handle. To add to the confusion, the helmsman is shouting to get the genoa sheeted in.

Sound familiar? Probably all of us have seen it happen once in a while. And although most of us are no longer novices and are not going to make the bumbling mistakes of a rank beginner, it is still helpful to review the steps involved in the proper operation of a genoa winch during a tack. The basic procedure is quite simple:

1. Find a place for your feet so that you can maintain your balance *throughout* the tack.
2. Make sure you know which direction is high gear for the particular winch you are operating and wind that way first.
3. Start winding when the clew of the genoa has cleared the mast and is approaching position D in figure 17.1.
4. If the tailer shouts for more turns, take the winch handle out of the winch so he can get the turns on easily and quickly.
5. As soon as the turns are on, put the handle back in the winch and get that genoa in.

But even if a person is following these steps, he may still not be operating the primary winch to best advantage, simply because he is not winding in the most efficient way possible. How do you wind a winch efficiently? When starting to wind, your movement should be all arm motion. The object is to get the drum turning as quickly as possible. This reduces friction and helps the tailer get as much sheet in as he can before the genoa fills and winding becomes difficult. (See figures 17.2a and 17.2b.)

So far so good. But as the load increases, so does the effort required to operate the winch. Although you may be tempted to switch to that lower speed right away, don't do so yet. Instead of working with just your arms, begin to use your shoulder and back muscles. Do this by locking your arms and getting your chin over the winch.

There is a limit, however, to how long you can continue to wind in high gear. On larger boats, the sheet loading can be in excess of 10,000 pounds, so it is clearly impossible for a winch operator to get the genoa fully in without switching to a lower speed. In lower gears, of course, it is easier to turn the winch handle, but it takes more

Figure 17.1   Tacking a genoa. The sail is sheeted home on the starboard tack (A). When the boat comes up into the wind the sheet is eased out about a foot. As soon as it starts to break (B) the sheet is thrown off completely and the sail is blown across the foredeck (C). The crew should help the sail around the mast and shrouds until it can be wound in (D). Finally, the sail is fully home on the port tack (E).

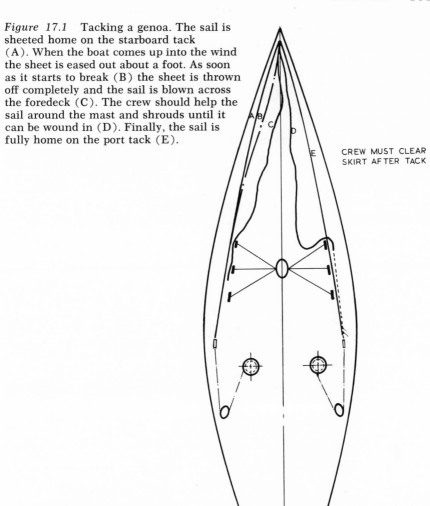

CREW MUST CLEAR
SKIRT AFTER TACK

turns to get one revolution of the drum. The manufacturer's name for the ratio between handle and drum revolutions is gear ratio. The other phrase often used by winch makers is power ratio, which depends to some extent on the gear ratio.

$$\text{power ratio} = \frac{\text{gear ratio} \times \text{length of winch handle} \times 2}{\text{diameter of winch drum}}$$

For fast tacking, both these ratios must be optimized by the manufacturer, and the designer must select the winches that best suit the sail plan of the boat and the future crew's ability.

How should winch gears be used to get the genoa sheet in as quickly as possible on a tack? Begin winding in high gear, the most effective gear ratio being one to one. Then, when the handle revolu-

Figure 17.2a To insert a winch handle quickly, always use both hands. *17.2b* This crewman has little control over the handle and takes longer to get it into the winch.

tions begin to slow, snap into second gear to wind the rest of the sheet in. The exact point for switching to lower gear largely depends upon the strength of the individual crewman. Although the winch you are operating may have a third gear, you should only have to use this speed for trimming—that is, as long as the tailer is doing his job properly!

THE WINCH TAILER'S JOB. To tail a winch easily and quickly, the following technique works best:

1. On the order "prepare to tack" or "ready about," the tailer pulls the lazy sheet tight, with no more than two or three turns on the drum, as in figure 17.3 b. (After a tack, place the lazy sheet ready on the drum if another tack is expected.)

2. As soon as the old sheet is let go, the tailer pulls on the new sheet, so that when the boat comes head to wind the sail is pulled around.
3. Another crewman clears the bowlines off the shrouds and mast and attends to the skirt. The tailer then pulls with an elbowing motion, as shown in figure 17.4. *Be sure to keep tension on the sheet at all times.*
4. The winch operator winds as explained earlier. Remember, this is a partnership between tailer and winder. When the partners work together, the tack will be fast and smooth.

Figure 17.3a Too many turns on a drum can override or slide down the winch base, as in this picture. *17.3b* To tail a winch fast, two or three turns make the job easy.

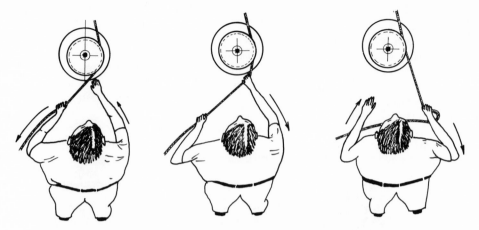

Figure 17.4 Tailing a winch as seen from above. *17.4a* The crewman pulls aft with his left hand while reaching forward with his right. *17.4b* He starts to pull with his right hand while maintaining tension on the sheet with his left. Note that the only body movement involved is a swivel from the hips. *17.4c* The man is pulling aft with his right hand and reaching for the sheet tail with his left. A bight of rope piles up in front of him, ready to run out when the sheet is cast off.

5. As soon as the load is on the sheet and the winder begins to slow down, the tailer takes more turns on the drum and continues to pull, in order to aid the winder a little. If the sheet slips at this stage, it means more work for the winder.

On boats with linked winch systems, a somewhat different procedure is used. Here, two crewmen are needed to operate the remote drive pedestal, and one of them often faces aft. It is usually best for the tailer to call the tack, since he can see when to trim and when to stop winding. But once again, he must watch the sail clew carefully as it comes around and avoid telling the winders to start too soon, or they will be out of breath before the sail is fully in.

Helming during a Tack

Next we bring into the game yet another player, the helmsman. He has the difficult job of watching virtually everything that goes on during the tack. For example, if the sheet fouls anywhere, the helmsman can hold the boat head-to-wind for a few seconds to allow the snag to be freed.

The helmsman must also be careful about the speed with which he tacks. He can tack fast or slowly, depending upon how quickly he thinks the cockpit crew will get the genoa in. A powerful crew can put the genoa aback and stop the boat in the middle of the tack. With a powerful crew, therefore, the helmsman will probably put the helm hard over and spin the boat around quickly. There are some possible problems with this technique, however. Unless the man at the wheel knows what he's doing, the boat will fall off, and several yards to windward can be lost on each tack. If the boat does not point too well, or if the helmsman has difficulty locating the "groove," letting the bow sag off a little may be the way to go. But this does lose yards, which on a long beat may be important.

If a boat is lightly crewed, holding the bow up in the tack for a moment to allow the sail to come around is often a help in getting the genoa home. But this too, loses speed and yards to windward.

The best helmsmen use different techniques for different boats and different crews. You should practice tacking until you find which techniques suit your boat and crew. Using a stopwatch, clock each tack from the moment you say "Helm's alee!" until the genoa is fully home on the new heading. Then look at your wake to see if the boat made a clean, right angle without any sags or bumps.

Tacking the Mainsail

Having reviewed all the other operations involved in tacking, the simplest one remains—tacking the mainsail. With the small mainsail on a modern racer, the main sheet rarely requires adjustment. Usually, only the traveler is moved to a new position, corresponding to its position on the old tack. For example, if the traveler was four inches to weather, then as the boat is tacked and the main momentarily flogs, the traveler should be moved four inches to weather on the new tack. On some one-design boats or on boats with larger mainsails, however, you may also have to ease the sheet or vang in order to help the boat around.

Although tacking the mainsail is an easy operation, it is surprising how often it is poorly performed. One potential problem has to do with where the crewman involved positions himself. It is essential for the man tacking the mainsail not to interfere with the cockpit crew tacking the genoa. This means that the mainsail trimmer often has to be forward of the crew's working area. Timing is another aspect of tacking the mainsail that needs more attention on some boats. The sail should be adjusted when it is flapping, because it is easier to move then than when it is filled on the other tack. The mainsail trimmer should then look up the sail to see that it is drawing and that the telltales are streaming out as they should be.

By now even the novice will have gathered that there is much more to tacking a racing boat than simply saying "Lee ho!" When you are out there on the racecourse, why not try putting some of these suggestions to use and see if your fleet position doesn't improve.

18 *Spinnaker Handling*

When was the last time you prepared to set a spinnaker, only to find it hadn't been packed properly? Or when did you last start to hoist a chute and suddenly discover that the halyard had been carefully hooked to the clew? If such foul-ups are easy to remember, now is the time to review your spinnaker handling techniques. You may find that your problem is not so much a lack of knowledge and skill as a lack of good planning and attention to detail. With a little extra effort, made well in advance, some of the difficulties you so often encounter on the race course can easily be avoided. In this chapter I'll discuss three important aspects of spinnaker handling on racing boats: packing a spinnaker, setting a spinnaker, and changing spinnakers.

Packing a Spinnaker

A good spinnaker set at the weather mark can often gain you boat lengths. But before the sail can be set properly, it must be packed properly. There are several methods. The sail can be either stopped or flaked and then stowed in a turtle, or it can be rolled and stowed in a sausage fastened by a zipper or velcro strip. It is useful to review each of these techniques, and the accompanying checklist shows where the most common mistakes are made.

STOPPING. The days when sailors used rotten cotton to stop their spinnakers are long gone. Today a far quicker and more efficient method has been found. It calls for an old plastic bucket with the bottom cut out (see figure 18.1), plus a handful of elastic bands about three inches long and fairly wide. Figure 18.2 shows how these are used to stop a spinnaker. First, place the elastic bands around the bucket. Then, keeping the luff tapes together, slide the bucket down the sail, starting at the head. Cast off the bands about every four to six feet, until you reach a point about two-thirds of the way down the sail. Next, remove the bucket and use the same technique to make "legs," starting at each clew. When you are finished, the sail should look like figure 18.3. You are now ready to place the spinnaker in the turtle. The two clews should be held outside the turtle while the

Figure 18.1 A stopping bucket. Note the glued-on wooden strip, to make it easier to lift off the bands.

Figure 18.2 An elastic band in place on a spinnaker. Notice how the luff tapes are parallel down the entire sail.

rest of the sail is fed into it, as shown in figure 18.4. When the entire sail has been packed, the corners should be folded on top and tied off. Figure 18.5 shows how.

FLAKING. Only your heavier spinnakers should be stopped by the method just described. Light wind sails should simply be "flaked." Starting at the head or at one of the clews, work around the sail, folding the edge tape back and forth on top of itself. The technique is illustrated in figure 18.6. Eventually, all the edges will be folded in a single pile. Then, holding the tapes and corners, stuff the rest of the sail into the turtle. The tapes go in last, and the three corners are tied off as before. (See figure 18.7.)

Figure 18.3   A fully stopped spinnaker with "legs."

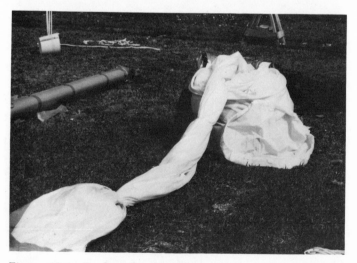

Figure 18.4   Feeding the spinnaker into the turtle.

Figure 18.5   The three corners of the sail should end up on top of the pile and be tied off.

Figure 18.6
A spinnaker
when flaked
down should
look like this.

Figure 18.6   A spinnaker when flaked down should look like this.

Figure 18.7   The three clews are tied off inside the bag.

STOWING IN A SAUSAGE. A sausage is really just a rectangular wrapper the length of the spinnaker. To stow the sail in it, first tie the head of the sausage to the spinnaker swivel or shackle. Then, starting at the head, bring the luff tapes together and roll the spinnaker up as if you were going to stop it. Work a yard or two at a time, wrapping the sausage around the rolled sail and fastening it with the zipper of velcro. Keep working down the sail, rolling and wrapping, until the entire spinnaker is firmly packed. Tie off the ends of the sausage and fold it, snake-like, into a bag or turtle. When you are ready to hoist the sail, remember to remove the ties. Once the sail is aloft, a pull on the sheet peels back the sausage, which collapses to the deck.

Setting a Spinnaker

No matter which method you use to pack and stow a spinnaker, careful planning is always needed to execute a proper set. Here we'll review the two most common types of spinnaker sets—the bear-away set and the gybe set.

A BEAR-AWAY SET. Suppose you are racing on a conventional thirty-five-to forty-foot boat with a guy and sheet on each side. You are approaching the weather mark and the next leg is off the wind. You know that a bear-away set is required because the boats in the class ahead already rounded the mark. What are some of the things that can go wrong?

One of the most common errors is being late setting up. This is usually caused by either a tactician who cannot decide whether the mark is actually being laid, or a navigator who has not yet worked out where the wind will be coming from on the next leg. The solution, then, is proper planning and quick action as the boat approaches the mark. Obviously, this involves making the right decision about which spinnaker to use. If the class ahead has already gone around the same mark, the decision is easy. If not, the question must be answered by the tactician or the navigator, who must then take enough bearings on the relative wind to be sure that the sail he has selected can still be carried.

As the mark is neared, each man should have a clear understanding of his job. For a bear-away set, the crew assignments on our one-tonner are as follows:

1. The present genoa sheet trimmer prepares the spinnaker sheet on the secondary winch. After the hoist, he will trim the spinnaker.
2. A second crewman prepares the spinnaker guy on the weather primary winch. After the set, he will trim the pole and foreguy as required.

3. A third man, usually the navigator, tends the mainsheet. This involves easing first the traveler, then the sheet, and putting the vang on.
4. Two other men take care of the halyards, raising the topping lift and the spinnaker halyard, and lowering the genoa halyard. On a boat where the halyards are led aft, one of these men must be in the cockpit.
5. The man at the bow makes sure that the spinnaker is properly hooked up, and he also gathers the genoa when it is dropped.
6. The last crewman is the helmsman. Hopefully, he manages to get the boat around the mark without hitting it.

A GYBE SET. Now let's look at the tasks required as the same boat rounds a mark for a gybe set. First, the preparation stage, which should take a competent crew only a few minutes to perform to windward.

1. Decide which spinnaker you will set and pass it forward to the bow man, who until now has been sitting on the windward rail. He takes the sail forward and clips it down.
2. Another man goes aft and uncleats the sheets and guys, easing them to the man at the bow as required.
3. The bow man next rigs the pole; he pulls the downhaul out about six feet and recleats it, raises the inboard end of the pole, clips the topping lift on, and holds it back to the mast.
4. A third man makes sure that a winch is clear for the spinnaker halyard, and that the genoa halyard is free to run.
5. The navigator goes forward and places the blooper immediately below the forehatch, with all three corners on a specially placed hook within easy reach of a person on deck.
6. The genoa sheet trimmer looks to see where the guy is.
7. On the weather side, another crewman places the spinnaker sheet on the secondary winch and takes a turn on the primary winch which holds the lazy genoa sheet.

It is now apparent that the boat is laying the mark. What are the crew assignments for the set?

1. As the boat rounds the mark, the navigator gybes the mainsail and then eases out the traveler and the mainsheet.
2. The genoa sheet trimmer lets go of the sheet on the gybe and places the guy on the primary winch. He then starts pulling the spinnaker guy aft.
3. The man on the other side of the cockpit—the side opposite the genoa sheet trimmer—hauls the genoa sheet in after the gybe, cleats it, and stands by the spinnaker sheet.
4. On the bow, there are two possible ways of hoisting the spinnaker. The more conventional method is to top the pole, and then hoist the spinnaker and drop the genoa. A faster but riskier method is to start the spinnaker up on the weather side and let it be blanketed by the

genoa, ignoring the pole, which will be lifted when the spinnaker fills.

5. When the spinnaker is almost up, sheet it and bring the pole fully aft. The timing of the sheeting is important. If it is done too soon, the sail may fill before fully up. To avoid this, it is customary to have one man tailing the winch as a safeguard, while another hauls on the halyard. On the other hand, of course, the sheeting must not be done too late, or else the sail will hourglass.

6. Now that the sail is up and drawing, drop the genoa. Ease the main outhaul, cunningham, and halyard. And finally, prepare the blooper and hoist it.

7. When all the sails are pulling, the crew should settle down in the most advantageous position and concentrate on getting the best speed possible. Only one man should be designated to clean up.

All these steps can be performed in a matter of a few minutes. In fact, on a one-tonner, it is possible to have the spinnaker up and pulling within a boat's length of the mark!

Peel Changing

In many races, I have watched boats lose places as they made bareheaded spinnaker changes. If you are skipper or crew on one of those boats, you are probably well aware of the disadvantages of dropping one spinnaker before raising another, but you may simply never have learned how to do a peel change. Yet this operation is not difficult. As long as you have two spinnaker halyards and an extra sheet, you can easily make the change with the aid of a short strop, as in figure 18.8.

While making a peel change, always make sure that the crew who are manning the sail already up carry on trimming and ignore the change preparations. If the present sail collapses, then any time saved with a peel change is lost.

For the actual change, here's the method I like to use:

1. Take the new sail forward and tie the turtle down.

2. Run off a new sheet and clip it to the clew of the new sail. Remember that different sails often sheet to different positions.

3. Rig the new halyard. If the original sail is hoisted on the leeward halyard, then the new sail will go up on the weather halyard, which *must be passed around the headstay* prior to hoisting. This means that the new sail will go up on the *inside* of the old one. (More about an *outside* spinnaker set later.)

4. Pull the new tack out of the turtle and clip it into the peel change strap. (I do this to make sure that this part of the sail does not fill with air and pull the rest of the spinnaker out of the turtle, with disastrous results.)

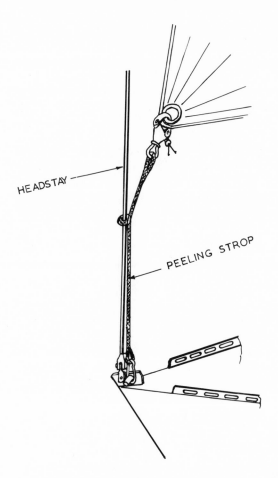

Figure 18.8 Spinnaker peeling strop tied in position around the headstay and attached to the spinnaker.

5. The remaining crewmen should be at their stations: one man in the pulpit; one to hook the new halyard on and to help at the mast; one to lower the pole, if required, and to raise the new halyard and lower the old; one to operate the foreguy and afterguy; and one to operate the old sheet and to change to the new. Other crewmen should be detailed off as "gatherers." If your boat does not carry this many crewmen, some people can be assigned more jobs, and certain things can be done prior to the actual set.

6. Before hoisting, check: Is all clear aloft? Is the sheet clear? Is the new tack clipped on? Is everybody in position and ready?

7. When the order is given, hoist the new spinnaker, cleat the halyard, and set the sail. There are now two spinnakers flying, hopefully both setting.

8. The next step is to lower the pole and bring it forward to the man in the pulpit, who unhooks the old spinnaker, allowing it to peel back, ready to be taken down. The pulpit man then hooks the guy into the new sail. (It is important to give him plenty of slack in the guy at this stage.) As soon as the guy is clipped on, the pole should be

wound aft, giving the bow man time to unhook the changing strap. Remember to ease the sheet as the pole comes aft.

9. While all this is happening on the bow, the old sail should be gathered, cleared off the deck, and repacked.

10. Finally, rerun the sheets and guys for the next change. And that's it.

Now for some variations on this theme. If the original spinnaker has been hoisted on the weather halyard, the change must be made in such a way that the new sail goes up *outside* the existing sail, using the leeward halyard. Some sail makers do not like this method, fearing that a snag in the new halyard could rip the old sail. But if the new halyard is passed outside the sheet and is hooked onto the spinnaker, I have found that it rarely touches the old sail when hoisting. If you use this technique, remember to sheet the old sail in hard just before unclipping. This will pull it inside the new spinnaker, ready to be taken down in the lee of the mainsail. From here on, the change is done exactly as outlined above; simply follow steps 8–10.

These methods are fairly easy and will take a competent crew very little time to learn. With a little planning and practice, almost any crew will be able to execute a smooth, efficient peel change.

CHECKLIST
to Avoid Common Errors

Packing

- Are the elastic bands used for stopping the spinnaker strong enough?
- Are the luff tapes together?
- Are the corners of the spinnaker clearly labeled, so you don't hoist the sail upside down?
- Has the spinnaker been stopped with "legs" so it does not fill too early when hoisted?
- Are the corners of the spinnaker properly tied so that they don't get lost when the turtle is moved?
- When stowing a flaked spinnaker in a turtle, did you pack the luff tapes and corners last?
- Did you take care not to pack any extraneous objects with the spinnaker? (We once packed the cook's pajamas!)

Setting Up

- Are there any split pins or sharp edges around the pulpit or in the area where the spinnaker will be hosited?
- Do the crewmen know their positions and assignments well before the hoist?
- Does the afterguard know what the foredeck men are doing and vice versa?
- Do you have the correct spinnaker on deck?
- Are the halyards clear?
- Is the genoa sheet *over* the pole and topping lift?
- Are the sheet and guy led *over* the lifelines and not through them?
- Is the genoa halyard ready for the sail to be lowered?
- Do you need the jockey pole?

Hoisting

- Is the turtle tied down?
- Are the tapes at both ends of the sausage undone, so that it will drop back to the deck?
- Do you have at least one turn on the spinnaker halyard winch?
- Do you have the proper amount of tension on the sheet? (Too much tension will cause the spinnaker to fill early, but too little tension may cause it to wrap.)
- Is the foreguy cleated off?

Peel Changing

- Are the halyards clean and not twisted?
- Is the peeling strop rigged properly?
- Is the new sheet ready and led through a block in the correct position? (Usually a reaching spinnaker should be sheeted further forward than a running spinnaker.)
- Are all crewmen in position?
- Is everything clear aloft?
- Is the sail in danger of snagging or ripping when hoisted?
- Is the afterguard ready to gather the old spinnaker?
- Is the man trimming the guy ready to give the bow man *plenty* of afterguy?
- As soon as the guy is clipped on, trim the sheet and guy to the desired position. Repack the old spinnaker and rerun the old sheet and halyard. Note that on an outside set the sheet of the old sail should be trimmed in hard before releasing it in order to pull the old sail inside the new one.

19 Working the Foredeck

There is a certain mystique about a good foredeck man. He is the person who, when the wind is blowing thirty knots, manages to execute a flawless spinnaker set. He is the person who, when the sea is breaking over the bow, changes from the number four genoa to the storm jib with seemingly effortless speed and precision. He is the person with the aura of complete confidence no matter what the sailing conditions.

How does one become a top-notch foredeck hand? Fortunately for the average sailor, a good foredeck man is largely made, not born. The skill he displays is the result of a sound knowledge of the boat he is sailing, coupled with the experience needed for quick and flexible decision-making. With enough investment of time and effort, then, almost anyone can become a good foredeck hand.

What Does a Foredeck Hand Do?

The foredeck man, as everyone knows, is the crew member who works in the portion of the deck forward of the mast. On boats smaller than three-quarter ton, there is usually only one foredeck man; on boats from one ton to Admiral's Cup size, there are typically two; and on larger boats there may be even more foredeck hands. But regardless of boat size, the work of the foredeck crew remains generally the same. What, exactly, do the foredeck men do? Their job entails a series of very specific tasks before, during, and after the race.

Before the Race

The work of the foredeck man begins long before the race. When he arrives on the boat, his first task is to get out the sheets and guys. Depending upon the particular boat, these may be rigged immediately or left on deck to be rigged later, when the boat is clear of the dock. Once he has the sheets and guys out of the forepeak, the foredeck man should repack the sails as required. All the spinnakers should be flaked or stopped, and all the genoas should have their luffs flaked and be placed ready in their turtles. The sails should then be stowed in their bins, or on the cabin sole.

During the Race

While racing, the foredeck hand performs many different jobs. Here we'll look at the major ones and outline the basic tasks required for each.

CHANGING GENOAS. When genoas are changed, it is the foredeck man's job to carry the new sail up to the bow, hook the tack on, and attach the halyard to the head of the sail. If a twin luff groove device is used, he should make sure that the tack and the halyard are on the same side, ready for the sail to be hoisted. Then, when the new genoa is up and sheeted, he must pull the old sail down and either flake it in preparation for being used again, or stow it and flake it later.

If a bareheaded change with hanks is required, the foredeck man should clip the new genoa onto the headstay below the lowest hank of the old sail. When the old sail is lowered he must undo the tack, undo each hank, and then put the same halyard on the new sail. Now he is ready to give the order to hoist. As the new sail goes up, he should make sure that the hanks do not foul. Finally, he must clear the old sail off the deck and make it ready for use again.

HOISTING THE SPINNAKER. When approaching the weather mark, the foredeck man should set up the spinnaker pole and lead the sheets and guys to the turtle. The turtle, in turn, should be clipped to the leeward rail for a bear-away set, and to the weather rail for a gybe set. He must then make sure that the guy passes through the pole end (not through the pulpit), that the sheet is clear aft, and that the halyard is clear aloft.

At this stage he is ready to set the spinnaker. For a bear-away set, he can hoist and secure the pole when the boat is laying the mark. Note that the genoa sheet should cross over the top of the pole. For a gybe set, on the other hand, he should hold back the topping lift at the mast, to allow the genoa sheet to cross the pole without fouling. The pole can then be topped up as the spinnaker is being

Figure 19.1 Foredeck men readying the spinnaker for a set. The guy has been led around the back of the genoa and will be hooked onto the spinnaker.

hoisted. For this operation I like to allow a few feet of slack foreguy and let the spinnaker lift the pole; later I tighten the topping lift.

When the spinnaker is up and drawing, the foredeck man should gather the genoa and flake the luff in preparation for the next hoist, or he should make ready the sail required on the next leg. Needless to say, he should finish cleaning up the foredeck and get off the bow as quickly as possible.

CHANGING SPINNAKERS. A spinnaker change will usually be done as a peel change. This means that the foredeck hand must set up the peeling clew (see the section in chapter 18 that discusses peel changing) and reeve a new sheet. By bringing the halyard forward, the new spinnaker is made ready for hoisting.

Once the new sail is up, it is the foredeck man's job to unclip the old sail from the guy and clip the guy into the new tack, ready for the pole to be taken aft. Often, he then moves back to the mast

Figure 19.2 Foredeck men hoisting a spinnaker. One man hauls on the spinnaker halyard where it emerges from the mast while another (hidden behind the mast) takes up the slack on the halyard.

to lower the old spinnaker. And finally, he must bring the turtle aft and get the old spinnaker sheet ready again.

GYBING THE SPINNAKER. To execute a spinnaker gybe, needless to say, the staysails or blooper must first be taken down. Beyond this, however, the method of gybing varies, depending upon such factors as the size of the boat and the skill and preferences of the foredeck crew.

In an end-for-end gybe, the pole is passed through the foretriangle. This technique is only used on smaller boats. The foredeck man's role in the drill is first to trip the guy out of the pole, and then to take the pole off the mast. (The reverse procedure could result in driving the pole through the mainsail.) Next, the foredeck hand hooks the mast end of the pole onto the new guy (the old sheet) and reclips the pole onto the mast on the new gybe.

In a dip-pole gybe, the outboard end of the spinnaker pole is unhooked from the guy, swung forward, and dropped into the pulpit. The foredeck man, therefore, must sit in the pulpit and pull the foreguy toward him while the pole dips under the headstay. He then hooks the new guy into the pole and pushes the pole out on the new gybe.

For the third type of spinnaker gybe, a twin-pole gybe, the foredeck man first rigs the second pole with its new foreguy, topping lift, and afterguy. Then, when the order is given to gybe, he usually works at the mast, either tripping the old pole or topping the new one. After the gybe is completed, it is the foredeck hand's job to remove and stow the old pole and to clear the guy if desired.

TAKING DOWN THE SPINNAKER. When approaching the leeward mark, the foredeck hand must be ready to drop any blooper or staysails that may have been set. He then attaches the genoa halyard in preparation for hoisting. As the boat nears the mark, the genoa is raised and the foredeck hand goes to the bow to unclip the tack of the spinnaker for the takedown.

After the Race

Although the race may be over, the foredeck man's job is not. Often, there are sails to dry and pack, lines to coil, and gear to repair. A good foredeck man performs these tasks while the boat is on the way back in, and if any equipment must be sent out for repair, he makes a note of it. With all this finished, his work is over for another race.

What Makes a Good Foredeck Hand?

The accompanying checklist summarizes the major things a fore-deck man must remember when executing basic drills. Obviously, if he is to perform his job well, he must be mentally alert at all times. The crewman who pays more attention to what the other boats are doing than to what is happening on his own deck can never make a good foredeck hand.

Beyond this, there are several general qualities that make for a first-rate foredeck crew.

KNOWLEDGE OF THE BOAT. There is no substitute for knowing the boat one is sailing on. When sailing on a new boat, a good fore-deck hand always makes a thorough inspection as soon as he arrives, because every boat is set up differently. It is essential that he knows how everything on the deck is laid out well before the race gets underway.

EXPERIENCE. The more a person has sailed, and the more varied the conditions he has encountered, the more effective he will be on the foredeck. With experience comes the ability to be flexible in executing drills and the confidence to try out new ideas. The result can be seconds saved here and there which together can make the difference between winning and losing.

STRENGTH AND AGILITY. To perform well on the foredeck it helps to be physically fit and well coordinated. And because of the lifting and pulling involved, sheer strength is also a plus. Still, some of the required brawn can be compensated for by the ability to think quickly and to improvise.

PRACTICE. The flawless foredeck drill is usually one that has been performed over and over again. Simple practice is essential to develop dexterity and speed. And if there are two crewmen on the foredeck, practice is needed to build a smooth working rapport. When foredeck partners are working together properly, each one knows exactly what the other is about to do at any moment. A foredeck crew composed of odd hands picked up on the dock just before the start almost never wins races.

CHECKLIST
for a Foredeck Hand

Drill	*Points to Remember*
All drills	Check aloft and keep the halyards clear.
Changing genoas	Check that the tack and the hayard are both on the same side (both to port or to starboard).
	Check that the sheet lead is correct for the new sail.
	After the change, make sure that the new sheet is clear for a tack and that it is tied onto the genoa.
Hoisting spinnakers	Make sure the genoa sheet is over the top of the pole.
	Check that the sheets and guys are clear and not twisted or passed under the pulpit or lifeline.
	On a gybe set, keep the topping lift back to the mast.
	Make sure that the head of the sail is above the lifeline so that the halyard shackle cannot catch on the lifeline and open.
	On a gybe set, hoist the sail to weather as the bow of the boat is level with the mark.
Changing spinnakers	Keep the peeling strop short.
	On an outside set, pull the sheet on the old spinnaker in hard to get the old sail inside the new one.
	Make sure that the new sheet is led inside or outside the old one, depending upon the type of set.
	Be careful not to cross the halyards. Check aloft and mentally work out the sequence of operations before hooking up.
Gybing the spinnaker	Clear the staysails or blooper, but have them ready to hoist on the next gybe if required.
End-for-ending	Take the pole off the sail first, and then off the mast. On the new gybe, put the pole on the sail first, and then on the mast.
	Ease the foreguy if necessary.
Dip-pole gybe	Make sure that the babystay is removed.
	Check that the new guy is led forward and put in the pole the correct way around.

	Make sure that the genoa is kept low enough so that it doesn't prevent the pole from passing through the foretriangle.
	Run all halyards back to the mast or forward of the headstay.
Twin-pole gybe	Make sure that the poles will not interfere with one another and that all lines are led correctly.
After gybing	Check that the genoa sheet and halyard are clear and that the genoa is on the correct side for hoisting.
Taking down spinnakers	Clear the staysails or blooper.
	Hoist the genoa and make sure that all the sheet leads are clear and that the genoa sheet is over the pole.
	Let go of the spinnaker at the tack.
	Get the pole down, clear the topping lift, and be ready to tack if required.
	Rerun the weather sheets and guys.
	After tacking, rerun the other sheets and guys and make sure that the halyards are ready to use again if required.

20 Operating the Mainsheet, Traveler, and Vang

Proper mainsail control is much more important to winning a race than most people think. When sailing to windward, the mainsail can be adjusted to balance the helm and significantly increase boat speed. And easing the traveler when a puff hits can also help to balance heel angle. To get the most out of your mainsail, you should know when and how to use all of its controls—the main halyard and the cunningham for adjusting luff tension, the outhaul for tensioning the foot, the mainsheet for positioning the boom and tensioning the leech, the vang also for adjusting leech tension, and the traveler for controlling the sail's angle of attack.

For best results, the mainsail shape should approximate that of the genoa. To understand why, imagine that you are sailing to windward with a mainsail alone. The mast disrupts the flow of air over the sail. So although the streamlines on the weather side tend to straighten, those to leeward remain turbulent until they reattach about two-thirds of the way back from the leading edge. Now suppose a genoa is placed in front of the main. The air flow passes through the slot between the two sails and helps reduce the turbulence on the leeward side. It stands to reason, therefore, that when the shape of the main conforms to the shape of the genoa, the air flow through the slot will be fairly constant from top to bottom. As a result, both sails will be approaching maximum efficiency.

The mainsheet, the traveler, and the vang do a great deal to keep the mainsail shape similar to that of the genoa. In this chapter

176

we'll take a look at what each one does and how it should be adjusted under different conditions. In addition, we'll review how these three controls can be used together to best advantage.

The Mainsheet

Mainsheets come in various shapes and sizes. Figures 20.1a and 20.1b show simple two-part and four-part mainsheets which can be led to a winch or pulled in by hand. The windage they create can be reduced by using a wire strop to lower the height of the top block, as shown in figure 20.2. These arrangements are extremely efficient when used with a traveler and taglines, or when linked to a single fixed point on the deck. But often they have one big disadvantage. The block leading to the winch must be positioned on the centerline so, under load, the boom tends to be pulled toward the center. This can be remedied by taking the sheet forward, as illustrated in figure 20.3. The additional blocks, however, introduce extra friction and make the sail slower to trim. Another, more minor drawback to two-part and four-part mainsheets is the amount of rope they require to swing the boom fully out—two to four times the amount required by a single-part tackle.

Many other mainsheet systems are possible. Most of them unduly complicate matters. The layout shown in figure 20.4, for example, may look efficient, but all the blocks must turn when the traveler is moved. Under load this is often next to impossible. To my mind, a single-part tackle led to a powerful winch, as seen on twelve meters, is the simplest and most efficient method of trimming a mainsheet. And when a rope sheet is fitted a self-tailing winch will help make the job even easier. The cost of the winch, however, is quite high, which is a considerable disadvantage.

Whatever the design of the mainsheet, its major function is to shape the sail, and its tension is critical: too little allows the sail to twist off at the top, while too much pulls the leech up tight and stalls the air flow out of the sail. In both cases, boat speed declines. To know when the mainsheet is set properly, it is easiest to watch the telltales. These should be sewn into each batten pocket, with one or two more in the belly of the sail. The trimmer then adjusts the mainsheet until all the telltales are streaming aft.

The amount of mainsheet tension varies with the mast characteristics and cut of the sail. For example, some sail makers cut mainsails with a very large roach, to gain extra unmeasured sail area and increase efficiency by having more of the sail behind the air flow reattachment point. This large roach is notoriously hard to control,

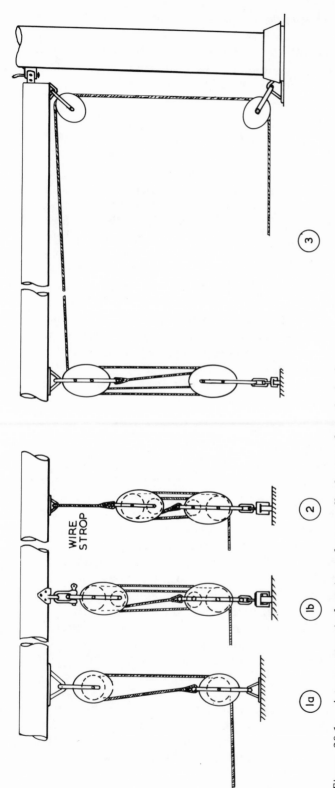

Figure 20.1a A two-part mainsheet is used on smaller boats, where the loads are fairly small. *20.1b* On larger boats, a four- or six-part sheet is often used, although this increases windage substantially.

Figure 20.2 One way to reduce windage is to insert a wire strop between the boom and the sheet. The strop is long enough so that the sheet is still not quite two-blocked under maximum load.

Figure 20.3 Often the mainsheet is led forward to the gooseneck end of the boom and back to the operator or winch along the deck.

requiring high mainsheet tension even in light airs. It also requires careful positioning of the mainsheet. When the mainsheet is attached to the end of the boom so that it pulls vertically downward, tensioning the leech of the sail is easier. In contrast, when the sheet is attached to the middle of the boom, or when it is led aft, as in figure 20.5, controlling the leech is more difficult. You may want to check the position of the mainsheet on your own boat to see if it might be altered for improved efficiency.

Figure 20.4   This method of leading the mainsheet may look efficient, but if the traveler is moved, all the blocks must turn and this is sometimes next to impossible under a high load.

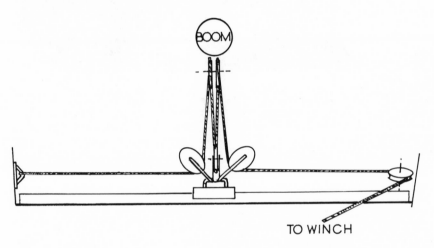

Figure 20.5   The position of the mainsheet often governs its effectiveness. Position A is the most efficient and position B the second most efficient. Also note that the attachment shown would make it very difficult to control leech tension in heavy winds.

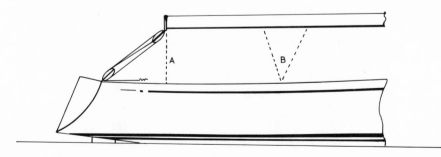

Figure 20.6 A mid-boom sheeting track. This is a good system for a boat with a low boom. It also removes the need for a vang.

The Traveler

Positioning the boom is easier when the lower block of the mainsheet is shackled to a traveler which moves along a track. The track should be long enough to allow the traveler to be taken well to windward in light airs. On stock boats, the traveler is usually positioned by means of moveable stops, but these are often difficult to adjust and do not give very accurate trim control. A better arrangement uses taglines, which are typically in one, as shown in figure 20.7, or two parts.

While the mainsheet helps to obtain the best possible sail shape, the traveler sets that sail at the optimum angle to the wind. To find the ideal angle of attack, watch the speedometer and the helm and heel angles, and adjust the traveler and mainsheet accordingly. When the traveler is pulled too far to windward, both helm and heel angle increase and the boat begins to slow. On the other hand, when the traveler is eased out too much, the sail starts to luff, the helm and heel angles decline, and boat speed also drops. In addition to these routine adjustments, special attention should be given to the traveler under certain kinds of conditions. In sloppy seas, for example, the traveler can be eased slightly more than usual, to get a bit more drive from the mainsail. Or in gusty winds, the traveler can be slid down to leeward to reduce heel angle, and then pulled back to its original position without affecting sail shape.

The Vang

When the boom is eased out further than the end of the traveler, it is held down by a vang and held forward by a preventer. Vangs can be rope tackle, adjustable steel bar, or hydraulic, depending on how much you want to spend.

A rope vang is usually a three-part or five-part tackle similar to the mainsheet. It may either be attached to the mast at one point, or it may run on a circular track. Obviously, the circular track arrangement is more efficient, because the pull of the vang is straight down from its attachment point on the boom. An adjustable steel bar vang has the advantage of supporting the boom in addition to adjusting the mainsail. But it is slow to operate and adds extra weight above deck. A hydraulic vang is almost always attached at a single point, usually to the mast and as near as possible to the deck. Its big

Figure 20.7 Single-part taglines on a quarter-tonner.

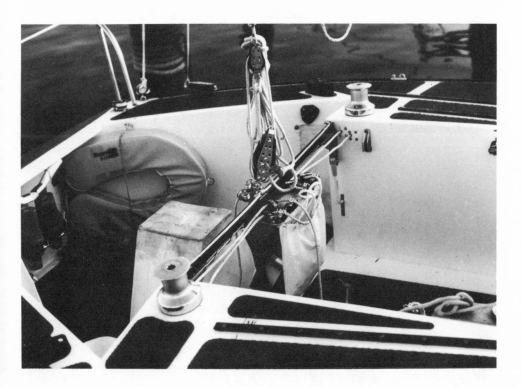

Table 20.1 What to Do When

Conditions	Mainsheet	Traveler	Vang	Other Remarks
SAILING TO WINDWARD				
In very light winds	Ease mainsheet to obtain some twist, but maintain enough tension to stop the leech from falling off.	Take to windward.	Set hydraulic vang to hold boom up, making mainsail fairly full.	Use preventer, mainsheet, and vang or topping lift to stop boom from bouncing. Ease main halyard slightly. Ease the outhaul. No cunningham.
In light winds	Tension enough to hold boom on centerline with plenty of twist.	Take to windward.	Tension leech but allow plenty of twist.	Make sure all telltales are streaming aft from the batten pockets. No cunningham. Some outhaul. Use runner to get some reverse mast bend and make the mainsail fuller.
In medium winds	Use enough tension to get correct leech shape, with all telltales streaming.	Take to centerline or just above, ready to be eased if conditions are gusty.	If boom is bendy, use vang to bend it and remove some of the sail's fullness. Also shorten the vang to get good leech tension.	Make sure all telltales are streaming aft. Some cunningham. Outhaul fully, or almost fully, out. Zippers may be in or out, depending on sea conditions. Some babystay for mast bend.
In heavy winds just before reefing	Use plenty of tension to flatten the sail and stop leech	In steady winds, put the traveler slightly to leeward	Use vang to flatten sail.	Make sure all telltales are streaming aft. Cunning-

	Use plenty of leech tension. Set boom to leeward, amount dependent upon sea conditions.	twist. Hold the boom slightly to leeward of the centerline.	of the centerline. Watch the helm and heel angle and ease the traveler if one or the other increases too much. If traveler must be eased more than 50 percent of the time, reefing would be a better solution.	ham should be fully down. Flattening reef may be in. First reef lines rigged. Outhaul fully extended. Use babystay and **midstay** for maximum mast bend. Use runners to hold the mast securely.
In heavy winds when reefed		Take slightly to leeward. Be ready to ease as **required**.	Use vang to stop boom from lifting or bending.	Use babystay, midstay, and runners for mast bend and mast support. Have second reefing line ready.
SAILING ON A REACH				
In light to medium winds	Ease mainsheet as required if wind is gusty.	Take to leeward.	Use vang to hold boom down and to tension leech.	Ease outhaul. Use a preventer to hold the boom forward. No cunningham. No reefs. Telltales streaming.
In medium to heavy winds	As above, but have a man ready to ease the sheet in the gusts and let go if any danger of broaching.	As above.	As above, but have a man standing by to ease the tension if any danger of broaching.	If boom must be eased out often, it may pay to put in a reef. Watch helm and heel angles carefully.
SAILING DOWNWIND				
In all wind strengths	Ease all the way out.	Take to leeward.	Ease slightly.	Ease outhaul. Use a preventer to hold the boom forward. No reefs. No cunningham.

advantage is the ease and precision of adjustment it allows. But it is expensive and requires a pump.

The vang has always been thought of as a device for tensioning the leech of the mainsail, but it has more uses than this alone: it can also support the boom, and on smaller boats it can bend the mast or boom to help flatten the main. Figure 20.8 shows the mechanics of such a system. Another use for the vang is to prevent the boom from rising during a gybe. For instance, if the mainsail is handed across without a vang and without pulling the sheet in, it could fly high enough to hit the backstay, thus breaking either it or the stay. And finally, on older boats with their much longer booms, the vang is used to stop the boom from bending upward in the middle and making the mainsail fuller than it really should be.

When properly used, the mainsheet, traveler, and vang work together to maintain good mainsail shape and present the sail to the wind at the best possible angle. There are other mainsail controls, of course. But these three are the ones that the mainsail trimmer needs to adjust most often, becuase they are also the ones that can make the most difference to the speed of the boat on the racecourse.

Figure 20.8   The vang can be used to help bend the mast or boom depending upon its position and the design of the spar.

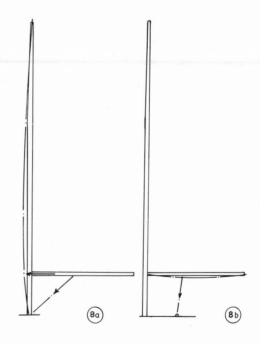

21 *Helming*

The helmsman is clearly one of the most important members of any racing crew. With poor helming, even the fastest boat will seldom be found leading the fleet. Fortunately, though, the secrets of good helming are not difficult to master. Most crewmen can perform quite well at the wheel, as long as they know the basic techniques involved and are willing to invest a little practice and concentration.

But what if your helmsman is perfectly capable yet is still having difficulty controlling the boat? It may be that something is wrong with your steering equipment. Stiff and unbalanced steering are among the most common design flaws on modern racing boats. And when these flaws are serious, they can lead to poor performance from even the best of helmsmen. What's more, steering system problems can be due to many different factors, so it is often difficult to pinpoint the exact cause of a particular trouble.

Good helming, then, is influenced by two things: the skill of the helmsman and the quality of the steering system on the boat he is driving. Only when both are working at peak efficiency can top helm performance be achieved. We will now consider both the techniques and the design characteristics that contribute to successful helming, paying particular attention to common problems and how they might be solved.

Characteristics of a Good Steering System

Let's start by looking at the design side of the picture. What are the characteristics of a good steering system from the helmsman's point of view? Perhaps the most obvious quality is a proper "feel" to the tiller or wheel—easy to move without being stiff or sloppy, and light to the touch rather than heavy and resistant. Two other qualities are good balance and good control. Specific design features contribute to each of these.

EASE OF MOVEMENT. If the helm is too stiff, then the tiller or wheel will tend to stick when put over, and this could prove dangerous when sailing in close company. On the other hand, if the helm is too loose, then everything will feel slack, meaning that small movements of the tiller or wheel will probably have no effect on the rudder.

Fortunately, stiffness or slackness in the helm are often among the easiest mechanical defects to remedy. If stiffness is the problem on a boat with tiller steering, the possible causes are few. Most likely the bearings or pintles are stiff, and the solution is to remove the rudder and ream them out a bit. On the other hand, if slackness is the problem, the reason may be looseness where the rudder blade or tiller join the rudder stock. A loose rudder blade attachment is the more serious problem and probably requires yardwork to fix. A sloppy tiller attachment usually calls for a simple tightening, which can be done with shims or padding. Occasionally, though, when the tiller is keyed to the stock, the trouble is due to a worn key or keyway. Here the solution is to fit a new key and repair the keyway either by welding and remilling, or simply by milling out a larger keyway.

Figure 21.1 Some different rudder shapes. *21.1a* The center of pressure (*p*) of this rudder is well aft of the rudderstock, making the helm feel "heavy." *21.1b* This shape is better, but the helm will still have a heavy feel. *21.1c* With the center of pressure just aft of the rudderstock, this rudder is fairly well balanced. The helm will feel light and comfortable. *21.1d* This shape will not work well unless the boat is going astern, because the center of pressure is forward of the rudderstock.

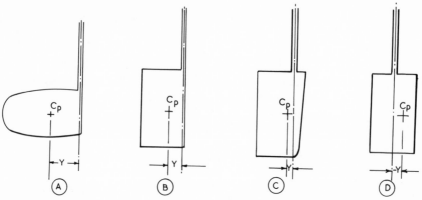

On a boat with wheel steering, stiffness or slackness in the helm are more difficult to diagnose and cure due to the many components of the system. To start with, the quadrant is subject to the same possible problems as a tiller on a tiller-steered boat. And on top of this, the wires, sprocket, chain, and steering wheel all require proper adjustments of their own. There are so many types of wheel steering mechanisms that it would be impossible to detail a method of tuning each. Suffice to say that for easy movement of the helm, the steering cables should be reasonably tight, with the wheel, sprocket, rudder, and quadrant all secured firmly to their respective shafts.

LIGHTNESS. In addition to being easy to move without being stiff or slack, a good helm should also feel fairly light to the touch. When the helmsman pushes the tiller or turns the wheel he should not experience a heavy and persistent counterforce that increases with rudder angle. If he does, the problem may well lie in the shape of the rudder itself, or its positioning on the rudder stock.

Consider, for example, rudders a and b in figure 21.1—on a high-aspect ratio modern type, and the other the kind of lower-aspect ratio rudder sometimes found on catboats and dinghies. The two are equal in area. Each rudder has a center of pressure where the force of the water may be said to act. The center of pressure is nearer the rudderstock in rudder b than in rudder a. Consequently, rudder b will feel lighter, meaning that the helmsman will have to exert less force to turn it.

Quite often a heavier rudder, such as the one in drawing a, will be compensated for by a longer tiller, which gives the helmsman extra leverage. (The relationship between the pressure on the rudder blade, the length of the tiller, and the hand pressure needed to move the tiller is shown in figure 21.2a.) But a longer tiller can be tedious to use because the helmsman must make larger movements to turn the rudder a given amount. And it can also cause problems in a crowded cockpit—on a tack, for instance, when the tiller is put hard over and the crew have to trim the genoa and mainsail sheets.

Perhaps a better way to lighten the helm is to adjust the position of the rudder blade along the stock. Various positionings are shown in figure 21.1. Rudder b, with the blade positioned so that the center of pressure is well aft of the stock, would give a heavier feel to the helm than rudder c. Alternatively, if the blade were moved far enough forward so that the center of pressure coincided with the stock, the tiller or wheel would have no "feel," and the helmsman would have difficulty gauging the pressure on the rudder. The positioning of the rudder in drawing d is even less desirable. Because the center of pressure is ahead of the stock, steering would be extremely difficult. The rudder would constantly try to turn itself off-center—in the same way that the rudder keeps tending to go hard over to one side when a boat is going astern. The rudder blade po-

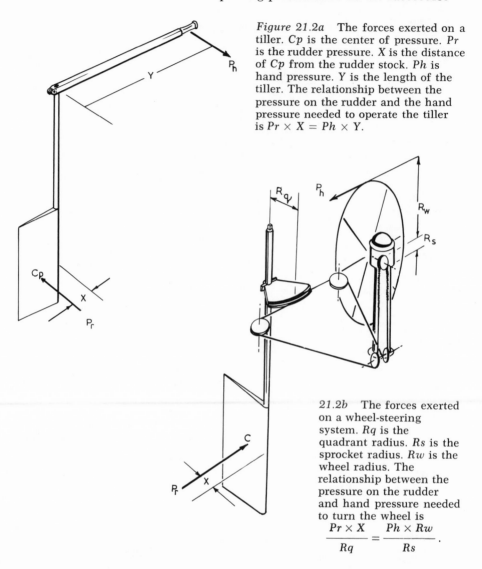

Figure 21.2a The forces exerted on a tiller. Cp is the center of pressure. Pr is the rudder pressure. X is the distance of Cp from the rudder stock. Ph is hand pressure. Y is the length of the tiller. The relationship between the pressure on the rudder and the hand pressure needed to operate the tiller is $Pr \times X = Ph \times Y$.

21.2b The forces exerted on a wheel-steering system. Rq is the quadrant radius. Rs is the sprocket radius. Rw is the wheel radius. The relationship between the pressure on the rudder and hand pressure needed to turn the wheel is
$$\frac{Pr \times X}{Rq} = \frac{Ph \times Rw}{Rs}.$$

sitioning in drawing c, then, where the center of pressure is slightly aft of the stock, makes for the lightest and most effective helm.

BALANCE. Beyond ease of movement and lightness, a third quality of a good helm is balance. If a boat is well-balanced, the helmsman will be able to keep tracking in a straight line with about three or four degrees of rudder angle and a minimum amount of movement of the tiller or wheel. What contributes to a well-balanced boat? Essentially, balance is the result of an interaction between the sail area, hull, and keel of a boat. (See figure 21.3.) A bit of design theory will help explain how.

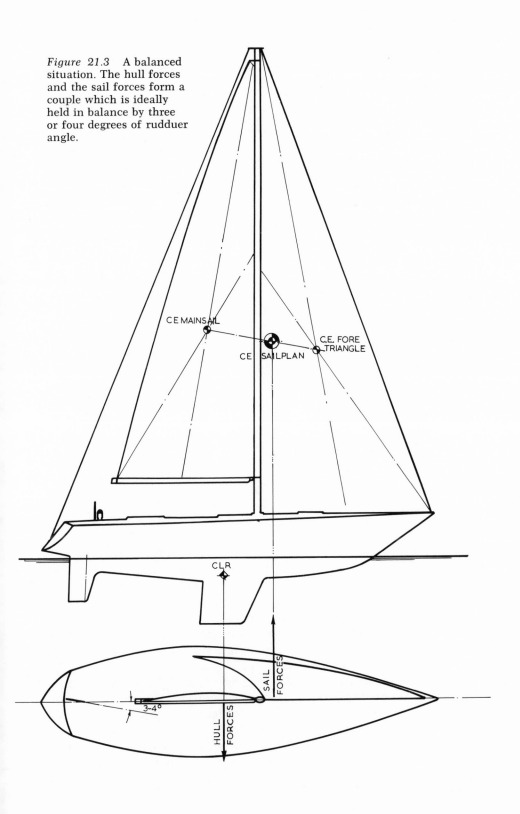

Figure 21.3 A balanced situation. The hull forces and the sail forces form a couple which is ideally held in balance by three or four degrees of rudduer angle.

C E MAINSAIL

C.E. FORE TRIANGLE

CE SAILPLAN

CLR

SAIL FORCES

HULL FORCES

3-4°

If a rope were attached at the correct point on a boat's under-water profile, the boat could be towed sideways without the bow or stern swinging toward the person doing the towing. This point is known as the center of lateral resistance (CLR). There is also a center to the sail plan of a boat (CE), which can be found as illustrated in figure 21.3 a. A designer projects both these points to the waterline, where they are measured and expressed as a percentage of the waterline length. The distance between them, known as the lead, should be between 15 and 18 percent of the LWL for most boats. If the lead is smaller than this, it is likely that the boat may have weather helm; conversely, if the lead is larger, the boat may have lee helm.

From the helmsman's point of view, excessive weather helm means that to keep the boat tacking, he must constantly hold the tiller or wheel further to weather than the three or four degrees of rudder angle required for optimum lift. This increases drag. Weather helm might be eliminated by reefing the mainsail, but if wind conditions do not warrant less sail area, then the suggested remedy is to rake or move the mast forward. A far more complex and expensive cure is to move the keel aft. The characteristics of lee helm are precisely the opposite of those describing weather helm, and the solutions are also the reverse: moving the mast aft, or alternatively moving the keel forward. It is possible, of course, for weather or lee helm to occur only in heavier winds. If so, your sail combination (mainsail and genoa) is incorrect. Reef the main or change headsails until you obtain the optimum rudder angle.

CONTROL. Sudden heavy puffs of wind can reveal another serious steering problem—namely, the tendency for a boat to get out of control. If a steering system is not well-designed, extreme heel angle can easily cause a boat to broach. One feature that can affect the likelihood of broaching is the depth of the rudder. Generally, the helmsman's control can be improved if the rudder blade is made deeper, but this has the advantage of increasing wetted area and hull drag. Another feature related to the tendency to broach is the shape of the afterbody. On some boats, the run aft is distorted to give a better rating, and this has resulted in pinched areas or abrupt curves, usually in the front of the rudder. Figure 21.4 shows such a hull with the buttock lines sketched in. A disturbed flow of water typically starts in the notch and proceeds over the rudder blade, reducing its efficiency. When this feature is combined with a large bustle, control, especially at higher speeds, may be reduced considerably. The only cure is to redesign the aft end of the boat.

On a boat with pinched ends and a large bustle, the bustle is often faired into a skeg located in front of the rudder. In theory, the skeg decreases the chances of losing control of the boat because the

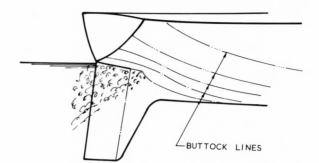

Figure 21.4 A distortion in the aft end of a hull can create turbulence and reduce the effectiveness of the rudder.

BUTTOCK LINES

leading edge of the skeg maintains a constant angle to the water flow; therefore the rudder is less likely to stall out. A skegged rudder, however, may have several disadvantages: it adds extra wetted surface and it may also slightly reduce the boat's handling qualities. Indeed, with a very large skeg, the major steering problem might be slowness in turning rather than loss of control. A spade rudder, on the other hand, often rates particularly high in responsiveness of helm and easy control. But at larger rudder angles it may stall out, with consequent problems of handling.

So far we have covered some of the major contributions that careful design can make to good helming. If the design of a steering system is faulty—if the tiller or wheel is too stiff or too heavy, if the rudder is improperly balanced, if it lacks control—then the helmsman's ability to drive the boat is seriously handicapped. But once design requirements are met, the responsibility for performance at the wheel shifts to the helmsman himself, his knowledge and skills.

Table 21.1   Tiller Steering Fault Finding

Fault	*Reason*	*Cure*
Tiller moves small distance at head of rudder stock	(1) Tiller is a sloppy fit (2) Rudder blade may be loose	(1) Add washers or shims until snug fit is obtained (2) Take to shipyard for repair
Tiller is hard to move	(1) Bearings are too tight	(1) Remove rudder and ease bearings
Tiller is hard to move; appears to be too short	(1) This could be a fault of the rake of the rudderstock and too much rudder aft of stock (2) The tiller may simply be too short	(1) Redesign rudder (see text) (2) Increase length of tiller

Table 21.2   Wheel Steering Fault Finding

Fault	Reason	Cure
Can move the wheel with no rudder movement	Steering lines are too slack; wheel or quadrant improperly fixed on shaft	Tighten steering lines; tighten bolt holding wheel on; check splines/keys/bolts holding quadrant to stock
No feel on the helm in light airs. Wheel feels a little stiff	Steering lines are too tight	Ease steering lines slightly
Steering feels stiff (see text)	Steering gear bearings are too tight	Remove rudder and ease all bearing surfaces
When out of water, the rudder blade moves without moving the wheel	If stock does not move, rudder blade is loose on stock. If stock moves, check #1 above	Get shipyard to repair rudder
Helm feels loose enough but boat does not react until wheel is moved considerably	Flow over rudder may be too turbulent, thus the rudder will not act until it is turned beyond the turbulent flow	Refair the afterbody to get smooth water flow (this is a major job)

Table 21.3   Loss of Control Problems

Fault	Reason	Cure
Rudder blade stalls out early	(1) Thin rudder blade (2) Poor section shape (3) If rudder is near the water surface, it may be ventilating	(1) Thicken up blade (2) Revise section shape (3) Put fence at top of rudder blade just under water
Difficult to keep boat tracking in a straight line; boat rolls excessively	(1) Small lateral plane (2) Small or short rudder	(1) Increase lateral plane by increasing size of keel (2) Increase rudder area or deepen rudder
Spade rudder has very little feel and wants to go its own way in heavier winds	It may be too well balanced, with too much rudder blade in front of the rudderstock (see figure 1.)	Reduce blade area in front of rudderstock

Boat tracks well but is difficult to turn	Skeg is too big	Make skeg smaller
In higher wind strengths helm is heavy or hard to move	Center of pressure of rudder is too far aft	(1) Remove area from trailing edge of rudder (2) Redesign rudder, reducing rake of rudderstock
When reaching, boat broaches easily in high winds	(1) Lack of stability (2) An inattentive helmsman (3) Too small a rudder	(1) Add ballast, preferably as a shoe on the bottom of the keel, where it will act most effectively (2) Replace helmsman (3) Increase rudder size; deepen it first and then add area in a fore and aft plane

Helming Techniques

Helming a racing boat is hard work. If you think otherwise, you are certainly not steering your boat as well as you might. Helming is difficult, not so much because of the physical effort involved as because of the total concentration required. The skipper who takes the wheel for hours at a stretch, and between tacks entertains his crew with amusing stories, is seldom the one who wins races. To perform at his peak, a helmsman must pay close attention to everything going on around him, and this demands constant mental effort. No wonder, then, that the performance of even the best helmsman begins to decline after an hour or so on the wheel or tiller.

But however important mental alertness may be to good helming, it is not all that's involved. Performance at the wheel is also a matter of experience and skill. Such things as knowing how to compensate properly for undesirable heel angle and trim, and how to steer the boat most effectively on different legs of the course and in different kinds of wind and sea conditions are all involved. Here we'll review some of the techniques that can help turn an average sailor into a top-class helmsman.

PREPARING TO TAKE THE HELM. Good helming begins even before you take control of the boat. This is the time to acquire a complete picture of all the relevant facts. The present wind direction, for example, is easy to gauge. But to be thorough, why not watch the wind speed and direction indicators for a while to find out if condi-

tions are at all variable? Look around to see where the other boats
in the fleet are, and perhaps take a bearing on one or two of them
to give you something to measure future performance against. Ask
the navigator if any tactical considerations, such as rounding a mark,
are likely to arise during your trick. And are any major wind or
weather changes predicted? If it is night, and you are just coming
on deck, find out from the helmsman going off watch if any sail
changes were made while you were below, and what other sails are
now on deck. At night, it helps to arrive on deck a little early for a
watch change so that your eyes can get accustomed to the darkness
before you take over.

ADJUSTING HEEL ANGLE AND TRIM. Now you're ready to relieve
the present helmsman. With the wheel or tiller in your hands, you
can begin to feel the boat. The steering qualities you sense are the
result of several variable factors, two of the most important being
heel angle and trim. These, in turn, are influenced by other variables,
such as sail area and crew position. The combined effects give the

Figure 21.5 When a boat heels the CLR moves forward, increasing the
tendency toward weather helm.

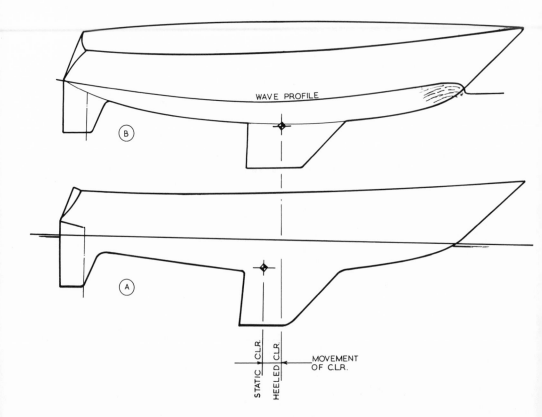

Table 21.4   Offwind Sailing

Fault	Reason	Cure
Fine-bowed, beamy-sterned boat loses control when heeled	As boat heels, bow is immersed and stern emerges, lifting rudder out, and CLR moves forward	Deepen rudder, sail boat more upright and maybe put a fence at the top of the rudderstock. Sail with crew aft
Tender boat loses control when heeled	CLR may move forward due to heeled effect	Deepen rudder blade or sail boat more upright
When reaching, boat broaches easily in higher winds	(1) Mainsheet may be too tight (2) Too much sail up	(1) Ease mainsheet and then vang in the puffs (2) Reduce sail

Notes

LIGHT AIR

Crew slightly forward and to weather.
Small helm corrections.
  Reach up to gain speed (see text).
  Sheets eased.

MEDIUM AIR

Crew keeping boat level, weight aft.
Helmsman tries to avoid big waves or troughs without wandering.
Steers course but sails up in the lulls and down in the puffs.

HEAVY AIR

Sails led forward, crew aft.
Helmsman tries to avoid big waves or troughs and to prevent the boat from
  rolling.
Helmsman steers course; probable large helm movements.
Change helmsman frequently.

helm a certain feel and set a limit to the boat's maximum possible
speed.
   No single factor affects steering qualities more than heel angle.
As a boat heels, the shape of its lateral area changes, often quite
dramatically. Figure 21.5a shows a typical boat upright. Note where
the center of lateral resistance (CLR) is. Heeling the boat causes
the bow to sink slightly and the stern to rise a little; the entire boat,
because of the volume of the immersed wedge, tends to lift out of
the water somewhat. Consequently, the CLR moves forward, as indicated in figure 21.5b. In general, the greater the heel angle, the larger
the forward movement of the CLR and the smaller the lead becomes.
From the helmsman's point of view, these progressive changes are
experienced as an increasing tendency toward weather helm.

Table 21.5 Upwind Sailing Problems and Notes

Fault	Reason	Cure	Notes
LIGHT AIRS			
Excessive lee helm	Too much sail area forward of the CLR or mast too far forward	Move or rake the mast aft	Crew sits to leeward
Slight lee helm. No helm in light air	That's O.K.	No change	Make very small and gentle helm corrections
Weather helm in light air (it usually gets worse as the wind increases)	Mast too far aft	Move or rake mast forward	Helmsman sits to leeward or where he can watch for any puffs
MEDIUM AIRS			
Excessive lee helm	(1) Mast is too far forward (2) Too much sail area forward	(1) Move mast aft (2) Use a longer boom and more mainsail area or change to a smaller jib	Crew to windward far enough to keep boat heeled a few degrees
No helm or slight weather helm	That's O.K.	No change	Helmsman positioned where he can see waves and wind approaching the boat
Excessive weather helm	(1) Mast is too far aft (2) Too much sail area aft of CLR	(1) Move mast forward (2) Reef mainsail or, if permanent result desired, shorten main boom and reduce main sail area	Helm corrections should be small; there should be a litle weather helm, which can be eased in the puffs by easing the main traveler
HEAVY WINDS			
Excessive lee helm*	Too much sail forward of the CLR	(1) Change to a smaller jib, or (2) Shake the reef out of the mainsail	Helmsman watches seas and tries to steer around waves (see text)

| Slight weather helm | That's O.K. | No change | Probable large movements of helm; sails to be reefed sufficiently to give slight weather helm |
| Excessive weather helm | Too much sail aft of the CLR | (1) Reef mainsail, or (2) Change to a larger jib | Main traveler and then sheet eased in the puffs |

As the wind increases, this condition becomes more dangerous as the wind increases.

* If this condition exists throughout the wind range, move the mast aft. This condition becomes more dangerous as the wind increases.

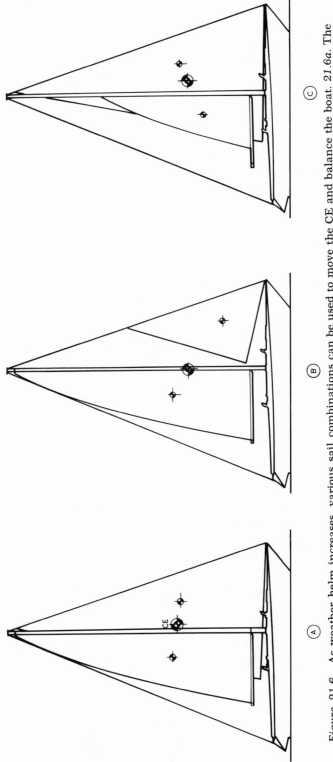

Figure 21.6 As weather helm increases, various sail combinations can be used to move the CE and balance the boat. 21.6a. The standard rig, showing the CE. 21.6b With a small headsail, the CE moves aft. 21.6c A reefed mainsail moves the CE forward.

Changing sails, of course, helps to correct weather helm. (See figure 21.6.) As heel angle increases and the CLR moves forward, a forward movement of the center of effort (CE) will keep the boat in balance. The first change in this direction is made by reefing the mainsail, which reduces sail area and moves the CE forward. After this, a crew usually switches to a smaller jib, which reduces heel angle and thus moves the CLR aft. If the new jib is sized properly, the boat will remain in balance.

A change in a boat's trim also moves the CLR and so has an influence on the handling characteristics of the helm. Crew weight fore or aft is one thing that can affect trim. Its detrimental effects are especially noticeable when a boat is sailing downwind and the crew goes forward to prepare for the next sail change. The bow is already being pressed down by the spinnaker, and the crew's position forward only worsens the situation. The result is not only a forward movement of the CLR, but also a lifting of the rudder, which renders it less effective.

Going upwind, on the other hand, crew weight should be kept on the weather rail to reduce heel angle and the accompanying movement of the CLR. This is particularly important on a wide-sterned boat, with its tendency toward increased bow down trim with greater heel angle. Typically, a wide-sterned boat must be sailed as upright as possible to obtain maximum speed, and proper crew positioning can help.

STEERING THE BOAT. Part of the technique of good helming, then, is careful adjustment of such things as sail area and crew positioning, which directly affect heel angle and trim, and indirectly the steering qualities of a boat. But calling these adjustments is not the main part of a helmsman's job. The task that is the sole responsibility of the helmsman is the skillful handling of the wheel or tiller in varying wind and sea conditions. We will now consider steering techniques for upwind and downwind sailing, and how they should be altered for different kinds of weather.

SAILING UPWIND. When sailing upwind in light airs, the helmsman should sit so as to be able to keep an eye on the luff of the genoa and the compass, preferably to weather, where he can see any puff of wind or lulls moving across the water toward him. This advance warning of approaching wind fluctuations allows the helmsman to luff the boat slightly and thus gain a few more yards to weather in the puffs, or to bear off slightly and thus keep up boat speed in the lulls. He should also glance frequently at the compass to check for major windshifts, so that the boat can be tacked on a header.

Because there is usually very little sea in light airs, small movements of the helm should be used to control the boat. This, of course, will only be possible if the boat is well balanced. One of the primary aids to proper balance in light air sailing is the mainsail, which ideally should be trimmed to give three or four degrees of weather helm, or at least neutral helm. But be careful not to overtrim the main.

In medium winds there will be slightly more sea, and the helm will require a little more movement. But always keep wheel or tiller movement to the minimum needed to stay on course. As the winds rise and the seas build even further, the helmsman should use the large waves to best advantage. He can, for example, gain an extra yard or two to windward by luffing slightly into a big sea and allowing the boat to slide down the back of it.

With increases in wind strength, a boat will have more helm— usually weather helm. To compensate, the crew can ease the mainsheet a little or put the flattening reef in. As the wind continues to rise, sail changes are needed to reduce heel angle. The helmsman, of course, will feel the effects of these adjustments in sail area: reefing the mainsail reduces weather helm, while a jib change can affect the helm either way, depending upon the shape and size of the replacement sail.

SAILING DOWNWIND. The helmsman doesn't have much to do when sailing downwind in super-light conditions. In fact, he may not even be able to control the direction of the boat! But as soon as the wind begins to pick up, so does the helmsman's work.

Boat speed can often be increased by coming up slightly onto a reach, and then, when the boat is moving nicely, sailing off a little and gradually easing down to course. If the speed starts to fall when the boat is back on course, reaching up again will help regain it. In fact, when sailing downwind in very light winds it often pays to reach above the course line and then gybe back down to it.

One common downwind helming problem is excessive roll. Initially, roll is caused by the fullness of the spinnaker, but the condition is often exacerbated when the helmsman steers with the rolls. To reduce rolling, move the spinnaker sheet well forward—say, by the shrouds—and then overtrim it as well as the spinnaker guy. These adjustments should give the helmsman greater control. If rolling starts again and the helmsman has nerve enough, he can steer against the roll—that is, turn the rudder in the opposite direction to the way it really wants to go. This will effectively stop the rolling, unless the spinnaker is just too full.

When sailing downwind in a large sea, the helmsman can increase boat speed by skillfully using the motion of the waves. The tendency of the boat to surge on the back of a wave can be prolonged by going down the wave at a slight angle. Then bear off again to get to the crest of the next wave as quickly as possible. Naturally, the helmsman must sail an equal distance on either side of the course.

Getting the timing of this technique requires careful observation of wave patterns, so that keeping a constant eye on the compass is difficult. One solution is to find a reference object in the distance. When the boat is on the correct course, check for something directly ahead—a buoy, one of the boats in the class ahead, or a star perhaps —that can serve as a point to steer for. This should enable you to refer to the compass less frequently.

Good helming, under any conditions, is only part of the formula for winning a race. The condition of the boat and its equipment and the efforts of all the crewmen play significant parts as well. But the helmsman, as the person in control of the boat, is undoubtedly one of the most critical ingredients for top racing performance. Helming ability can be improved by following some of the suggestions outlined here. There is no substitute, though, for experience, mental alertness, and good teamwork.

22 The Causes and Cures of Broaching

Broaching. The very word conjures up visions of white-knuckled crewmen hanging on grimly while their boat charges off on a course of its own. It is a scene no one wishes to go through. But can broaching really be avoided? Many racing sailors would reply that occasional broaching is like occasional foul weather—inevitable. Are they right? Or can the experienced crew prevent the problem? To answer this question, we must first review what actually causes a boat to broach under different sailing conditions.

Broaching on a Reach

First, consider a boat that is sailing upright in very light winds, as shown in figure 22.1. Several forces are acting on it. Heeling force and driving force are acting through the center of effort (CE) of the sail plan, while side force and drag are acting through the center of lateral resistance (CLR) of the underwater part of the hull. When the resultants of these forces are drawn in and projected (dashed lines), they are separated by distance a. Now suppose this boat is ideally balanced, which means it would sail to windward with three to four degrees of weather helm. Any reduction in a would then give the boat excessive weather helm, and any increase in a would give it lee helm.

When a spinnaker is set, heel angle increases, the wave pattern changes, and the boat has slightly more bow-down trim. All these

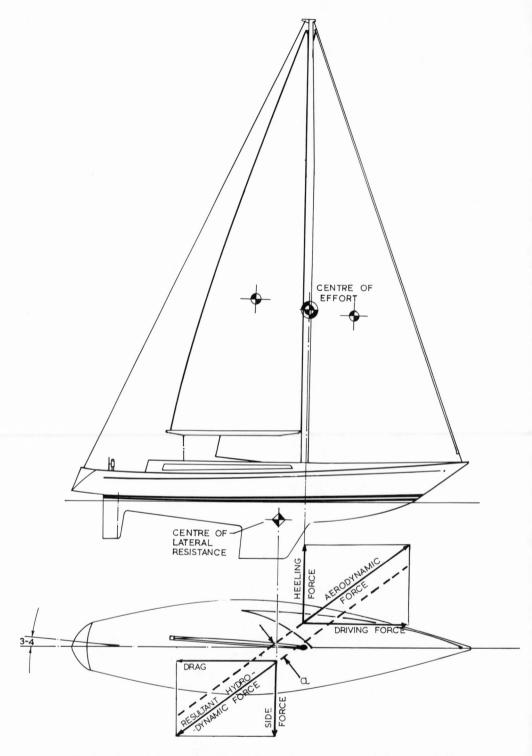

Figure 22.1   The forces acting on a boat in a balanced situation. As long as distance *a* remains the same, the boat will remain balanced. If *a* decreases, weather helm will increase. Conversely, if *a* increases, lee helm will result.

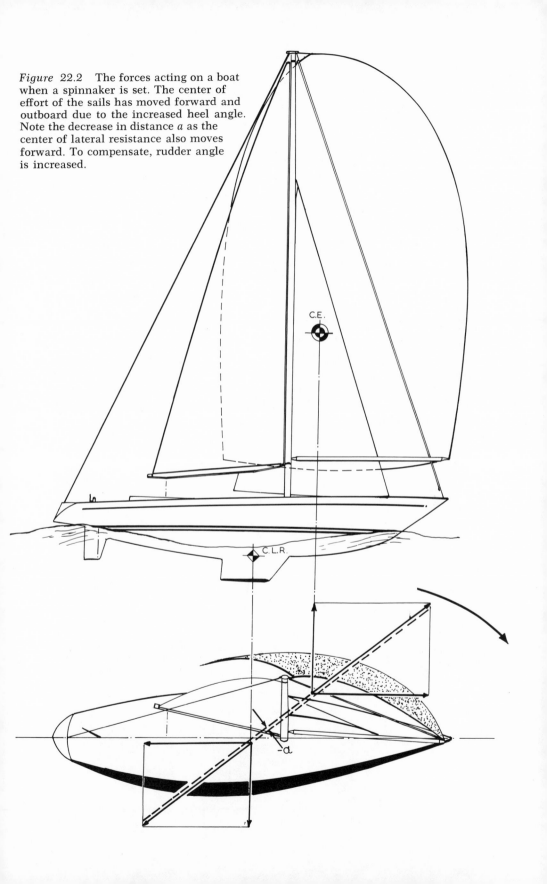

Figure 22.2   The forces acting on a boat
when a spinnaker is set. The center of
effort of the sails has moved forward and
outboard due to the increased heel angle.
Note the decrease in distance *a* as the
center of lateral resistance also moves
forward. To compensate, rudder angle
is increased.

C.E.

C.L.R.

-a

factors move the CLR forward. Due to the additional sail area, the CE also moves forward, although not by as much as the CLR. Distance a is now somewhat smaller, reflected in the increased rudder angle needed to keep the boat on course.

As the wind strength increases, heel angle increases. This moves the CE further outboard and the CLR further forward. The result is a continual decrease in a, until eventually the rudder is hard over and overpowered. In this condition the boat broaches, or stalls out, as illustrated in figure 22.2. Note also that the increased heel angle has reduced the effective rudder angle.

A broach of this type can be controlled by a combination of good crew work and helming. When the boat begins to heel excessively and the rudder is almost hard over, release the mainsheet and vang; this will reduce the power aft of the CE; if the boat continues into a broach, let go the staysail sheet. The man trimming the spinnaker sheet should be aware that with excessive heel the wind is no longer entering the spinnaker from the front. Instead, it is entering from the bottom. This means that if the sheet is let out several feet as the boat heels, a complete broach can usually be prevented. But a lot of muscle is needed to bring the spinnaker sheet back in quickly as the boat comes upright again. Slowness here will cause the spinnaker to collapse—almost as bad as broaching in the distance lost!

Figure 22.3 Sailing downwind. The aerodynamic driving force is acting straight ahead, while hydrodynamic drag is acting straight aft.

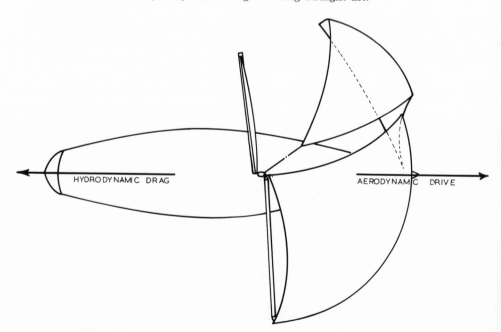

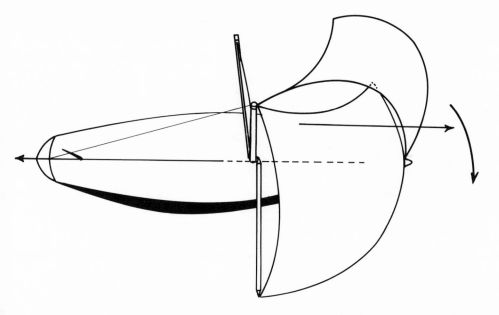

Figure 22.4   As the boat rolls to port, the aerodynamic force moves away from the axis of the hull. A couple is formed, which tends to turn the boat to starboard.

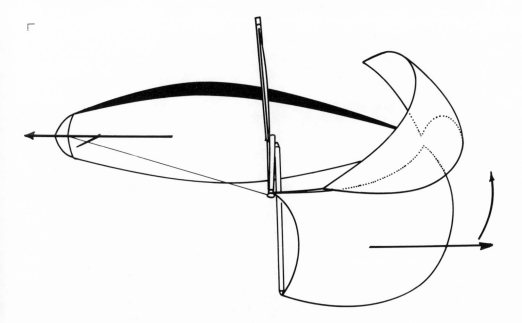

22.4b   The same thing happens as the boat rolls to starboard.

Farther Bruin (K5218) has a slight bow down attitude. Notice the amount of rudder out of the water. It looks as if wave action may have helped to start this broach. The spinnaker is collapsing, but the mainsail is still driving her around. Notice, too, that K3486 still has her mainsail reefed. Unreefing the main would help blanket the spinnaker for an easier takedown and increase boat speed on the run. Her blooper also needs sheeting.

Farther Bruin has almost no control. The rudder is barely in the water. It looks as if the blooper is holding the boat over and preventing a quick recovery. Note that the mainsail is now luffing.

Farther Bruin has now regained some control. But the mainsheet has still not been thrown off completely and the sail is starting to fill again, making it difficult to get back on course.

Dumping the mainsheet entirely would let the main flag and prevent the boat from being pushed into the wind. Having missed K3486, I wonder if the crewmen are looking for another victim! Note also the distance lost to K3486.

Rosie III has rolled to leeward with the mainsail sheeted hard in on the centerline. She might have been able to get back on course had the mainsail been fully out and had the helmsman not lost his balance. Note the tiller on the centerline.

To summarize, then, you should observe the following rules to avoid broaching on a reach under marginal conditions:

1. Never cleat the main, staysail, or spinnaker sheets.
2. Throw off the main, staysail sheets and vang as soon as the helmsman calls.
3. Ease the spinnaker sheet out as the boat heels. Then trim it quickly back in as the boat comes upright again.

The main has filled on the lee side and is now pushing *Rosie III* around further. The spinnaker, which is filling from the foot, is holding the boat over. Fortunately, the spinnaker is about to collapse. If it had stayed full, it might have pulled the boat over and dragged it along sideways. The best thing to do in this situation would be to let the sheet run and collapse the sail, thus helping to right the boat.

The spinnaker has collapsed, but the blooper and mainsail are still holding the boat over. Both these sheets should have been let go immediately.

Broaching When Sailing Downwind

Is a broach on a downwind leg caused by the same factors as a broach on a reach? Not entirely. The downwind broach, which occurs either to windward or to leeward, is triggered by its own set of circumstances. To obtain a practical cure, let's look again at some sailing theory.

When sailing downwind, the forces on the sail are usually acting straight over the bow, and the boat's drag is all that holds it back. (See figure 22.3.) But as the wind and seas increase, the spinnaker often starts to oscillate and the boat begins to roll. As you can see in figures 22.3 and 22.4, this rolling motion moves the center of effort of the sails away from the centerline. The couple formed by the CE and the boat's drag tends to turn the bow in the direction indicated.

Once this couple becomes large enough, it will overpower the force exerted by the rudder and cause a broach.

The helmsman, of course, can contribute to the problem by not reacting fast enough as the boat rolls, and by actually steering into a broach. Or an inexperienced helmsman may mistakenly steer with the roll, thus accentuating it and eventually causing the boat to broach.

Waves can also contribute to broaching. Sometimes, when sailing down a wave, the rudder partially emerges while the bow submerges. If this situation coincides with a good roll, there may not be enough submerged rudder area to provide the counterforce needed to right the boat again. Then, too, in a wind against tide state, waves can actually push the bow of a lighter boat off course. This moves the aerodynamic and hydrodynamic forces out of equilibrium and starts a broach.

To avoid a downwind broach, first make every effort to stop the spinnaker from oscillating. Either fly your flattest spinnaker, or make a fuller sail flatter by lowering the pole and trimming it aft a little, taking the sheeting point forward and overtrimming the sheet, and making sure the halyard is two-blocked. And strange as increasing sail in heavy weather may seem, a blooper set opposite the spinnaker will also help reduce oscillation.

The helmsman can help prevent rolling by making a conscious effort to predict the motion of the roll and steer out of phase with it. This requires both skill and nerve on the helmsman's part, but it is the most effective way to stop a broach. Also, to avoid unnecessary fatigue and helming errors, change helmsmen every half hour when sailing downwind in heavy weather.

To summarize, follow these rules to prevent a downwind broach:

1. Fly your flattest spinnaker.
2. Make the spinnaker as flat as possible by lowering and trimming the pole aft and by sheeting in a little more than usual.
3. Put the best helmsman on the wheel for short periods of about half an hour.
4. Concentrate your crew weight aft to keep the rudder immersed as much as possible.
5. Don't cleat the sheets.

These are essentially the causes and cures of broaching, both on a reach and downwind. Fortunately, with good crew work and helming, most broaches can be avoided—even the spectacular ones we have become so accustomed to seeing.

$\mathscr{23}$ What You Can Learn from Wake Watching

How often during a race do you look at your boat's wake? Probably not very often. Yet the characteristics of a wake can provide a great deal of useful information. It can alert you to possible design problems, tell you how well your crew is handling the boat, and even supply essential navigational data—all this for the price of a quick look over the transom.

For wake watching to pay off, however, the observer must have an educated eye. To begin with, it helps to understand what causes a wake to form. Essentially, a wake is the result of two combined factors—frictional drag, and a reduction in the relative velocity of the water flowing past the stern.

The first of these means that the boat is actually towing water behind it. As the hull moves through the water, the friction of its surface causes surrounding water to be pulled along. The size and velocity of this forward-moving current increases toward the stern, thus creating the wake that can be seen trailing the boat.

Augmenting the effects of frictional drag is the second factor. As the streamlines on either side of the hull converge at the stern, the pressure there increases. This causes the relative velocity of the water passing by the stern to drop below the boat's speed. The result is seen as a forward-moving wake.

The Wake as a Guide to Locating Design Problems

Knowing what causes a wake to form helps a designer to plan the stern shape of a boat. For maximum speed, the designer should

210

Figure 23.1 The stern wake of the Swan 47 *Alvorada* when the boat is running at close to maximum hull speed.

obviously draw a stern that creates as clean a wake as possible. But unfortunately, this is not always done. The pressures of racing rules often force designers to try to get a lower rating by distorting the after-girth station in the case of an IOR boat, or cramming extra displacement into the bustle to gain more sail area in the case of meter boats. Such distortions or enlarged bustles increase wetted area and cause a more turbulent wake. And if these design features are in front of the rudder, they also reduce rudder efficiency, thus necessitating a larger rudder with additional wetted surface to do the same job.

An owner can get some idea of the extent to which stern shape is hindering or helping boat speed simply by glancing over the transom. A turbulent wake is easy to spot: increased wave action with plenty of bubbles and foam, or in extreme cases, breaking water. If this describes your wake, you should probably inspect the after end of the boat next time it is hauled out of the water. If your boat is an IOR design and you no longer race under that rule, you may be able to make the boat faster by fairing out any hollows or notches you might find. And if you discover that as a result the boat handles better, you may also be able to reduce rudder area. For those who are still racing under the IOR and do not want to lose a rating advantage by fairing out hollows, at least make sure that the stern area is as smooth as possible. The fastest boats are usually those with a fair

THE IDEAL WAKE SHAPE

Figure 23.2   Various wake shapes.

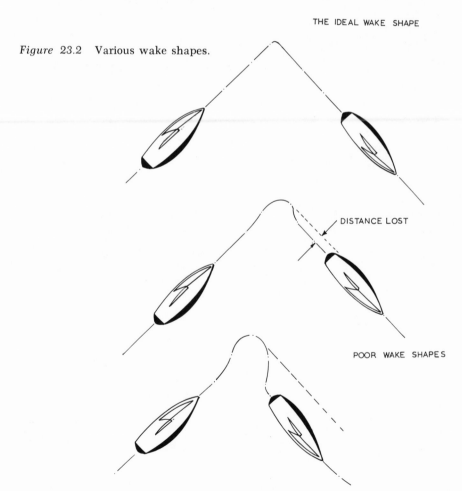

DISTANCE LOST

POOR WAKE SHAPES

run aft and hence minimum wetted surface and low friction. These are the boats that tow very little water behind them.

The Wake as a Guide to Helming

When racing downwind, your wake can tell you whether you are sailing the shortest distance between two marks, or a straight line. In lighter, steady air the wake should obviously be straight. (Note that if the wind is fluctuating, the helmsman should sail up in the light patches and down in the puffs.) Not only does a straight wake downwind indicate that you are sailing the shortest distance required, it also indicates that you are probably getting reasonably good boat speed because the helmsman is keeping rudder movements to a minimum.

When racing upwind, the helmsman should be following the fluctuations in wind direction, which will probably mean that the wake makes a series of curves. The crewman watching the wake should note any tendency it may have to curve downwind (if the helmsman has not already observed the header!) and any necessary corrections to the course should be made. Conversely, if the wake is seen curving upwind, the boat is lifted up and the appropriate corrections (easing the sheets to lay the mark) should be made.

Tacking is still another situation in which watching the wake of a boat can improve performance. When a boat is tacked, the wake should form a sharp angle without any hollows or bumps. Figure 23.2 shows the optimum tacking wake.

The Wake as a Guide to Navigating

A wake can provide valuable information not only for a helmsman, but for a navigator as well. For one thing, the navigator can obtain an estimate of the leeway by taking a bearing on the wake and comparing it to the centerline of the boat. In addition, he can calculate a wake course, which can serve as a check on the ship's course. In this case he simply takes the reciprocal of the ship's course (course minus 180°) and subtracts an estimated leeway angle. Then, too, when crossing a tidal stream, the navigator can use bearings taken on the wake to tell when the boat is out of the strongest current—a calculation that can be critical in many situations.

A wake, then, can provide a large amount of practical information to an observant and knowledgeable crew. By casting that occasional glance over the transom, you may well be able to increase your sailing performance this season, and consequently place better on the racecourse.

$\mathcal{24}$ Tips for Beginning Navigators

Noah never had celestial tables. He never used a radio direction finder or knew what a black and white striped buoy means. Yet he managed to keep the ark afloat and eventually to find land—or so the story goes. If Noah did this well as a rank beginner, maybe the job of a race navigator isn't so difficult after all?

Although the inexperienced navigator may wish he could believe such reasoning, he knows that its logic is hopelessly flawed. For one thing, Noah didn't have to find his way around a racecourse. For another, he didn't have to stay in the lead of a fleet of competitors, many with highly skilled crews. The truth is that in yacht racing the work of the navigator is never easy. Fortunately, however, practice can help to make it a little less than impossible.

Usually a navigator's hardest race is the first one. Without the experience of several races behind him, a beginning navigator often lacks the confidence, precision, and speed that can make the difference between winning and losing. In this chapter I'll review how a navigator can prepare for that all-important first race and what his responsibilities on the racecourse will be. Since the navigator's job differs depending upon the length of the race, this section will be divided into two parts: first, navigating a round-the-buoy race or overnighter, and second, navigating a long offshore event.

Short-Distance, Coastal Navigation

PREPARATION PRIOR TO THE RACE. The navigator's job starts early in the week before the race, when he receives the race circular. He is the one person on the boat who *must* read the circular carefully and know exactly what it says. Inattention to details can carry a high price tag. For instance, some committees require boats to observe certain channel buoys and pass on the correct side. Make sure you are aware of such rules since ignorance of them can cost you the race. You might even want to make a list of marks to be observed and post it somewhere on the boat where the crewmen can easily read it. Included on this list might also be information such as courses and times of tide, as shown in figure 24.1. This will help make sure that everyone on the boat knows what to expect and will not be endlessly asking the navigator for basic information.

Once you have read the race circular and know where you will be sailing, you can begin to plot the course. Suppose it is now Tuesday and you will begin a 200-mile race on Friday afternoon. Get out your chart of the area and indicate on it the turning marks, as well as any other buoys or obstructions that must be observed. Then look up the relevant tide conditions, so that you can correct your course accordingly. To do so you must assume a boat speed, which will depend upon both the expected wind conditions and the size of the boat. Study long-range weather forecasts to get an idea of what the wind strength and direction are likely to be. Local newspapers usually publish weather maps and give useful long-range predictions. The latest satellite pictures can be seen on the TV news, while the radio of course gives regular shipping forecasts.

All this weather data must then be taken into account when calculating average boat speed. Under normal conditions, average speed will be approximately equal to $\sqrt{LWL}$. If LWL is twenty-five feet, for example, average boat speed would be five knots. For very

Figure 24.1   A crew information sheet such as this could be taped up somewhere in the cockpit.

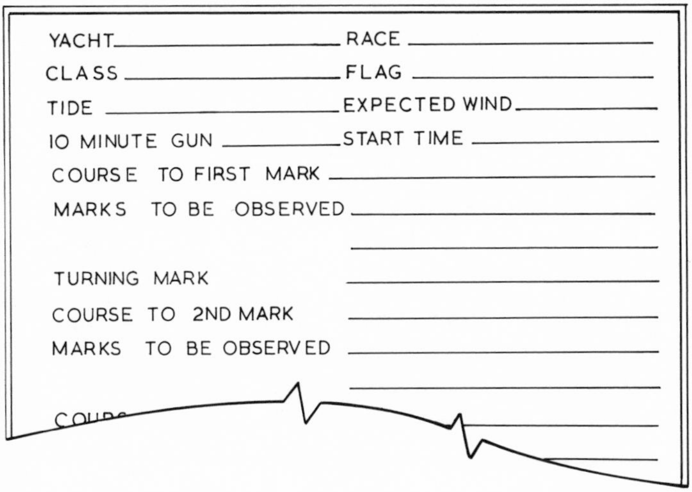

YACHT_____ RACE _____

CLASS _____ FLAG _____

TIDE _____ EXPECTED WIND_____

IO MINUTE GUN _____ START TIME _____

COURSE TO FIRST MARK _____

MARKS TO BE OBSERVED _____

_____

TURNING MARK   _____

COURSE TO 2ND MARK   _____

MARKS TO BE OBSERVED _____

_____

COU

heavy expected wind conditions, this figure should be multiplied by a factor up to 1.3, which will give you maximum boat speed. For very light conditions, on the other hand, $\sqrt{LWL}$ should be multiplied by some factor less than 1. Many navigators use $\sqrt{LWL} \times 0.5$. Thus, by plotting your couse at various speeds, you can get a reasonably good idea of where the boat will be at any given time under any given conditions and make allowances for the tide or current you'll encounter. You should also take special note of any areas of very strong tide and try to avoid them if foul or use them to your advantage if favorable.

As a final prerace preparation, the navigator should go down to the boat and familiarize himself with its instruments and equipment. Read the operating manuals or use a hands on approach to learn all you can about the navigation gear on board. If you are already familiar with the boat's equipment, it is still good practice to check for malfunctions, so that repairs can be made before race day or a backup unit can be supplied. The following are some of the things you should look for:

- Check the batteries on the ship's radio and the RDF. Are you getting powerful signals?
- Check the speedometer log for accuracy. If in doubt, verify it over a measured mile.
- Make sure that the Loran, Omni, or Omega is giving an accurate plot of your position.
- Make sure that your slide rule or hand-held calculator is in good working order and that you know how to use it properly.
- Make sure all the things you need to plot a course (parallel rules, triangles, compasses, pencils) are on board and in good condition.
- Make sure you have all the charts you are likely to need.
- Check your hand-held bearing compass against the ship's compass for deviation.
- Make sure you have a stop watch on board and that it works properly.
- Make sure you have fog horns, flags, and a radar reflector on board and that they are not damaged.
- Check to see if there is a racing rule book on board.
- Make sure that emergency flares are available. If they are old, you might want to try one out in the backyard to be certain they work.

Don't leave the boat until you are assured that everything is in order.

AT THE START. The navigator's responsibilities on a race begin even before the gun. It is he who determines the most advantageous point to cross the starting line, and a good start, as every sailor knows, can give you the lead for the rest of the race. The decision about where to start should be made as carefullly as possible. Here is the procedure most navigators use.

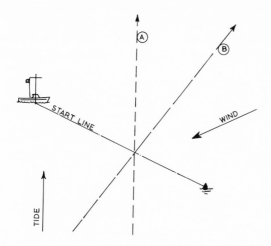

Figure 24.2   If line *A* is the course, a boat must start on starboard and reach to the mark with the tide. Because the line is biased, most boats will start at the committee boat end. The ideal position is just to windward of the majority of the fleet. If line *B* is the course, on the other hand, a boat must sail close-hauled, with the tide pushng it past the mark. The alternatives in this case are to start on starboard and stay on that tack in the hope of a wind shift, or to tack after the start, get clear air, and hope that the wind will not shift.

Have the crew sail the boat down the line while you record the time elapsed and take a bearing. Next have the crew put the boat head-to-wind while you check the wind direction. Plot this information, together with the course to the first mark and the state of the tide, and determine the best approach to the line. (See figure 24.2.) You may want to modify this choice due to tactical considerations, such as what you think your competitors will do. But once your final decision is made, adhere to it as closely as possible.

Now you are ready to make several trial runs to the line. Establish a point from which to begin, as shown in figure 24.3. Remember that you should always try to start on starboard tack. On every trial approach you make, note the time taken to reach the line, so that you can pace your final approach perfectly, crossing the line at maximum speed just as the gun goes off.

Of course, knowing exactly when the gun will fire is also critical. A good navigator is aware of the signals used to start the classes in front of his so that he can check his own time accordingly. With ten minutes left before the start, you should begin to call out the remaining time at thirty-second intervals. Then switch to ten-second intervals with two minutes to go until you begin your final ten-second countdown. If all goes well, the boat will hit the line at full speed precisely on the gun. Enter the starting time on the ship's chronometer into the log, together with other pertinent data. It is often helpful to record the boats on either side, particularly in a pro-

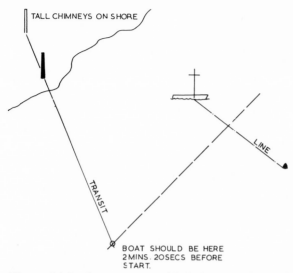

Figure 24.3 One way to establish the point from which to begin your run to the line. Another method is to sail back from the line for one or two minutes and then time how long it takes the boat to reach the line again.

test situation. Immediately after the start, also listen to the ship's radio or watch for recalls.

ON THE RACECOURSE. On each tack of an upwind leg you should keep a log of compass courses to see if a pattern of lifts and headers develops. Also record tacking angles, sea states, and wind conditions for future reference. On longer races the crew can help you keep up the log. In addition to the information recorded after each tack, log in, every half hour or hour, the data needed to maintain a dead-reckoning position. Figure 24.4 shows the entries in a typical log.

In the cruising world, knowing where the boat is at all times is often enough to make a good navigator; in competition it is not. The race navigator has the added responsibility of keeping the rest of the crew fully informed. What marks and lights are expected along the course? What will their probable bearings be and their estimated times of sighting? Such information is critical to good crew work. Similarly, the helmsman must know on which side to leave each mark as it is neared, and what the course for the next leg will be. And the skipper must be advised about the wind angle and probable boat speed, so that he may select the correct sails. If this information is inaccurate or provided too late, poor decisions can be made which can cost you the race.

Finally, several other tasks fall to the navigator on a short-distance race. First, you should be aware of where your boat is in relation to the rest of the fleet, and you should keep a careful eye on competitors for any wind, sail, or tide advantages they may have. Second, you should immediately log any protests that may occur, describing the situation fully, or even sketching it if time allows. And third, you should listen to weather forecast updates to keep abreast of any unusual weather activity that may influence the race.

As the boat nears the finish line, the beginning navigator may conclude that his responsibility has now ended. It has not. The navigator is expected to advise the skipper and crew about the characteristics of the finish line and also about any special rules (such as flashing a light on the sails or calling the race committee on the radio) that must be observed. In addition, he should recommend the best approach to the line, and when the line is crossed he should record the finish time by the ship's chronometer, and if possible note the boats that finished ahead or astern. Finally, the navigator must get the boat safely to the dock. And in a strange harbor with numerous rocks or reefs, this may be no easy task, particularly after a long hard race.

Long-Distance, Offshore Navigation

All the things a navigator must do on a round-the-buoy race he must also do on a long-distance race—plus others. When navigating an event like the Bermuda, Fastnet, or Sydney-Hobart for the first time, here are some of the tasks you should be aware of.

PREPARATION PRIOR TO RACE. For long-distance races you must check your celestial navigation equipment carefully. Accurate time keeping is essential. Make sure that the ship's chronometer is work-

Figure 24.4   Some typical log entries. Each navigator may want to include additional columns, to record such items as sea state, sails used, and so forth.

TIME	LOG	COURSE STEERED	WIND SPD	WIND ANGLE	BAROM PRESS	SEA TEMP	BOAT SPEED	REMARKS
0100	654.9	075	8 K	S	1006	72	6.3	TANKER TO PORT
0130	660.2	075	8 K	S	1007	72	6.4	
0200	666.7	075	7.8K	SSE	1006	72	6.4	TRIED STAYSAIL. SPEED INCREASED

YACHT _____ RACE _____

DATE _____ SKIPPER _____

ing properly and that the radio can pick up regular time checks. Also check the sextant for error. Does the boat carry an emergency sextant? An inexpensive plastice sextant can serve as a backup in case the primary one gets broken. Finally, make sure all the other gear you'll need is aboard, including the nautical almanac, sight reduction tables HO 229 or 249, universal plotting charts (these should be prepared in advance, using the required longitudes or latitudes, and the rhumb line should be marked), light lists/radio beacons, coastal pilots, and pilot charts.

At home you can prepare in a number of other ways. First, you can write out the headings for your rough log, as shown in figure 24.4. The data required will probably vary, depending upon the race. Sea temperature, for example, is essential for the Bermuda, where you'll be entering the Gulf Stream, but on the Fastnet all you need to know about temperature is that the water is *very* cold! Other items included in a typical log are barometric pressure, apparent wind speed, apparent wind angle, and depth. Second, you can compute sunrise and sunset times and the probable positions of navigational stars and planets, based on anticipated boat speed. Be sure to select stars that will give both a latitudinal and longitudinal fix—that is, stars ahead and astern of the rhumb line as well as along it. Finally, consult a light list and mark on your charts the maximum radius within which each light along the course should be visible in clear weather.

ON THE RACECOURSE. From the navigator's point of view, starting a long-distance race is not different from starting a round-the-buoy race. The responsibilities and techniques are exactly the same. Once the race begins, however, the picture changes, for a number of new duties fall the navigator's way. One is monitoring the radio to obtain current weather information, to check the time ticks or radio Canada against the ship's chronometer, to find out where freighters and fishing fleets are located, and to discover which boats in the race, if any, have already finished. In addition, the navigator must keep his dead-reckoning plot up to date and check it regularly against his celestial fixes, to determine if the boat is being driven off course by ocean currents.

Bear in mind that on most boats it is not the navigator's job to decide where the boat *should be*, but rather to keep the crew informed as to where the boat actually *is* at any given time. Needless to say, this in itself is no easy task. To develop the ability to navigate quickly and accurately under the most intense competitive pressure and in the worst kind of weather conditions requires a great deal of experience. So the next time someone asks you to navigate a race, prepare carefully and give it a try. After all, even the best race navigators were beginners at some time in their lives.

$\mathbb{25}$ Race Cooking

How well does your crew eat on a long-distance race? Do you survive on slapped-together meals, supplemented with occasional candy bars and sodas? Many crews do. And even those who are fortunate enough to eat better than this may not be planning, preparing, and serving meals as well as they could. Does it take your cook forever just to make a simple dish because food and utensils have been carelessly stored? When a hot meal is served, is it likely to be cold before it arrives on deck? Do you often find yourself running out of food by the end of a race in spite of your efforts to keep the galley well supplied? Although race cooking on most boats will probably never be a gourmet affair, problems such as these can usually be avoided. All that's needed is good meal planning, plus good preparation and serving techniques.

Meal Planning

When I sailed on *Morning Cloud* several seasons ago, I cooked as well as stood a watch. Good meal planning was essential. My preparations usually started on Monday or Tuesday, when I made out the menus for the weekend. Here is a typical plan for a Friday/Saturday race:

FRIDAY

Dinner   Raw carrots

Broiled steak with mushrooms and onions

Boiled potatoes with butter and chopped parsley
Peas (or mixed green salad in warm weather)
Fruit salad
Coffee/tea

Snack   Cookies/biscuits
Hot chocolate/tea/coffee

SATURDAY

Breakfast   Grapefruit
Cereal with milk
Eggs with bacon and broiled tomatoes
Toast with butter and marmalade
Coffee/tea

Lunch   Ham and cheese sandwiches
Fresh fruit
Coffee/tea/soda

Dinner   Beef stew
Rolls with butter
Canned pears
Coffee/tea

Snack   Cookies/biscuits
Hot chocolate/coffee/tea

In addition to planning the food I knew would be served, I always allowed for a few additional meals, in case the race ran late.

All these food requirements were then entered on a shopping list, like the one shown in figure 25.1. This simple form was a big help in making sure that nothing was forgotten. Before leaving the boat after a race, I would check the lockers and stowage compartments and make a note of all the nonfood items and staples—such as soap, paper towels, salt, or cooking oil—needed for the following week. Later in the week I would add the major food requirements, taking into account whatever canned goods were already on board. In this way, very little was left to memory.

One question new cooks frequently ask when sitting down to plan their menus is "What kinds of foods are best for a racing crew?" Two factors should be taken into account. First, consider the digestibility of the foods you serve. Steer clear of rich sauces and fatty foods, which are difficult for the stomach to handle. Meals that offer a balance between protein-rich foods (lean meats, fish, eggs, dairy products) and good sources of carbohydrates (fresh fruits, vegetables, whole grains and cereals) are best. Second, consider the expected weather conditions when selecting menus. A hearty stew may be just right for a cool evening, but far less appealing when the temperature hovers in the nineties. In very hot weather, salads and cold dishes may make more sense.

In addition to considering what kinds of meals are best for the crew, you should also consider what kinds of meals are best

DATE_____ RACE_____

Qty.	Type		Qty.	Type	
		Meats			**Bread & Cereals**
_____	_____	steak	_____	_____	breakfast cereal
_____	_____	chicken	_____	_____	bread
_____	_____	chops	_____	_____	crackers
_____	_____	bacon	_____	_____	rice
_____	_____	sausage	_____	_____	_____
_____	_____	_____			**Dairy**
_____	_____	_____	_____	_____	butter
		Vegetables	_____	_____	milk
_____	_____	tomatoes	_____	_____	eggs
_____	_____	lettuce	_____	_____	cheese
_____	_____	mushrooms	_____	_____	yogurt
_____	_____	onions	_____	_____	_____
_____	_____	potatoes			**Beverages**
_____	_____	carrots	_____	_____	coffee
_____	_____	peas	_____	_____	tea
_____	_____	_____	_____	_____	chocolate
_____	_____	_____	_____	_____	soup
_____	_____	_____	_____	_____	beer
		Fruits	_____	_____	soft drinks
_____	_____	grapefruit	_____	_____	fruit juice
_____	_____	apples	_____	_____	_____
_____	_____	pears	_____	_____	_____
_____	_____	fruit salad			**Paper & Soap**
_____	_____	_____	_____	_____	toilet rolls
_____	_____	_____	_____	_____	kitchen rolls
		Staples	_____	_____	toilet soap
_____	_____	salt/pepper	_____	_____	dishwashing soap
_____	_____	cooking oil	_____	_____	scouring powder
_____	_____	jelly/jam			**Snacks**
_____	_____	ketchup	_____	_____	cookies/biscuits
_____	_____	mustard	_____	_____	candies
_____	_____	mayonnaise	_____	_____	nuts
_____	_____	_____	_____	_____	_____

Figure 25.1 Using a form like this one is an easy way to compile a shopping list. The most commonly purchased things are listed on the form and blanks are left for other items. The cook simply writes in the quantity and type needed—*3 lbs. stewing steak*, for example.

for the cook. One of the secrets of successful race cooking is selecting dishes that can be prepared with a minimum amount of fuss. Casseroles made ashore, which simply need to be reheated, are always easy, as are precooked meats such as baked ham, which can be served either hot or cold. For lunch, Cornish pasties, which originated in my native area of Cornwall and Devon, are also easy. (Sailors who have done the Fastnet may have eaten them in Plymouth pubs.) A recipe for pasties is given at the end of this chapter. Sixteen to twenty pasties, enough to feed a hungry crew of eight, can be made very inexpensively the day before a race. Because pasties can so easily be held in one hand, they are a practical lunch for even the busiest crewmen.

Another simple meal idea for long-distance races is Chinese wok cooking. A wok, for those who don't already know, is a deep, round-bottomed cooking container specially designed for frying food quickly over a high heat—called stir-frying. A ring-shaped base supports the wok on the stove and a metal spatula is used to toss the food as it cooks. All the ingredients for a wok dinner can be diced, cubed, and sliced ashore, so that the actual meal preparation on the boat takes only a few minutes. (Food is never cooked long in a wok; vegetables should always remain slightly crisp.) A few easy wok recipes are given here, but part of the fun of Chinese cooking is using your own imagination to produce new and different combinations. Virtually any kind of food—beef, chicken, fish, vegetables, fresh ingredients or leftovers—is appropriate for wok meals.

Working in the Galley

Meal planning, of course, is only a first step in successful race cooking. The most difficult part comes when you are on the race course and must prepare three good meals a day, regardless of sea and wind conditions. There are many small tricks to achieving success which one gradually learns through experience. Some of the most basic requirements, however, are good stowage techniques, good organization while preparing food, and good attention to safety.

STOWAGE IDEAS. A cook who has trouble finding or reaching what is needed can never be efficient. This includes cooking utensils as well as food supplies. Stowage problems are particularly acute on a boat where space is very limited. But with a little ingenuity intelligent solutions can be found on even the smallest boats, making the cook's job that much easier. Here are some of the techniques I recommend.

1. *Packing the ice box.* Always make sure that frozen foods are packed in the order in which they will be used. This saves a lot of rummaging around and keeps foods colder longer. A good way to prevent crewmen from constantly opening the icebox is to pack beverages in a separate styrofoam ice chest. (Also remember to keep a large supply of drinks on board, since dehydration can be a serious problem at sea, especially in hot weather. This does not include alcoholic beverages, which tend to contribute to dehydration.)
2. *Stowing cans.* Cans can often be stowed in the bilge, where they also contribute to stability. But before using this stowage place, remove all labels and write the contents on the cans with a felt-tip pen. This avoids the dismay of lifting the sole boards and finding a bilge filled with half-dissolved paper, blocked bilge pumps, and a clutter of unidentifiable canned goods. Another stowage idea when space is

tight is to put cans, as well as paper goods, in unused lockers in the head.

3. *Stowing utensils.* The trick to utensil stowage in a galley is to have a place for everything and to keep everything in its place. Chap 6, on galley design, suggests some possibilities.

ORGANIZATION TIPS. Many of the truly terrible meals you have had on the race course were probably the result of poor organization. All good cooks are reasonably well organized; they know what they intend to do before they actually do it. The following simple guidelines for organization may be helpful to beginning cooks.

1. Whatever work can be done in advance, do ashore before the race. This includes preparing casseroles to be reheated, cooking meats which can be eaten cold, making sandwiches or pastries, and simply cleaning, peeling, and slicing ingredients for meals to be cooked on board.
2. Whenever possible, try to put things away as you use them in order to keep countertops clear. One of the things that can slow the progress of food preparation most is having nowhere left to work.
3. Know how long it will take to cook or prepare each food on your menu so that everything will be ready at once. It is disconcerting, to say the least, to discover that your steaks are done but your potatoes are still half raw. Accurate timing of cooking takes practice, but cookbooks can give you the basic information you need.
4. Since stove-top space is at a premium on most boats, think of ways to use fewer pots and pans. Many foods can be broiled or grilled rather than cooked on top of the stove. And several things that must be boiled can often be cooked in the same pot. When boiling potatoes, for example, peas can be added to the same water when the potatoes are almost done.

TIPS FOR SAFETY. Good racing cooks tend to have few accidents in the galley. They have learned how to prepare meals both quickly and safely. Although safe race cooking is very much a matter of common sense, a few general practices are wise to follow. First, in rough weather, wear your harness in the galley, so that you will not be accidentally thrown against the stove. Also wear your oilskin pants, so that if you hit a sea and hot food comes flying off the stove, you will be protected against major burns. Second, use good judgment in the utensils you select. For example, always choose wide, flat-bottomed pots rather than narrow or rounded ones; they are obviously much more stable. Third, make sure the crew gives advance warning when the boat is about to be tacked. This will allow you sufficient time to prevent spills. And finally, if something looks risky, don't try it. Nine times out of ten it won't work.

SERVING FOOD ON A RACE. After food is planned and prepared, the final step in successful race cooking is serving it efficiently. Most cooks have their own methods of serving major meals, but their ways of providing between-meal snacks are often more haphazard. Frequently, each crewman ransacks the galley, hunting up whatever he can. The result can be a bit chaotic. A simple solution is to put a large bowl of fruit, nuts, bisquits, and cookies in a place where crewmen can easily help themselves. At night the cook can also make up a thermos of coffee for the on-watch crew. Or during the day he can serve hot drinks from an aluminum cup tray fitted over the stove, as shown in figure 25.2. Cups of coffee, chocolate, or soup can be kept in the tray without spilling even in the roughest conditions. This provides the crew with hot drinks whenever they want them—something that's greatly appreciated on a cold, wet day at sea.

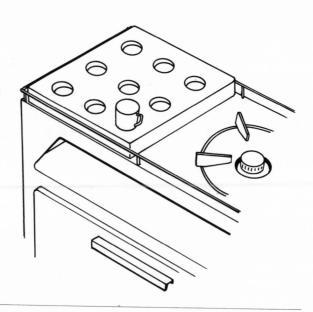

Figure 25.2 A nine-cup tray can be made to fit the top of a stove for ease of filling cups with hot drinks and serving them to the crew.

CORNISH PASTIES

The ingredients in a pasty vary depending upon the whim of the cook. In the old days, Cornish miners often lunched on "two-ended" pasties, with meat and potatoes in one side and fruit or preserves in the other. Here is a basic pasty recipe to which you can add your own touches.

> 2½–3lbs. *lean stewing beef, cut into half-inch cubes*
> 8–10 *medium potatoes, peeled and diced*
> 1 *large turnip or* 6–8 *medium-sized carrots, peeled and diced*
> 2 *medium onions, peeled and chopped*
> *salt and pepper to taste*
> *finely-chopped parsley*
> *pastry dough*
> 1 *egg, beaten*

Mix up pastry dough from a cookbook recipe or a packaged mix—enough for about eight to ten pies. Roll the dough out on a floured board and cut into sixteen to twenty circles with a baking dish nine inches in diameter. Fill half the pastry disk with equal amounts of potatoes and meat (previously browned in a frying pan or boiled in well-seasoned water). Also add a bit of turnip, some onion, a sprinkle of parsley, and salt and pepper to taste. Wet the edges of the pastry and fold the empty portion of the disk over the filling. (The pasty should be well stuffed, but not so full that it barely closes.) Press the edges together with a fork and glaze the top with a beaten egg. Bake at 350 degrees for about twenty minutes or until golden brown. Serve hot or cold. Sixteen to twenty pasties should be enough for a hungry crew of eight.

A Simple Wok Meal

Here are a few easy wok dishes which together make a respectable meal. All are for eight persons and can be cooked all at once or half at a time. For anyone who wants to try others, good Chinese cookbooks are available at any major bookstore. Or you can simply experiment on your own. But be sure to try any new dish at home first before serving it on a race.

CHINESE HAMBURGER

1 clove garlic, crushed	
1 medium onion, chopped, or	4 Tbs. oil
6–8 chopped scallions	¾ lb. mushrooms, fresh or
2 lbs. ground beef or	canned
hamburger	12 oz. peas, frozen or canned

Heat the wok over a high flame for about ten seconds. Add half of the oil and let it get very hot (about twenty to thirty seconds). Add the garlic and onions, stir-frying for two to three minutes. Add crumbled hamburger meat and stir-fry until brown. Add soy sauce, toss, and remove meat mixture from wok. Add remaining oil and heat. Add mushrooms, stir-frying for about two to three minutes. Then return the meat to the wok. Add peas and stir-fry until thoroughly heated (about one to two minutes). Keep warm until served.

SPINACH AND MUSHROOMS

This is a dish that goes well with Chinese hamburger. A careful cook could serve a spinach and mushrooms salad one night, and the next night make stir-fried spinach and mushrooms to use up the leftovers.

4 Tbs. oil   2 lbs. spinach
4 cloves garlic, crushed   1 lb. sliced mushrooms
1 medium onion, chopped   salt, sugar, soy sauce to taste

Heat the wok over a high flame for about ten seconds. Add the oil and let it get very hot (about twenty to thirty seconds). Add the garlic and onion, stir-frying until light brown. Add the mushrooms, lightly salted, and stir-fry two to three minutes. Add the spinach and about a teaspoon of sugar. Stir-fry until the spinach becomes deep green. Sprinkle with soy sauce. Keep warm until served.

FRIED RICE WITH GREEN PEAS

Most Chinese dinners are served with some kind of rice dish. This is a basic recipe that can easily be modified—for example, by substituting another vegetable in place of peas, or by adding a cooked diced meat (chicken, pork or ham) or baby shrimp.

1 clove garlic, crushed
1 small onion, chopped fine
3 Tbs. oil
9–10 cups cold, cooked rice
1 12–oz. can peas (frozen peas are better if you have them)
4–5 eggs
4 Tbs. soy sauce
1½ Tbs. sherry
1½ Tbs. corn starch   } mix together to form a sauce
salt and pepper to taste

Heat the wok over a high flame for about ten seconds. Add the oil and let it get very hot (about twenty to thirty seconds). Add the onion and garlic and stir-fry until light brown. Add the rice and then the eggs, slightly beaten. Stir-fry for two to three minutes. Drain the peas and add to the rice mixture, stir-frying for another three to four minutes. Add the sauce and stir-fry for one minute more. Serve.

26 Improving Crew Efficiency

How many boats have you raced on over the years? If you're like most sailors, the number is quite large. Now how many of those boats would you say had truly first-rate crew work? Probably only a handful. Many factors can contribute to crew inefficiency. I shall discuss two of the most common ones—the failure to instruct new crewmen about the layout of your boat, and the failure to practice crew rotation—and some possible solutions to them.

Instructing New Crewmen

Every skipper has a number of new hands sailing on his boat each season, but how many skippers prepare these men well to join the existing crew? When a new crewman arrives on your boat late Friday evening for an overnight race, do you offer him a drink rather than a tour around the boat? If so, it should come as no surprise when he drops the main instead of the spinnaker in the middle of the night, or when he ends up spending most of his time asking "Where's the ——— ———————?"

With a little forethought on a skipper's part, all the inefficiency of an uninformed new crewman can be avoided simply by giving the right answers on an early tour of the boat. So the next time a new man joins your crew, offer him that drink but don't let him sit down with it; instead, take him for a walk around the boat. Tell him what his position on deck will be and spend a few minutes familiarizing him with the locations of the nearest ropes, handholds, stowage places, and other fittings. Encourage him to try out the gear. By actually undoing the halyard or sheet, he will probably remember where it leads much better than if he simply looks at it.

At the start of next season, you might want to write out lists of essential information which can be distributed to newcomers on the boat. The following are some of the questions that new crewmen most frequently ask.

FOREDECK MAN
- Are port and starboard halyards color-coded at the shackle and winch end? (If so, what are the colors?)
- How is the spinnaker pole hooked up/released?
- Where are all the sails and sheets, spare shackles, blocks, and so on stowed?
- What method of spinnaker set/takedown is usually used?

MID-DECK HAND
- In what order do halyards exit from the mast?
- What method of raising/lowering/gybing the pole is usually used?
- Where do the halyards lead? What cleats take which halyard?
- Where is the vang stowed, or if hydraulic, where are the pump and handle, and how does it work?
- Where is the nearest winch handle stowage?

AFTERGUARD
- Where do all the sheets lead?
- What happens on a spinnaker set, gybe, takedown?
- Where are the handles and spare gear stowed?
- Is there a "short" sheet aboard? It is used?

ALL CREWMEN
Where and how are the following items stowed:
emergency tiller
flashlights
life raft
flares
spares
toolbox, including emergency tools
life jackets
harnesses
man-overboard poles and horseshoes
beer

Practising Crew Rotation

One thing to keep in mind when showing a new crewman around a boat is the need to familiarize him with the entire layout, not just a single area. This is because efficiency can be improved by having crew members rotate positions. Rotation is especially important for the helmsman. On many boats the skipper, because he is the most experienced, takes the helm for several hours. If you want to win, however, you must break this habit. Studies have shown that the maximum period of concentration for the helmsman is under forty minutes; after fifteen minutes, concentration begins to ebb. By changing helmsmen every thirty minutes, it will soon become apparent how much you gain over a crew whose helmsman steers for three or four hours at a stretch.

But knowing the optimum length of time a crewman should perform a particular task is only one part of solving the problem of crew rotation. Often crews have no set method of rotating duties. Here I've suggested a method for a four-man watch, but this can be modified to suit a two-man or a six-man watch. The skipper will probably be the best judge of how to modify a rotation system to suit both the size and the varied skills of his particular best crew. One man's duties over a four-hour watch:

> helm—thirty minutes
> weather rail—thirty minutes
> sheet trim—thirty minutes
> weather rail—thirty minutes
> helm—thirty minutes
> weather rail—thirty minutes
> sheet trim—thirty minutes
> weather rail—fifteen minutes
> This leaves fifteen minutes for the crewman to go below, put the kettle on, make hot drinks, and wake the other watch.

The theory behind this system is that a crewman helms for thirty minutes and can then rest for thirty minutes before he takes his turn calling sheet trim. If there are four men in the watch, each man has two tricks at the helm, two on the sheet, and four on the rail. This method alleviates any boredom that may result from one man sitting for four hours on the rail while the skipper steers for four hours. The final fifteen minutes, used to prepare hot drinks and wake the other watch, helps ensure that the new crew members arrive on deck alert and on time.

If there is no regular cook on board, a man can come off watch at 7:30 A.M. to make breakfast for the next watch. Again, a system can be developed to make the most of watch changes, as illustrated in table 26.1.

Such a system need not be rigidly adhered to, but it does provide a basic plan which a skipper can modify to suit his own style. It also gives everyone a chance at both the good and the bad jobs. And by making use of the on-watch men who are not busy, it ensures that the off-watch get enough sleep so that they can perform at peak efficiency on deck, where it counts. (For races up to 200 miles, all the crew would turn to for sail changes.)

After considering a rotation system like the one outlined here, you may have your doubts as to whether you or your crew would like the discipline involved. But it is this kind of organized approach that has won more races than any other.

Table 26.1

Watch change	Time	Galley duty for a man on the weather rail
12 midnight	11:45	Make hot drinks and wake the next watch.
	12:15	Clean up.
4:00 A.M.	3:45	Make hot drinks and wake the next watch.
	4:15	Clean up.
8:00 A.M.	7:30	Cook breakfast for next watch.
	8:30	Cook breakfast for off-watch crew.
	9:00	Clean up.
12:00 noon	11:30	Make sandwiches for next watch.
	12:30	Make sandwiches for off-watch crew.
	1:00	Clean up.
4:00 P.M.	3:45	Make snack and hot drinks if required.
	4:15	Clean up.
8:00 P.M.	7:00	Cook dinner.
	7:30	Serve dinner to next watch.
	8:00	Serve dinner to off-coming watch.
	8:30	Clean up.

Table 26.1 At each of the times designated, one of the on-watch crewmen on the weather rail performs the galley duty indicated.

Part IV

Racing Boat Maintenance

Introduction

Some people think that maintenance is complete when routine chores are finished. They scrub the deck, pump out the bilges, clean the interior, and consider the day's work done. But proper maintenance involves much more than this. Overhauling the engine, removing and inspecting the mast, checking out winches and hydraulics are some of the more difficult tasks that should be included on every owner's maintenance schedule. A racing boat, like a highly tuned racing car, requires a tremendous amount of care. In fact, it would not be excessive for a good paid hand to put in sixty to seventy hours a week keeping a boat in tip-top shape.

The first three chapters that follow are organized around the major areas of boat maintenance—hulls, decks, and interiors; sails, rigging, and deck gear; and mechanical and electrical equipment. The coverage given, of course, is not meant to be all-inclusive, for an entire book could be written on each subject. But the information presented should indicate the types of maintenance chores required on a boat, how to go about performing them, and how to organize a system to avoid neglecting any task. Finally, the last chapter in this section gives owners some advice on the various maintenance jobs that can be done over the winter, when a boat is laid up.

27/ Maintaining Hulls, Decks, and Interiors

When you head for the start of a race, are you sure your boat is 100 percent prepared? Or do you just hope that the winch you didn't have time to check will hold up? If you and your crew know your boat is fully maintained, the chances are your performance will be better, because you are feeling completely confident. Boat maintenance, of course, is a large and varied topic which can take years to master completely. Here I'll simply review the basics of caring for hulls, decks, and interiors, with a checklist at the end for a review of the jobs to be done.

Organizing Your Maintenance Program

Thorough maintenance takes time even for the most experienced owner, but good organization helps to get many jobs done more efficiently. With a well-planned system you should always know what needs to be done when and how to do it. Here is the method I use.

For every job on board I make out a 3″ × 5″ card; a typical one is shown in figure 27.1. This particular card deals with a winch check. On the front is the job title and method. I tab it with a color-coded tag which tells me whether this is a daily, weekly, monthly, or less frequent job. Whenever possible, I include a list of the tools that are needed to do the work required.

On the back of the card is a list of all the winches on board, and

RED TAB →

WINCH CHECK

CHECK FOR FREE RUNNING. REMOVE DRUM. CHECK PAWLS
CLEAN GREASE OF BEARINGS, CHECK SPINDLE FOR WEAR
(ROCK SHAFT GENTLY) PUT HANDLE IN AND WIND. LOOK
FOR COGS BENT OR MISSING. WIPE OFF GREASE, (MIND
THE DECK, LIGHTLY LUBRICATE COGS BEARING CAGES
AND PAWLS. REPLACE DRUM, CHECK FOR FREE RUNNING
BY WINDING WITH HANDLES, LISTEN FOR PAWLS
CLICKING (SEE ALSO LEWMAR TECHNICAL MANUAL)

FRONT OF CARD

WINCHES		23 JUNE	25 JULY	7 AUG									
SPIN. SHEET	P	✓	✓	✓									
	S	✓	✓	✓									
GEN. SHEET	P	✓	✓	✓									
	S	✓	REPLACE PAWLS	✓									
SPIN. HAL.	P	✓	✓	✓									
	S	✓	✓	✓									
GEN. HAL.	P	✓	✓	✓									
	S	✓	✓	✓									
MAIN SHEET		✓	✓	✓									
FOREGUY		✓	✓	✓									
TOPPING LIFT		✓	✓	✓									
UTILITY		✓	✓	✓									
MAIN HAL		✓	REW	✓									
SPARES KIT		✓	PAWLS USED	✓									

BACK OF CARD

Figure 27.1 A set of 3″ × 5″ cards can be used to keep track of maintenance jobs. This is a sample card for a winch check. The front describes what needs to be done and the back records the dates completed. A red tab indicates that this is a weekly job. Yellow, green, and blue tabs indicate daily, monthly, and more frequent jobs respectively.

columns that show when they last were checked. I leave a space to show whether the spares are complete, and also include a space for any other comments. The back of the card in figure 27.1 shows that the main halyard reel winch was replaced on July 25 because it was slipping and potentially dangerous.

I file all the cards in a card box, which is divided into two main sections: summer and winter jobs. Each main section is then divided into daily, weekly, monthly and less frequent jobs. At the beginning of each week, I take out the weekly cards and a number of monthly cards for work that is to be done that week. (After a short period of time the daily jobs become routine, but the cards still should be kept in case a helper does the work.) As soon as the jobs are completed, the cards should be updated and refiled in the back of the section, so that all jobs come up again in the correct order.

This system has several advantages. First, it ensures that each job on your boat is brought to your attention regularly. Nothing is neglected simply because it is overlooked. Second, it makes it easy to distribute jobs among helpers. If an owner can persuade his crew to arrive a few hours early before a race, he can give each one a job card and not have to waste time explaining what needs to be done. In fact, if it's a morning after the night before, he doesn't even have to speak to anyone. The job cards contain all the necessary instructions.

Of course, any such system is only as good as the information contained on the cards. So let's turn to some of the jobs that must be done to maintain hulls, decks, and interiors. Owners should tailor my suggestions to the needs of their own individual boats.

Hull Maintenance

TOPSIDES. Most modern hulls are made of fiberglass and, apart from an occasional polishing, not much work is needed to maintain a fiberglass hull above the waterline. Most people don't bother about polishing unless they are selling the boat. But what is better at the beginning of the season than to see the topsides looking shiny and unmarked?

To polish a fiberglass hull, first wash the topsides with soapy water. I always use a household dishwashing detergent and a soft brush. If there is oil around the waterline, try hot water and a concentrated detergent. If this fails, use scouring powder on a damp sponge. But a word of warning: scouring powder can scratch, so beware of using it in highly visible or reflective areas. After you have finished washing down, you can start polishing. The topsides of a thirty-footer should only take a couple of hours. Spray polishes are helpful here.

Bad scratches in fiberglass hulls—often the result of hitting a buoy—should be refilled with resin that is color-matched to the original hull. If the scratch is deep, the job should be left to an expert, because the surrounding area may have to be ground away to form a good base for the filler. Minor marks and scratches, though, can often be polished out or touched up with a little paint or resin filler.

Paint can also be used to cover scratches on an aluminum hull. But be sure the paint you use is not lead-based, or it can set up an electrolytic action. If the scratch or dent is deep, an epoxy filler may have to be used. The filler can be sanded off fair afterwards and painted up to match the hull color.

Polishing an aluminum hull, as I suggested for a fiberglass hull, will improve the look of the hull. But don't rub hard with scouring powder. You may remove paint.

A steel hull can also be touched up with paint. But if the scratch is deep, remember to use an antirust primer before applying the top coat.

BELOW THE WATERLINE. While a boat is in the water, not much can be done below the waterline unless you happen to be a diver. The frequency with which you haul your boat out to work on the underside depends in part upon how keenly competitive you are. If the boat is lifted out regularly, the hull can be kept almost like new. But unless you are racing often, it is not likely that you will do this.

When the boat is out of the water, one of the first things you might check is the rudder. Do all the bolts on the rudder fit snugly? Is there play in the rudder stock? Also check that all through-hull fittings are clear and not fouling. Then make sure that the antifouling paint is intact, and touch it up where required.

If the boat is wood, check all the underwater fastenings. Any signs of corrosion should be dealt with as quickly as possible. If the corrosion is very bad, don't hesitate to get a qualified opinion. It may save you a lot of money, and possibly even your life! Check the caulking, if possible, and make sure it is not falling out.

Once you have inspected the exterior of the hull, now may be a good opportunity to hose out the bilge. If the boat does not have a drain plug, disconnecting the lowest through-hull fitting can make a useful drain hole. But remember to connect it up again afterwards!

When you think the bilges are clean, scrub them down and get them really clean. Check the keel bolts, interior fastenings, and all through-hull fittings. Can you move all the seacocks easily? If not, dismantle them and grease or renew. Check that you don't have a brass fitting in a steel or aluminum hull. Or—an even more likely source of future trouble—a steel fitting on a steel hull fastened with brass bolts. Such things have been done and they cause electrolytic corrosion.

Your next step, after you have checked through the bilge, scrubbed it down, and removed all the oil, grease, and shavings, is to let it dry out thoroughly. Now, if you like, you can paint through

Figure 27.2   A simple hull scrubber.

WET & DRY

the bilge. I always use white or light gray paint, because any dirt shows up clearly and can be easily cleaned away. Another boat owner I know always uses black paint for just the opposite reason! But I feel that if the bilge is clean, any bilge water that slops up into lockers will also be clean and so will not leave a dirty residue.

At this point, the racing sailor may want to put in the effort to obtain that extra bit of polish. A clean and highly polished hull gives not only top performance but also a psychological edge over competitors with slimy undersides. If the yard is agreeable (some yards do not allow crews to work on the hull below the sheerline when the boat is out of the water), polishing can be done with 400-grade wet-and-dry emery paper. Figure 27.2 shows a simple scrubber that can be made to hold the emery cloth or paper. Use long horizontal strokes, working from the bow area toward the stern. The theory is that the bow needs to be smoothest to carry laminar flow as far aft as possible, so if you work from forward to aft your early energy and enthusiasm are likely to be concentrated where it is most important. When using the wet and dry, lubricate with water that has some washing-up soap in it. This makes for easier work. Put a polyethylene bag over your hand and fasten it with elastic bands around your wrists. This stops the water from running up your arm and down inside your shirt.

Fairing strips around the rudder need checking often if you are to obtain optimum performance from them. Sometimes these bend and foul the rudder. At other times filler that has been used can flake or break off. Try to make the leading edge of your rudder as smooth as possible, again to improve laminar flow over the rudder. Remember, the rudder is what steers the boat and it needs all the help it can get; that means not just above the waterline.

If there is a trim tab on your boat, the same rules apply. If the trailing edge is not knife-sharp, the next best thing, and some say it's better, is to file a ⅛-inch flat on the trailing edge at right angles to the water flow. (See figure 27.3.)

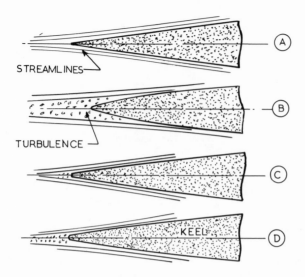

Figure 27.3a The ideal trailing edge shape. *27.3b* What often happens when an inexperienced person is asked to clean up a keel. *27.3c* A flat trailing edge is the next best alternative if your keel arrives from the yard looking like *27.3d*.

Deck Maintenance

CLEANING. Why bother to clean a deck? It will only get dirty again as soon as someone walks on it. This is the argument you often hear. But just remember that your sails are placed on the deck before hoisting, and what looks worse than dirty sails?

Fiberglass is easily cleaned by simply washing it down. As I mentioned earlier, dishwashing liquid makes a perfectly good cleaner.

Laid teak decks require a little more attention. Ideally they should be washed down with fresh water every day. If you are going to wash your deck once a week, there are teak cleaners available. The liquid form is best, because the powder solutions are more difficult to wash away. I have found that wetting the deck, then squeezing the liquid directly onto it and scrubbing hard with a good stiff brush makes a lather than can be easily washed off with a hose. Stains that cannot be removed with teak cleaner, scrubbing, and sanding, should be treated with oxalic acid, but have plenty of water available to rinse after use.

Natural teak oil is sometimes used after sanding a laid teak deck. However, I don't recommend it. When the oil is applied, planks of different grains and textures may absorb different amounts, causing a streaky effect.

Painted decks are usually marine plywood with nonslip deck

paint applied. The final result is often like sandpaper—both to the touch and to the seat of your oilskins! Painted decks are difficult to clean because the dirt lodges in the crevices of the paint. The best way to clean them is to scrub hard with a stiff brush. Regular cleaning will remove most of the dirt, but regular repainting is also needed to maintain good looks.

Another item on decks that needs attention is the tread strip. The diamond-patterned Trak-Mark is easily cleaned by brushing in the direction of the diagonals. The 3M's Tread Strip, however, is another game. In texture it is like nonslip deck paint, and it's equally as wearing. To clean it, use the same technique you would for nonslip deck paint. Where the dirt collects around the edges, a little turpentine will usually remove the layer of glue that causes the trouble.

Metal decks should be scrubbed, and any damage to the paint work quickly retouched. On a steel deck, if there is a deep scratch, touch it up with primer first and then apply a topcoat. On wooden plywood decks, if the paint is flaking, follow the same treatment, but make sure you give the deck time to dry after scraping off as much loose paint as possible. Once it is dry, you can touch it up with primer and topcoat.

VARNISH WORK. A good varnish job requires just the right kind of weather and plenty of hard work. If you are working with bare wood, try a first coat of 35 percent varnish and 65 percent turpentine. The second coat can be half and half, and the third coat 65 percent varnish and 35 percent turpentine. The next four layers can be all clear varnish.

Here's a tip given to me by an old hand whose varnish work was his pride. Once you have put a layer of varnish on, let it dry to the "tacky" stage. Then, without rubbing it down, apply the second coat. But never apply more than three coats without allowing twenty-four hours for it to harden off. Once the varnish has hardened, it should be "cut" (rubbed down) with 400-grade wet-and-dry paper before applying the next layer. The rubbing down is only to give a base for the next coat to adhere to, so remember to use a tackcloth to wipe off the white sediment before varnishing.

During a season I like to get about ten to twelve coats on the bare wood. This, incidentally, helps protect the wood if the boat is stowed outside during the winter. The next spring the varnish should be cut back hard, almost to the bare wood, and the cycle started again. The really crucial factor in getting that high sheen is the time of day when you apply the varnish. If the sun is too hot, the varnish will dry too quickly. If it is too cold or damp, the varnish will dull because of the overlong drying time.

Interior Maintenance

Interiors are treated in so many different ways that it is impossible to cover everything here. In general, my comments about varnishing, painting, and fiberglass maintenance still apply. In addition, cabin sole boards should be scrubbed at least once a month, and far more often in the galley, where grease and food (at least with my kind of cooking) tend to make the floor slippery.

After every long offshore race, I always remove all the bedding, mattresses, seats, sails, and other easily movable items onto the deck and scrub the interior thoroughly. This effectively removes any accumulated salt and makes the boat seem less damp. On a shorter overnight race, a quick freshwater hose-through and pump-out will usually suffice to get the boat clean and fresh, ready for the next race.

CHECKLIST

HULL MAINTENANCE

In the water
- touch up scratches and dents
- polish occasionally

Out of the water

check the following:
- caulking on a wooden boat
- hull/keel joint, touching up as required
- rudder bearings
- pintles
- fairing strips
- propeller, shaft, and strut for cracks and misalignment

make sure that:
- trailing edges of keel and rudder are knife-sharp or ⅛-inch flat
- there are no irregularities in the keel (especially near the bottom after you have gone aground)
- all through-hull fittings work efficiently and are of the correct metal, so as not to cause electrolytic corrosion
- the speed recording device is clear of seaweed
- the bottom of the hull is polished to a racing finish

DECK MAINTENANCE

- scrub regularly, at a minimum after each race
- remove stains from teak decks with oxalic acid, washing down well with water afterwards
- make sure there is plenty of nonslip on potentially slippery areas
- touch up any varnish work as required, trying not to allow the varnish to be rubbed down to bare wood
- touch up any scratches on a metal deck

INTERIOR MAINTENANCE

- clean regularly, scrubbing out completely after every race
- touch up varnish work as required
- clean cushions and berth linen regularly
- clean and disinfect the head and icebox, leaving the icebox lid off when not in use
- pump out the sump tanks and bilge
- make sure the electrical equipment and engine ignition are turned off
- open all lockers and doors if boat is to be left unattended (this ensures good air circulation)

28 Maintaining Sails, Rigging, and Deck Gear

Now let's look at preparing and maintaining some of the equipment aboard an ocean racer. The checklist at the end will outline the details.

Sail Maintenance

During an ocean race it is not uncommon to drop a sail in the water. Since salt is hygroscopic the sail will remain damp, making it heavier to hoist. If it's left unwashed for a week it will start to smell. Therefore, after every race, I thoroughly wash all the sails that were used with fresh water and, if it's a windless day, hang them from the mast to dry. When doing this, though, be sure to note the proximity of other masts and dock posts. I've seen a spinnaker catch on a metal sign post in a light breeze and then have watched the remains drop into the water as the luckless skipper tried to take it down in a hurry!

When drying a spinnaker, I attach both clews together rather than just one, to avoid letting it flap. Flapping can make the cloth panels move and this may break stitches, much to the delight of your sail maker. If you dry the spinnaker this way, make sure your dock-lines are secure, in case a breeze comes up. If it is a windy day, merely spread the sails on the foredeck and around the boat, turning them over once or twice before putting them away.

Everyone has his own technique for repacking headsails and

spinnakers. Some fold them carefully, which makes for a more compact and easier to stow sail bag. Others just stuff them in.

Now is the time to stop your heavier spinnakers. The technique I use is to take a plastic bucket and cut out the bottom (you can buy a device that is specifically made for this purpose) and put a bunch of elastic bands (say, 3″ × 1/16″) around the outside. Make fast the head of the spinnaker to the pulpit or dock and pull out the clews to keep the two luffs straight and together. Then slide the bucket down over the spinnaker and, starting about five feet from the head, flick the bands off about every three or four feet. Alternatively, you can attach the head to a spinnaker halyard and pulling it up through the bucket. (For an illustration of this basic technique, see chapter 18 on spinnaker handling.)

Any torn sails should be sent back to your sail maker immediately. Once in a while check each sail over for chafe or worn stitching and if necessary send it back to the sailmaker for repairs. In your bosun's kit you should always carry assorted needles, sail cloth in various weights, and spinnaker tape for running repairs. If you have mildew on the sail, there are one or two aerosol sprays that will remove it.

Rigging Maintenance

After a race, all sheets and guys should be washed with fresh water and hung over the boom or lifelines to dry. Check them all for bent pins and slack springs in the shackles. Halyard shackles should also be checked, and occasionally oiled lightly. Inspect the splices for wear.

Often, little "hooks" appear in a wire halyard, a sign that the halyard needs replacing. But to save your hands (and sails) temporarily, the hooks can be removed by rubbing a spike or the back of a knife up and down over them until the metal fatigues and drops off.

Periodically, your halyards should be withdrawn from the mast and cleaned and the splices should be redressed. I usually immerse the wire part of the halyard in preboiled linseed oil to preserve it a little longer.

The remainder of the rigging also should be checked regularly. Look for toggle pins starting to bend. If you have rod/wire rigging, check the swage fittings. Because of the pressure used in fitting the swages, they sometimes crack.

Many racing skippers wax their standing rigging to help retard corrosion and to get a little less air resistance. You can use ordinary wax polish for this.

Make sure there are split pins in all turnbuckles. Rod Stephens prefers them to be cut off fairly short and opened only about ten degrees. Many people prefer to fold the pin back against the thread of the turnbuckle. But if the pin has to be removed, bending it straight again fatigues it and reduces its life. Check that all cotter pins and other projections that may tear sails (and hands) are well taped, or have a blob of silicone sealer on them.

If you have closed turnbuckles, replace them with the open-center type. Closed turnbuckles keep you from seeing how much thread is inside, and this could be dangerous. (See figure 28.1.) Before installing a turnbuckle, grease it lightly with anhydrous lanolin or vaseline. This makes later adjustments easier.

Use any opportunity to go up the mast for a thorough check of all the components. Starting at the top, check the wind-vane alignment. Check sheaves and sheave boxes for free movement and wear. Are all screws tight? Check the tangs, tang bolts, and cotter pins. Coming down the mast, look at any navigation light fixtures and have them and the flood lights turned on. Look at the spreader roots, bolts, pins, and other fittings.

Once I went up a mast minutes before a race to check the wind vane and found on the way down that the spreader roots had cracked, leaving about an eighth of an inch of material still holding the spreader. We retired from the race, which later turned out to be a hard slog to windward. I doubt if the mast would have stayed up long in that kind of weather.

While you are up the mast, you should also check the padding on the spreader ends. Is it wearing thin? Have a look at the halyard exit boxes or slots. Does everything run freely? Oil lightly where necessary. Check the turning blocks on the deck for easy rotation and look for bent pins and shackles. Replace them if necessary.

Once you are down again, have a good look at the mast wedges and the boot around the mast. If the boot is canvas, is it watertight?

Figure 28.1 The open-center turnbuckle (A) is better than the closed-center type (B). With (A) the threads are visible and the ends can be pinned to prevent it from opening.

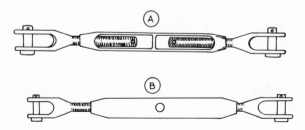

If it's rubber, are there any signs of it perishing? A smear of vaseline will help stop it from cracking, but it should be cloth covered for even better protection. If it does leak, some silicone compound liberally applied around the top of the boot will usually stop it. Apply silicone at the chainplates if they leak. If there are any other leaks, locate and repair them, if necessary by removing fittings. Relocate the fittings on a layer of silicone grease and smear the holding bolts or screws with anhydrous lanolin to facilitate later removal.

Finally, make sure the halyards are long enough to be made fast on the cleat with two or three turns on the winch.

Deck Gear

WINCHES. When I maintain winches, I like to remove all the grease by soaking them in kerosene. I then oil the winches once a week, usually on a Friday afternoon or immediately before a race. I've found that grease, when it's combined with salt water, eventually gums up the whole works, thus reducing efficiency. There are good greases recommended by winch manufacturers, but these should be used only if you plan to overhaul your winches about every three months.

If you follow this less frequent maintenance schedule, disassemble the winch completely, soak it in kerosene to get all the grease off, then dry it thoroughly. A compressed-air blower is useful for drying if you are in a yard, and even a hairdryer could be pressed into service. When the parts are dry, apply the recommended grease liberally and reassemble. Oil the pawls lightly and make sure they are seated correctly and are put on the right way around. It is maddening to find in the middle of a race that you have just acquired a reverse winding facility.

Never oil a reel winch, as oil may seep into the brake and render it useless. Use only recommended grease.

Winch spares such as pawls and springs should be carried at all times. Often, for a long important race, a set of spare winch innards can be "borrowed" from the manufacturer and returned if not used.

OTHER DECK GEAR. Pins on genoa cars often are a source of trouble. Check them for ease of movement and oil them lightly. All snatch blocks, locking or ratchet handles, vangs, and spare shackles should be checked for damage regularly and replaced if they are in critical condition. A faulty block can be extremely dangerous and it should either be returned to the manufacturer for repair or thrown out. Only if the damage is very slightly should any home repairs be attempted—replacing a broken key ring for example. Many people like to have a tail on a key ring. If this is done, it is a good idea to do it as shown in figure 28.2(*M*), for the loop shown in figure 28.2(*N*) can snag and open the snatch block or shackle.

Periodically dismantle all deck and mast movable parts and inspect them for cracks and wear. But beware of taking certain types of spinnaker pole sliders off the mast. You may spend the next week looking for the ball bearings!

Quite often the outboard end of a spinnaker pole can stick, and the time it usually happens is right in the middle of a gybe. These fittings should be carefully checked and lightly oiled or greased with WD-40 or a similar lubricant.

Another spot that is rarely noticed until something goes wrong is the outboard end of the main boom. A quick spray of WD-40 works wonders. But again, this mechanism should be periodically dismantled, cleaned, and greased. Also grease all stainless steel bolts and screws before putting them back in an alloy boom or mast.

HYDRAULICS. Check the hydraulic backstay pump. Is the ram dry and starting to rust, or is it slightly oily and operating smoothly? Check the pressure tubing. If the pump is operated from a remote station, are the connections starting to corrode? If they are, replace them or they may burst under pressure. If the hydraulics do give up, will there be enough adjustment in the backstay to take up the slack and keep the forestay tight? A bottle-screw above the cylinder is a good idea; it could help win that all-important race even if the hydraulics are gone.

Figure 28.2 When making tails for shackle pins, the looped version (N) can catch and open the shackle. A better technique is (M).

CHECKLIST

SAIL MAINTENANCE

- wash, dry, and fold all headsails that were used during the race
- check for torn stitching, repairing as required
- check headstay feeders and stay
- check the luff of each sail for tears, particularly where it enters and leaves the headstay device

RIGGING MAINTENANCE

- wash all sheets and guys after a race and check them, along with halyards, for bent pins, distorted shackles, and slack pins
- check halyards for wire meat hooks and deteriorating splices
- check chainplates, turnbuckles, and toggles after a hard race for any signs of distortion
- check and grease hydraulics and top up reservoir as required
- check that all split pins are taped
- check that lifelines are taut

MAST MAINTENANCE

- check mast from top to bottom, looking for damaged sheaves and loose or chipped screws and bolts
- inspect tangs and tang bolts, spreaders and spreader bolts
- inspect under the spreader end padding and check the padding itself for chafe
- check the halyard exit boxes for signs of wear and for sharp edges
- make sure all light fittings are working properly
- inspect all fittings around the base of the mast, including tracks, turning blocks, the mast collar, the mast step/base, and the tie rods under the deck
- check the boom, especially the outhaul and reefing gear, and check the spinnaker pole and its end fitting
- check the turnbuckles, toggles, and chainplates for corrosion and signs of elongation

29 Maintaining Mechanical and Electrical Equipment

Have you ever been late for the start of a race because your engine wouldn't work? Or have you started a race only to have your instruments fail? If so, you know how critical such equipment can be. I shall now talk about maintaining engines and electrical systems, two areas of a boat that are often overlooked.

Engines

One of the first things you should do after buying a boat is to note the engine make and number. This is an invaluable aid when obtaining spare parts, and it is also identification if the boat should be stolen.

Because there are so many different types of engines, it would be impossible to describe every aspect of maintenance in such a limited space. Therefore, I will give only some general guidelines for engine use and care, letting the operator's manual (which should always be kept aboard) provide more specific instructions.

STARTING AND SHUTTING DOWN ENGINES. Before starting an engine, whether diesel or gasoline, the following checks should be made.

1. Are all the seacocks open? If a butterfly valve is fitted on the exhaust system, is it open?
2. Check the coolant level in the engine if there is a secondary cooling system (there often is).

3. Check the engine sump and gearbox oil levels where required.
4. Check for plenty of fuel. Remember, diesels must be bled if they run out of fuel.
5. Also check the electrolyte level in the batteries if they will be charged when the engine is running. (More about batteries later.)
6. Release the shaft brake or remove the shear pin.
7. If exhaust or intake blowers are fitted for the engine compartment, be sure they are started.

Then, once you have started the engine, do the following:

1. If an oil pressure light is fitted, check to see that it goes out, and that the oil pressure gauge starts to read. (Pressures are usually given in the engine handbook.)
2. If a generator light is fitted, check that it goes out and that a charge is indicated on the ammeter or chargicator.
3. Look over the side to see that exhaust and engine cooling water, if used, are being discharged.
4. Check the RPM to see if the tachometer is working and to see at what speed the engine is running. Most engines don't charge batteries until a certain RPM is reached.
5. After running the engine a while, check the temperatures of the oil and cooling water if gauges are fitted.

Most diesel engines are equipped with a spring-loaded pull that decompresses the cylinder and stops the engine. When the engine is shut down, be sure to turn off the ignition. With gasoline and gasoline/kerosene engines, of course, shutdown is effected by turning off the ignition.

ENGINE MAINTENANCE. Engine maintenance should be done by a competent mechanic every few months or after a certain number of running hours. Usually, the following jobs are explained in the engine manual and are easy to do (about every three months or 500 miles):

1. Drain and replace the engine oil.
2. Change the oil filter.
3. Clean the air filter.
4. If the propeller shaft is lubricated with grease or oil, make sure the stern tube is fully loaded.
5. Check the belt tensions (often a monthly job.)
6. Clean the water trap and the bilge suction strum boxes if fitted. If the engine is lubricated with a closed-circuit cooling water system, check to see that there is adequate water.
7. Clean the starter and generator terminals and lightly smear them with petroleum jelly.

Other jobs which should be done seasonally are:

1. Check all the hoses and clamps.
2. Drain and clean the fuel tanks and fuel lines.
3. Change the gear box oil.

4. Check the engine mounting bolts and make certain the engine has not shifted on its bed, causing misalignment of the prop shaft. This could result in overheating and start a fire.
5. Check all insulation and lagging around exhaust pipes, particularly in areas where the pipes could come in contact with hands or clothing.

These are routine maintenance chores. In addition, you can eliminate the need for many major engine repairs simply by knowing the warning signs that indicate possible trouble. For instance, every time you open the engine box, look for telltable rust or oil streaks. These indicate where a leak may be starting.

Electrical Systems

STORAGE BATTERIES. The heart of every boat's electrical system are the storage batteries. If they do not work, the rest of the electrical and electronic gear on board is useless. Several kinds of storage batteries are available for marine use. The most common is the lead acid type, but alkaline batteries (nickel-iron and nickel-cadmium referring to the plate materials) are also used.

All batteries should have an isolation switch which is turned off when the battery is not in use. This switch must not be used to open-circuit a running alternator, because high-voltage surges are created which irreparably damage the alternator's rectifying diodes. The isolation switch and the batteries should be easily accessible. Check lead acid batteries regularly and top them up with distilled water to the level of the separators if the electrolyte level is low.

A lead acid battery's state of charge is determined by measuring the specific gravity of the electrolyte with a hydrometer. It should be about 1.25 to 1.3 when fully charged, 1.18 to 1.23 when half charged, and 1.115 or below when fully discharged. When charging a battery, hydrogen is given off, so ample ventilation should be provided and care taken to minimize the risk of explosion. Some larger boats have spark-proof ventilation fants, which should be run just before and during the charging cycle.

Certain aspects of your boat's storage batteries should be checked regularly.

1. See that battery terminals are clean, tight, and dry. A light grease applied to the terminals will help keep them dry and clean.
2. See that the battery space is well ventilated by natural or mechanical means.
3. Check the electrolyte level, as mentioned earlier.
4. Check that all switches or equipment that may cause a spark are not located in the battery space.
5. Remove all metal tools from the battery space. The boat's motion may cause them to land across the battery terminals.

6. Make sure the batteries are securely mounted, ideally in a lead-sheathed tray.

GENERATORS. Batteries are usually charged by an alternator, which is more efficient than the old-fashioned dynamo. If for any reason you must remove the alternator, make sure the leads are reconnected to the same terminals they were removed from, or damage to the rectifying diodes will render the machine useless. Periodically check the belt tension and alignment of the alternator or dynamo. The engine manufacturer usually ensures that the machine is installed in a position away from heat, but quite often it is up to the owner to keep water away from it. Remember: water and electricity are incompatible and can be fatal.

WIRING AND FUSES. If the generator and the battery are working properly, the next link in an electrical system is the wiring. It should be of adequate size and away from areas of extreme heat or chafe. All wiring systems should be of the two-wire insulated return type sometimes called fully floating. This means that all electrical components are fully insulated and that there is a current-carrying wire from the battery to the unit and back to the battery. Another type of wiring is that of positive or negative earth, such as used in an automobile. But in this system a short-circuit on the opposite pole can lead to electrolytic corrosion, which has been known to attack the hull of a metal boat. Therefore, check your system. Maybe you'll want the extra security of the insulated return type.

Occasionally check all fuses and fuse boards and all accessible connections. Very often the combination of damp, copper, and electricity proves extremely corrosive. Lamps and switches are particularly prone to corrosion and should be carefully checked and lightly greased at least once a season.

EQUIPMENT. Finally we come to a boat's electrical and electronic equipment. On larger boats proper maintenance of the refrigerator is extremely important, because an inefficient unit can create a substantial power drain. To maintain peak efficiency, check the water flow on water-cooled models. Also check the seawater strainer as often as possible to ensure a good flow of cooling water. On air-cooled units, make sure the condenser is clean and in an area where air can freely circulate. And on all refrigerators check the belt tension on the compressor periodically, and the motor brushes on low-voltage D.C. systems at least once per season.

Knowledge of how best to operate a yacht's refrigerator is also important. To keep battery drain as low as possible, restrict freezing of ice cubes to periods when you are running the engine. Also remove frost before it reaches a thickness of a quarter inch, for the same reason. And if the system is not being used over the winter, it should be either shut down and pumped down or run for fifteen to thirty minutes once a week.

Lights are another service which requires careful maintenance. Before every race, check the navigation lights. The bow or running light is one of the wettest places on the boat, and I think that no lights or very dim lights have contributed to more collisions than is generally acknowledged. Be sure that bulb sizes meet the recommended standards for the area in which you sail. Also ensure that your boat meets all other safety standards. Telephone your local Coast Guard or rating office for the latest information.

Last, electronic instruments. Most boats carry some form of electronic gear, even if it is only a depth sounder. The range of equipment can include a wind speed and direction indicator, a close-hauled meter, a hull speed indicator, radar equipment, a radio telephone, an auto pilot, a R.D.F., a navigation system such as Loran, Omni, or Omega, an electronic compass, sonar, and an emergency radio beacon. All these various types of equipment have their own maintenance and usage requirements, so read the operator's manuals carefully. In general, however, all electronic equipment that runs off the ship's battery should be wired efficiently, with all terminals clean and soldered where possible, to minimize power drain. For equipment that has its own batteries, make sure you carry spare batteries and store them in their original wrappers in a zip-lock plastic bag.

When you realize that the information in this chapter and the preceding two just covers the basics of boat maintenance, you'll understand how much work goes into keeping an ocean racer in first-class trim. Yet regular maintenance plays a critical role in winning races. If you do not now have a method for keeping your boat in top condition, work up a plan for next season and see if your performance doesn't improve.

30 Winter Work-Up

By now your boat is laid up, and your weekend interests may have turned to skiing or indoor sports. Although spring may seem a long time away, you should give some thought now to next season's racing. Do you intend to race seriously again, trying for more silver to enhance your trophy shelf? What was last year's record like? Did you launch your boat late and sail the first few races with the no. 2 at the sail maker's for repairs and the life raft at the manufacturer's? Was it only at the end of the summer that you were finally competitive with the leaders? If this sounds familiar, why not take time out now to visit your boat, check it over, and book an early launching date for next season? The major areas you should consider at this stage are sails, hull, rig, deck layout, instruments, interior, rating, and crew.

Sails

At the end of the season take all your sails to the sailmaker, so that he can clean them, inspect the seams for broken threads, repair any tears, install chafing patches, do any other necessary work, and finally store them. Clearly your chances of winning next year could improve if your sails are cleaned of salt, folded carefully, and stored in a sail loft rather than being stuffed in a sail bag in the damp air of a boat yard.

This is the time to get rid of your old blown sails. (Some sail makers have used-sail inventories, so you may be able to trade your old sails in against the cost of new ones.) Also establish where the gaps are in your sail wardrobe and fill them now, taking advantage of possible reduced winter prices.

Check the zips in the mainsail foot and in the sail turtles. They should all work smoothly. Order the battens you intended to get last year, and get more sail ties to replace those that were lost.

Finally, check out your sail maker's kit. Do you need more rip-stop, needles, or twine?

Hull

The condition of the underwater areas of your hull can make a difference in boat speed. Check to see if the bottom paint is in good order. Take particular care in examining the hull-keel joint and the surface around the rudder. If you need a new bottom job, get it done now, so that there is plenty of time for rubbing down before the spring rush starts.

Check the sacrificial corrosion zincs; they may have to be replaced. Check the rudder for ease of movement. Do you need fairing strips? Installing them can be tricky and is best done by a yard workman with plenty of time, rather than one who is rushing the job in order to get your boat in the water on schedule.

Rig

THE MAST. If your boat has been hauled out of the water this winter, the mast was probably removed. If so, this is a good opportunity to check it over carefully, reducing the likelihood of problems next summer. It often pays to completely dismantle the mast over the winter in order to locate any hidden damage. But remember to reeve in messengers when removing halyards.

When examining the mast, here are some things to keep in mind. Remove, if possible, the wind speed/wind direction arm. It may be damaged when the mast is replaced, and you will have to go up the stick to align it anyway. Check the light fitting. Is it corroded? Is the wiring all right? Look at the masthead sheaves to see if the blocks are worn or cracked. (See figure 30.1.) The edges of aluminum sheaves are often worn so sharp that they can cut halyards. Replacement is the only answer. Check the corners of the holes in the mast for stress cracks. (Figure 30.2 shows a typical crack.) Look also for loose bolts, bent shafts, and loose cover plates. Check the shroud

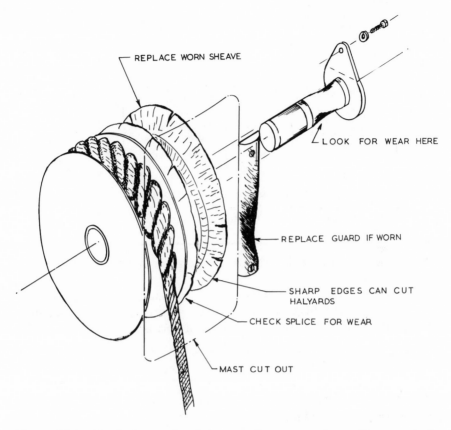

REPLACE WORN SHEAVE

LOOK FOR WEAR HERE

REPLACE GUARD IF WORN

SHARP EDGES CAN CUT HALYARDS

CHECK SPLICE FOR WEAR

MAST CUT OUT

Figure 30.1   Check the masthead sheaves after a season's use. You may find them looking like the one on the right.

tangs or attachment points, looking for signs of wear (metal being ground away). Check the shroud pins, even if it does mean cutting away all last season's tape. Check the spinnaker halyard entry holes or boxes. Do the chafing plates need replacing? Examine the spinnaker pole topping lift sheave boxes and the staysail sheave boxes. Do they move freely and can the pole move from port abeam to starboard abeam without the topping lift chafing on the mast or sheave box? Check the spreaders. Look for signs of wear and cracking on the mast attachment points and mainsail track, especially if you use a lot of backstay tension to bend the mast. Also check the spreader end fittings. Yes, you'll have to cut away all that padding from the spreader end, but what if a cotter pin is about to drop out? Look at the mast coat. Is the rubber getting worn and frayed? The best protection is to grease the rubber lightly with vaseline and then put a canvas mast coat over that. Also examine the electronics cables to see if they are broken or frayed. And finally, look at the mast foot for signs of corrosion. I was once on a boat where the foot of the mast

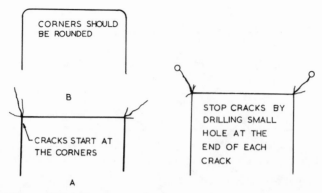

Figure 30.2 Cracks can start where
corners of mast holes are not rounded.
Inspect the mast carefully and stop cracks
as soon as possible.

corroded and simply splayed out, dropping about four inches onto
the mast step!

One last note to remember when working on a mast. If you
have to remove anything, it is a good idea to grease the screws before
putting them back. This will help prevent corrosion later.

STANDING RIGGING. In addition to checking the mast, check
over all the standing rigging. It may pay you to wipe it all down and
apply a light coat of grease, again helping to prevent corrosion. Also
check, clean, and grease all the turnbuckles. Do you need new cotter
pins? Why not order some spares now?

RUNNING RIGGING. Finally, examine the running rigging. Determine which sheets are worn or frayed and need replacing. You
may be able to use a frayed sheet as a dockline, but be sure to cut
out the frayed piece. It is amazing how many yachtsmen use old,
frayed sheets to tie up their boats. If a sheet breaks when you are
sailing, the race is lost; if it breaks when you are using it as a dockline, the boat may be lost. I know which I prefer!

Also look to see what lines need whipping or resplicing. Are all
the splices whipped properly? Check the halyards for wire hooks, bent
shackles, and mangled eye splices at the masthead end.

Deck

The deck is probably the most important area of your boat to be
checked before next season. And now is the time to do it, for as spring
approaches the manufacturers and their agents will be busier than
ever.

First, take a look at the stanchions and straighten or replace any that were bent when someone forgot the reaching strut. Then see if any winches need an overhaul. Or do they simply require a cleaning and regreasing? If you want to buy self-tailing winches for next season, order them now because they may be hard to get later. Check the fairleads. How about the halyard lead, where you always meant to have another padeye fitted but never got around to it? Are any genoa/spinnaker/mainsheet track cars sticking? How about returning the life raft for its annual overhaul? And do the flares still work? Is all other safety equipment still in good repair? Check the hydraulics. The rubber seals do corrode and it may be smart to return the gear to the manufacturer now for a quick turnaround. How about that annoying leak that got your bunk wet in the last race? Why not get it plugged now? Check over all your removable deck gear. Do you want any new shackles, blocks, or winch handles? Do any vents require attention? Are there any areas where nonslip is required? Check also the tack fitting, headstay leads, foreguy blocks (especially if underdeck), and the pulpit through bolts. Examine the lifeline terminals, in addition to checking the lifelines for wear and corrosion of the wire under the plastic covering.

Figure 30.3   Check all parts of the spreaders when the mast is removed.

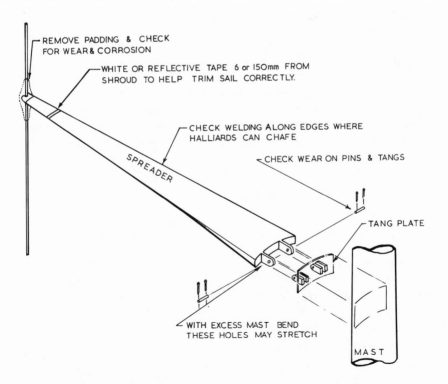

REMOVE PADDING & CHECK FOR WEAR & CORROSION

WHITE OR REFLECTIVE TAPE 6 or 150mm FROM SHROUD TO HELP TRIM SAIL CORRECTLY.

CHECK WELDING ALONG EDGES WHERE HALLIARDS CAN CHAFE

CHECK WEAR ON PINS & TANGS

SPREADER

TANG PLATE

WITH EXCESS MAST BEND THESE HOLES MAY STRETCH

MAST

Instruments

At the end of each season, have your deck instruments inspected by a qualified person. The log/speedo, wind speed/direction, close hauled meter, and fathometer should all be removed and returned to the makers for checking, cleaning, and calibration, if required. Examine the compasses for bubbles, and the next time you're out sailing, check them for accuracy. Do you have one or two compasses? A second one is always useful to check the first against, and as a spare if one is broken. Be sure also to inspect all the instrument lights and all the navigation lights. Replace those that are not working and make a note if you need to reorder light bulbs.

While thinking of instruments, don't neglect your most expensive equipment. Have you removed the Loran-C, SSB, and VHF radiotelephones for the winter? Not only can they be easily stolen, but a cold, damp boat is not the best place to store such sophisticated gear. This is also true of radio and stereo equipment, if fitted.

Interior

Over the winter, mildew commonly forms in the interior of a boat. It is best to remove all the berth cushions at the end of the season and wash them down thoroughly. All the locker doors should be left open to allow air to circulate. When the boat is hauled out, it is also a good time to wash the interior throughout. A little disinfectant in the washing water slows the formation of mildew, especially in fiberglass boats. While you're at it, you should also clean the freshwater tanks. Next check the engine over. Did you have any problems with it last year? Do you need an oil change or any other routine maintenance work? Finally, does the interior varnish/paint/bright work need attention? And do you need extra grabrails or more ventilation?

Rating

Now that it's winter, why not check with a designer to see if your boat's rating can be improved? Or perhaps you are contemplating hull changes to make the boat go faster. Now's the time to get an estimate of the work involved. Remember, every little bit helps. Rating improvements are not necessarily very expensive.

Crew

Have you lined up your crew for next season yet? It's no help telling yourself that you have Fred, Harry, and George if you haven't found time to tell Fred, Harry, and George yet. They may be making arrangements to sail on other boats next year. *Then* how many do you have?

Try to put together a crew of varied experience, age, and agility. The navigator should be very experienced and quick. You should find at least two good helmsman and a good foredeck chief. These people are essential to winning. Also consider how fit your crew is. On a boat, fitness shows up in small ways—like getting that last race-winning sail change made after being up all night, or having the strength to helm properly in rough seas.

Having read over this list of major areas to consider when maintaining your boat this winter, why don't you or your skipper visit the boat soon and see what needs to be done. You may be surprised how many things you forgot. But if the work is done properly now, next season will probably be longer and more enjoyable, and hopefully there will also be a bit more silver on that trophy shelf.

Index